FOUNTAIN OF PIERENE in
ruins of ancient city of Corinth.
Photo by Three Lions Inc.

STUDIES IN
SECOND CORINTHIANS

Other Books in the

BIBLE STUDY TEXTBOOK SERIES

- ACTS MADE ACTUAL
- SACRED HISTORY AND GEOGRAPHY
- THE CHURCH IN THE BIBLE
- ROMANS REALIZED
- HELPS FROM HEBREWS
- THE GLORIOUS CHURCH OF EPHESIANS
- THE GOSPEL OF JOHN
- GUIDANCE FROM GALATIANS
- THE GREATEST WORK IN THE WORLD
- PAUL'S LETTERS TO TIMOTHY AND TITUS
- SURVEY COURSE IN CHRISTIAN DOCTRINE VOL. I
- SURVEY COURSE IN CHRISTIAN DOCTRINE VOL. II
- LETTERS FROM PETER
- THINKING THROUGH THESSALONIANS
- STUDIES IN FIRST CORINTHIANS
- THE SEER, THE SAVIOUR, AND THE SAVED IN THE BOOK OF REVELATION
- SURVEY COURSE IN CHRISTIAN DOCTRINE VOL. III & IV
- STUDIES IN LUKE
- JAMES AND JUDE
- THE GOSPEL OF MARK
- GENESIS VOL. I

BIBLE STUDY TEXTBOOK

STUDIES IN

SECOND CORINTHIANS

T. R. Applebury

Professor of New Testament

Pacific Christian College

Long Beach, California

College Press, Joplin, Missouri

PREFACE

In these studies in the Corinthian letters and the Gospel of Luke, I have given particular attention to the Scriptural emphasis on the great doctrinal issues of the revealed Word of God. I have endeavored to bring other passages of Scripture to bear on these issues because the Bible is its own best commentary. I have written out the shorter quotations in full. I have cited many other references with the hope that those who use the studies may take the time to examine all the Scriptures that are given and also search for additional ones that may bear on the subject being studied.

A wealth of doctrinal material is to be found in Paul's second letter to the Corinthians as well as in the whole Bible which was written "for our admonition." This is true whether it be the carefully investigated truth about Our Lord which Luke has given in his gospel, or the teaching about the church which Paul presents in First Corinthians, or doctrinal issues such as the covenants, the atonement, heaven and other issues presented in Second Corinthians.

The charts are given to enable the student to see the whole epistle or some particular section of it at a glance. They are the road maps to guide anyone following the path of Paul's thoughts that range from sorrow to triumph, from expressions of great love to warnings of great danger.

The outlines constitute a paraphrase of the text in outline form. The comments are intended to explain the meaning of words, phrases, and other problems of interpretation. They have been prepared from a careful consideration of the Greek text for light that may be given to the meaning of the message of the inspired Word. They have been presented without needless use of Greek forms that might serve only to confuse the English reader. Since I am a preacher of the gospel, I have not hesitated to preach in the comments wherever I have believed that it might do some good.

The summaries and the questions at the close of each chapter are presented to help the student recall the content of the chapter and think through the meaning of the many concepts presented in it.

The BIBLE STUDY TEXTBOOK series is the result of a dream of Don DeWelt who has sought to extend the teaching program of the church through the printed page. He had been editor, counselor, and friend to me in preparing three books in the series. I pray that the Lord may bless us as we seek to teach His Word through this medium.

Department of New Testament
Pacific Christian College
February, 1966

CONTENTS

CHART OUTLINES OF SECOND CORINTHIANS

PAUL'S MINISTRY AND APOSTLESHIP

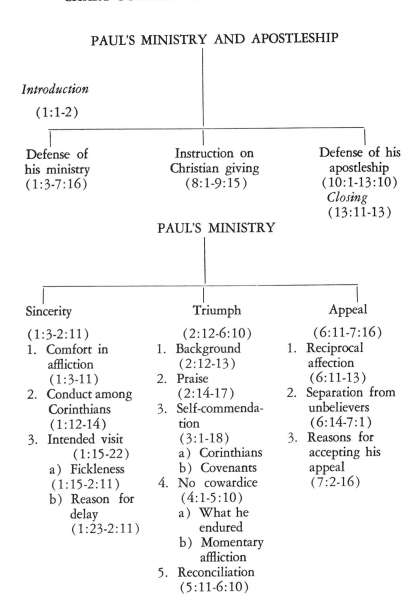

Introduction
(1:1-2)

Defense of
his ministry
(1:3-7:16)

Instruction on
Christian giving
(8:1-9:15)

PAUL'S MINISTRY

Defense of his
apostleship
(10:1-13:10)
Closing
(13:11-13)

Sincerity
(1:3-2:11)
1. Comfort in
   affliction
   (1:3-11)
2. Conduct among
   Corinthians
   (1:12-14)
3. Intended visit
   (1:15-22)
   a) Fickleness
   (1:15-2:11)
   b) Reason for
   delay
   (1:23-2:11)

Triumph
(2:12-6:10)
1. Background
   (2:12-13)
2. Praise
   (2:14-17)
3. Self-commenda-
   tion
   (3:1-18)
   a) Corinthians
   b) Covenants
4. No cowardice
   (4:1-5:10)
   a) What he
   endured
   b) Momentary
   affliction
5. Reconciliation
   (5:11-6:10)

Appeal
(6:11-7:16)
1. Reciprocal
   affection
   (6:11-13)
2. Separation from
   unbelievers
   (6:14-7:1)
3. Reasons for
   accepting his
   appeal
   (7:2-16)

9

THE GRACE OF CHRISTIAN GIVING

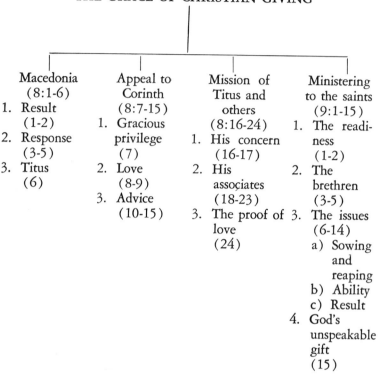

Macedonia (8:1-6)	Appeal to Corinth (8:7-15)	Mission of Titus and others (8:16-24)	Ministering to the saints (9:1-15)
1. Result (1-2)	1. Gracious privilege (7)	1. His concern (16-17)	1. The readiness (1-2)
2. Response (3-5)	2. Love (8-9)	2. His associates (18-23)	2. The brethren (3-5)
3. Titus (6)	3. Advice (10-15)	3. The proof of love (24)	3. The issues (6-14) a) Sowing and reaping b) Ability c) Result
			4. God's unspeakable gift (15)

HIS APOSTLESHIP DEFENDED

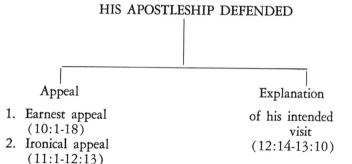

Appeal	Explanation
1. Earnest appeal (10:1-18)	of his intended visit (12:14-13:10)
2. Ironical appeal (11:1-12:13)	

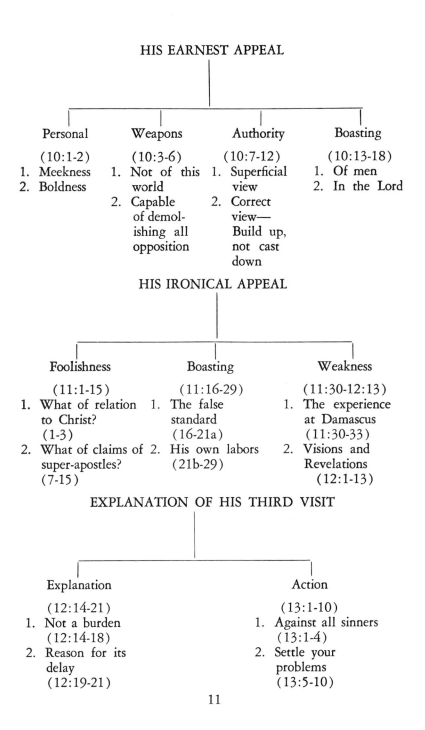

HIS EARNEST APPEAL

Personal	Weapons	Authority	Boasting
(10:1-2)	(10:3-6)	(10:7-12)	(10:13-18)
1. Meekness	1. Not of this world	1. Superficial view	1. Of men
2. Boldness	2. Capable of demolishing all opposition	2. Correct view— Build up, not cast down	2. In the Lord

HIS IRONICAL APPEAL

Foolishness	Boasting	Weakness
(11:1-15)	(11:16-29)	(11:30-12:13)
1. What of relation to Christ? (1-3)	1. The false standard (16-21a)	1. The experience at Damascus (11:30-33)
2. What of claims of super-apostles? (7-15)	2. His own labors (21b-29)	2. Visions and Revelations (12:1-13)

EXPLANATION OF HIS THIRD VISIT

Explanation	Action
(12:14-21)	(13:1-10)
1. Not a burden (12:14-18)	1. Against all sinners (13:1-4)
2. Reason for its delay (12:19-21)	2. Settle your problems (13:5-10)

THE COVENANTS

Promise (430)	Sinai Ex. 20	Pentecost Acts 2 New Covenant
To Abraham and seed—CHRIST. Gal. 3:8-14.	Law did annul the Promise Gal. 3:15-22 Old Covenant	Abraham's children Believers in Christ: Gal. 3:29 New Birth— John 3:3-5

(Gospels—Life of Christ)

ALLEGORY OF ABRAHAM'S TWO SONS
THE TWO COVENANTS
Gal. 4:21-31

	Gospel
Law	Gospel
Flesh Sinai	Promise (Zion)
Hagar	Sarah
Jerusalem	Jerusalem
(Ishmael)	above
Persecution	Isaac
JEWS CAST OUT	(Persecuted)
	CHRISTIANS HEIRS

THE KINGDOM OF HEAVEN
(God's Rule In Hearts)
↓

ISRAEL National and Religious OLD COVENANT David Psa. 89:3-4	CHURCH Spiritual kingdom of Christ. THRONE OF DAVID Lk. 1:32; Acts 2:29-36 NEW COVENANT	HEAVEN Eternal kingdom of Lord and Savior Jesus Christ. II Pet. 1:5-11 Rev. 2:10

Law and Prophets Gospels Points to Points to	Acts and Epistles Points to →	→ →

12

CHAPTER ONE

Analysis

A. Paul sought in his opening words to prepare his readers to receive the message of his second epistle (1-14).
  1. By his gracious salutation (1-2).
     a) The writer: Paul, an apostle of Christ Jesus through the will of God.
     b) Persons addressed:
        (1) The church of God, the one at Corinth.
        (2) The saints in the whole of Achaia.
     c) Salutation: Grace and peace from God our Father and the Lord Jesus Christ.
  2. By his praise to God for comfort in affliction (3-11).
     a) He identified God (3).
        (1) As the God and Father of our Lord Jesus Christ.
        (2) As the merciful Father.
        (3) As the God of all comfort—the compassionate God.
     b) He explained why God had comforted Him (4).
        (1) To enable him to comfort others in affliction.
        (2) To comfort others by means of the comfort God had showed him.
     c) He explained the relation between suffering and comfort (5-7).
        (1) Just as the suffering which Christ experienced came like a flood upon Paul, so the comfort that he experienced came through Christ also.
        (2) His affliction was for their comfort and salvation.
        (3) Paul's comfort was to comfort them and help them endure their sufferings.
        (4) His hope for them was firmly established, for he knew that as they had shared in the suffering so they would share in the comfort (7).
     d) He told them about his affliction in Asia (8-11).
        (1) Its intensity: It was so severe that he often despaired of life.
        (2) His attitude toward it: He put his trust in God who raises the dead.
        (3) His confidence: God will deliver us.

      (4) His deliverance: It was a gift from God.

        (a) The prayers of the Corinthians had helped to bring it about.

        (b) It had resulted in thanksgiving to God from many people.

3. By a brief explanation of his conduct and his writing (12-14).

  a) His conduct (12).

    (1) His conscience said he had conducted himself in a holy and sincere manner before God.

    (2) It was not in accord with fleshly wisdom, but with the grace of God who had granted him the privilege of living as a Christian.

    (3) This was true of his conduct in the world and especially before the Corinthians.

  b) His writing (13-14).

    (1) They were to understand that he meant by his writing exactly what they were reading.

    (2) They, in part, had understood that he was their reason for boasting as Christians and they were his reason for boasting in the day of Our Lord Jesus.

B. Paul explained why he had delayed coming to Corinth (15-24).

  1. What he had planned at first (15-16).

    a) Because of his confidence in their relation to Christ, he had planned to come to Corinth, then go on to Macedonia, and to return to Corinth.

    b) This second visit would prove his kindly feeling for them.

    c) It would have afforded them the privilege of sending him on his way to Judea.

  2. The defense of his plan against anticipated objections (17-22).

    a) Questions that required a negative answer (17).

      (1) In planning this, he didn't use levity, did he? No!

      (2) He didn't make plans according to flesh, as men do, did he? No!

      (3) His "yes" was not an absolute "yes" and his "no" an absolute "no" were they? Were not his plans made with this thought in mind: "If the Lord permits"? Yes!

b) Answers to possible objections to his plan (18).
(1) It was based on the principle that God is trust-worthy.
(2) Because of this he had not said an absolute "yes" or "no".
c) Arguments proving him trustworthy (19-21).
(1) Based on the reference to his preaching: The Son of God, Jesus Christ, who was preached by Paul and Silvanus and Timothy did not become a vacillating "yes" or "no" for in Him a "yes" is certain and trustworthy.
(2) Based on God's promises:
(a) The promises of God in Christ are trust-worthy.
(b) They can trust God and glorify Him through the things Paul had taught them.
(3) Based on God's approval of Paul's ministry (21-22).
(a) The One who establishes us along with you (in the Day of Christ) and anointed us is God.
(b) He also sealed us and gave us the guarantee of the Spirit in our hearts.
3. His reasons for delaying his visit to Corinth (23-24).
a) The solemn statement: I call God as witness upon my soul.
b) The plain reason: To spare you possible sorrow.
c) The explanation:
(1) Lordship: We do not have lordship over your faith; we are fellow-workers with your joy.
(2) Faith: You stand in your faith, that is, in your relation to Christ, for He is Lord of your faith.

Salutation
Scripture

1:1-2. Paul, an apostle of Christ Jeus through the will of God, and Timothy our brother, unto the church of God which is at Corinth, with all the saints that are in the whole of Achaia: 2 Grace to you and peace from God our Father and the Lord Jesus Christ.

Comments
Paul, an apostle of Christ Jesus.—In the first epistle to the Corin-

15

thians, Paul spoke of himself as a "called" or summoned apostle. Since the Corinthians were already familiar with this fact, it seemed unnecessary to repeat it in the second letter. They knew that they had heard the Word of God through him and that their position as Christians depended upon the fact that he was an apostle of Christ. He had made this known to them in the first epistle, but they were to be reminded of it again in this letter.

Paul wrote First Corinthians to correct certain problems that were present in the church. They were (1) those reported to him by members of the household of Chloe and (2) those about which they had written requesting information and instruction.

The second epistle was written to complete the reformation which he had begun through the first letter. Following a brief introduction, it tells (1) about the sincerity of his ministry in their behalf, and defends his change of plans that had caused him to delay his return visit to Corinth; (2) it gives further instruction about completing the offering for the saints in Judea; and (3) it defends his apostleship against the claims of those whom he called false apostles.

the will of God.—Because of the rebellious attitude of some who were disturbing the faith of the Corinthian Christians, it was necessary for Paul to remind them in both of his epistles that he had received his apostleship through the will of God. The teaching, correction, and instruction which he wrote to them was given by the authority of the Lord Jesus Christ. To rebel against the inspired writing was to rebel against the will of God.

and Timothy.—Sosthenes was associated with Paul in the writing of First Corinthians, but Timothy is in that place of honor in the second epistle. There is no reason to suppose that either of them had anything to do with the content of the messages other than being associated with Paul who wrote them under the direction of the Holy Spirit. Timothy is mentioned again in 1:19 along with Silvanus who was another of Paul's helpers.

After having learned about the problems in the church at Corinth, Paul sent Timothy, his beloved and faithful child in the Lord, to remind them of the things which he taught everywhere in every church. He instructed them to receive him with respect what was due one performing the work of the Lord even as Paul himself was doing. See I Cor. 4:17 and 16:10-11.

unto the church of God.—It was necessary to remind the Corinthians again that they were of the church of God, not of men. Paul had made it clear to them in the first epistle that the church was the temple of

God and that the Spirit of God dwelt in it. Anyone attempting to destroy that temple would be destroyed, for God's temple is holy. The Corinthian Christians were to conduct themselves in a manner befitting the saints of God. See I Cor. 3:16-17.

with all the saints.—As the church is holy because it is separated from sin and dedicated to the service of God so those who are members of that holy body are called saints. The Corinthians were reminded that they had gotten their sins washed away in baptism. They had been separated from sinful practices and set apart to the holy service of God. All this had been done in the name of the Lord Jesus Christ in accord with the instruction given to them through the Spirit of God. See I Cor. 6:11.

All of this was intended to remind the church at Corinth that God would tolerate no false teaching nor conduct that fell below the standard presented by His inspired apostle. The apostle Paul had set the example of holy living for them. See I Cor. 4:16 and 11:1.

in the whole of Achaia.—This suggests that, while the letter was addressed primarily to Corinth, there were other congregations in the area also. There was one church of God, but many congregations. There was one divine standard of teaching to regulate the life and conduct of all.

Grace to you and peace.—This conforms to the standard of greeting in all of Paul's epistles, but it is more than a mere greeting. Paul was aware of the hardships through which the church was passing. He knew about the ones who were troubling the saints of God. He knew how very much they needed the grace of God, His unmerited favor. The church had been torn by strife and faction; he knew how they needed peace from God the Father and the Lord Jesus Christ. The salutation was like a prayer that God's grace and peace from the Father and the Lord Jesus Christ might rest upon this congregation.

Comfort in Affliction
Scripture

1:3-11.   Blessed be the God and Father of our Lord Jesus Christ, the Father of mercies and God of all comfort; 4 who comforteth us in all our affliction, that we may be able to comfort them that are in any affliction, through the comfort wherewith we ourselves are comforted of God. 5 For as the sufferings of Christ abound unto us, even so our comfort also aboundeth through Christ. 6 But whether we are afflicted, it is for your comfort and salvation; or whether we are comforted, it is for your comfort, which worketh in the patient enduring of the same sufferings which we also suffer: 7 and our hope for you is stedfast; knowing that, as ye are partakers of the sufferings, so also are ye of the comfort. 8 For we would not have you ignorant, brethren, concerning our affliction which befell us in Asia, that we were weighed down exceedingly, beyond our power, insomuch that we despaired even of life: 9 yea, we ourselves have had the sentence of death within ourselves, that we should not trust in ourselves, but in God who raiseth the dead: 10 who delivered us out of so great a death, and will deliver: on whom we have set our hope that he will also still deliver us; 11 ye also helping together on our behalf by your supplication; that, for the gift bestowed upon us by means of many, thanks may be given by many persons on our behalf.

Comments

Blessed.—It is characteristic of Paul to sing praise to God in the presence of persecution and distress. When he and Silas were imprisoned at Philippi, they prayed and sang hymns to God. See Acts 16:25. His imprisonment in Rome resulted in Christ being preached. This led him to say, "Therein I rejoice and will rejoice" (Phil. 1: 18). He was fulfilling the standard about which he had written to the Romans that they were to be "patient in tribulation; continuing steadfastly in prayer" (Rom. 12:12). He wrote to the Colossians to say, "I rejoice in my suffering for your sake and I fill up on my part that which is lacking of the afflictions of Christ in my flesh for his body's sake which is the church" (Col. 1:24).

This attitude came, in part at least, from the fact that he had once been the chief persecutor—and chief sinner because of it— of the church. He now rejoiced that he had become identified with Christ. In no way was this more evident than in his suffering the same kind of affliction that Christ had suffered during His ministry.

Persecution and affliction do not always produce faithfulness and rejoicing. But those who have strong convictions about Christ and are fully assured about His resurrection and coming again rejoice in spite of hardships. See Rom. 5:1-5.

Paul began the letter on this note so that the Corinthians might understand when he listed some of the things he had suffered for that he was not asking for sympathy, but willingly enduring these things for their sakes.

God and Father.—This is not a repetition of verse two. There Paul wrote of "God our Father;" here, he writes of the God and Father of our Lord Jesus Christ.

We become children of God by being born of the water and the Spirit—the new birth. Our Lord Jesus Christ was designated Son because of the miraculous conception and by His resurrection from the dead (Luke 1:35; Rom. 1:3-4). His relation to the Father was unique, for He was the only begotten of the Father (John 1:14, 18). The writer of Hebrews quotes Psa. 1:7, "Thou art my son, This day have I begotten thee," and relates it, very likely, to the birth of Jesus Our Lord (Heb. 1:5). Paul used the same quotation in his sermon to the Jews in Antioch and related it to the resurrection (Acts 13:33). Hebrews, then, relates Sonship to the fact of His miraculous conception; Acts, to the proof of it.

Jesus made the distinction between His relation to the Father and ours when He spoke to Mary Magdalene, saying, "Touch me not (Greek: stop clinging to me) for I am not yet ascended unto the Father: but go to my brethren, and say to them, I ascend unto my Father and your Father, and my God and your God" (John 20:17).

We can call God our Father because of our relation to our Lord Jesus Christ. To those who accepted Him, He gave the right to become children of God—that is, to those who believed on His name and were born of God. See John 1:12-13; I Cor. 4:15; James 1:18. He called God His Father because of His miraculous conception. This is in harmony with the deity of Jesus, for John explained that "the Word was God" (John 1:1). So Paul speaks of the God as well as the Father of our Lord Jesus Christ—unique relationships in both cases. Paul, writing to the Philippians, explained how this One who was on an equality with God came to be in the likeness of men. See Phil. 2:5-11.

On the cross, Jesus as man cried with a loud voice and spoke the words written in Psa. 22:1, "My God, my God, why has thou forsaken me?" (Matt. 27:46; Mark 15:34).

Lord Jesus Christ.—The word "Lord" is used in many ways in the Bible. It is used in respectful address, like our word "sir." It may refer to the owner of a house or a master of a vineyard or to one who has the right to order his servants and expect them to obey. What did it mean in reference to Jesus Christ? In some instances it could well be rendered "sir." In others it suggests His right to command those who are to perform a service under His direction. But in addition to that, it refers to His deity. In the Old Testament God is called "Lord." It is well known that the LXX substituted the word "Lord" for "Jehovah." God told Moses that "JHVH" was the name of the God of Abraham, of Isaac, and of Jacob. See Ex. 3:15. The apparent reason for the substitution was to avoid using the ineffable name of God in vain.

Quotations from the Old Testament that refer to Jehovah (JHVH) are rendered "Lord" in the New Testament. One such is Isa. 40:3, quoted in Luke 3:4. It clearly refers to the work of John the Baptist who was to prepare the way for the Lord Jesus Christ.

On the Day of Pentecost when Peter declared that God had made Jesus both Lord and Christ it is very likely that the Jews who were used to this word for Deity understood him to say that Jesus is God.

"God and Father of our Lord Jesus Christ" contemplates Jesus in His unique relation to the Father in His deity, His office as Saviour, and as Messiah—that is, prophet, priest, and king.

the Father of mercies and God of all comfort.—God is the God of all comfort. Then comfort that comes from any other source is subject to question. This is not to say that God cannot use one whom He has comforted to comfort others. The Corinthians needed to remember that God is like a father who takes pity on his children in their distress. Corinth had its troubles and its troublemakers, but the Father knew all about them. The Old Testament has a significant word on this: "As a father pitieth his children, so the Lord pities those who fear him. For he knows our frame; he remembers that we are dust" (Psa. 103:13). But in the New Testament in the person of Our Lord, we see this demonstrated as He healed the sick, gave sight to the blind, and proclaimed the gospel to the poor.

The God of comfort is like one called to stand by the side of the helpless, the discouraged, and the oppressed. God comforted Paul as he faced death with the assurance that Christ lived and that after this body dies, he would have a building from God, eternal in the heavens. See II Cor. 5:1. Paul told the Thessalonians about the coming of Christ and the resurrection of the dead, and added, "Comfort one another with these words" (I Thes. 4:18). He comforts those in trial with the assurance that the way out is provided for them—that is, by following His direction just as our Lord did in the wilderness temptation. See I Cor. 10:13; Matt. 4:4; Heb. 4:15. He comforts those who are sometimes misunderstood by the assurance that God knows the hearts of all men. See Rom. 8:27.

that we may be able to comfort.—God came to the aid of Paul in all the pressures of life that brought distress, not for his sake alone but that he might in turn pass this blessing along to others. He told the Corinthians how God delivered him that they might find in the God of comfort the relief from their hardships, discouragements, and

20

trials, which, in their case, often came from their own sinful practices or the disturbing influence of false teachers.

For as the suffering of Christ abound unto us.—The sufferings of Christ are the sufferings He endured during His ministry for the sake of others—that is, to help others. He was persecuted, maligned, and in the end, crucified. All who would be His disciples face the need of bearing the cross, drinking the cup He drank, and suffering as He suffered. But the flood of sufferings that often swept over Paul was balanced by the flood of comfort that came to Him through Christ.

For your comfort and salvation.—The things which Christ suffered led to His death and resurrection which provided the means of salvation for all those who are willing to become united with Him in the likeness of His death that they might also be in the likeness of His resurrection. Paul's sufferings were in a sense like the sufferings of Christ, for they provided comfort and salvation for others. Christ's sufferings provided salvation from sin, for He shed His blood to blot out sin. Paul's sufferings brought comfort and salvation, not in the sense of blotting out sin, but by encouraging others to patiently endure the suffering which were like his own sufferings through which he had safely passed.

our hope for you.—Paul knew about the sufferings of the church at Corinth, for he was like a loving father who suffered when he knew that his children were suffering. But he also knew that this example of patience in tribulation would be followed by the Corinthians. His confidence in them and his hope for them, remained undaunted despite the fact that in both of the epistles to the Corinthians Paul shows how far short of the standard of Christ the Corinthian church had fallen. His hope was not based on any false notion that the Lord would accept them in their sin, but that they would correct their errors and imitate him, their spiritual father as he imitated Christ.

our affliction which befell us in Asia.—Paul mentions this to show them the extent to which he had gone in suffering in order that he might minister to them. We have no way of knowing the exact thing to which he referred. Luke tells about the riot which Demetrius and the silversmiths caused at Ephesus when Paul was there. But he also reminds us that Paul's friends kept him from getting involved. See Acts 19:30-31. Paul mentions the fact that he had fought with wild beasts at Ephesus. See I Cor. 15:32. But we have no way of knowing exactly what this meant.

The thing that happened to him in Asia was so beyond his ability to endure that he utterly despaired of life. In 4:10-11 he mentions the fact that he constantly faced death for Jesus. In 11:23-28 he listed many of the trials through which he had gone as an apostle, often being in danger of death. Constantly facing this sentence of death, he was led to put his trust in God who raises the dead. It was toward God, and not toward himself, that he directed his hope of continued deliverance.

by your supplication.—Paul had no doubt about God's ability to deliver him from this threat of death. But there were two other factors involved in the deliverance: (1) his own patient endurance of the trials that he suffered, and (2) the help which the Corinthians supplied by their supplication in his behalf.

This brings up the interesting subject of the place of prayer in connection with the providence of God. Paul urged the Colossians to pray for him that God might open a door for the word and that he might speak as he ought to. See Col. 4:2-4. Paul says that God's administration of the fulness of times bring all things together in Christ. This, evidently, is done to insure the success of God's plan of redemption. See Eph. 1:9-10. Abraham prayed for the deliverance of Sodom and Gomorrah from the destruction which God said was to come upon them, but they were not delivered because there were not even ten righteous men in those cities. Moses prayed that God would spare the nation of Israel when they sinned by worshipping the golden calf. The nation was saved, but the guilty ones were punished by being put to death. Jesus told Peter that Satan desired to have the apostles that he might sift all of them as wheat. He made supplication for Peter that his faith should not fail, but even the prayer of Jesus did not keep Peter from denying that he had ever known his Lord. Why? Because he would not listen to the warning which Jesus gave nor to the instruction which He had given him concerning the nature of His kingdom. Peter was sure that even if all the others should fail Christ, he wouldn't. But when Jesus meekly submitted to arrest in the Garden of Gethsemane, Peter lost all faith in Him. While the prayer of Jesus did not prevent Peter's denial, it did give him, because of the resurrection, an opportunity to find the basis of genuine faith which would not fail him. See I Pet. 1:3-7. Prayer must not only be offered in accordance with God's will, but those for whom it is offered must also be willing to conform to His will as revealed in His Word. See I John 5:14-15. The church ought always to pray for its minister, but their prayers won't keep him from teaching falsehood if he has not diligently studied and earnestly sought to handle the Word of God accurately. The church ought always to pray for their missionaries, but prayer won't keep the missionaries from mistakes of judgment if their judgments are not based solidly on the principles presented in the Word of God. Even if death for the sake of the gospel should be their lot as it was in Paul's case, the crown of life awaits those who keep the faith.

the gift bestowed on us by means of many.—Paul's deliverance from the trial which he faced in Asia was like a gracious gift from God. It had been made possible by means of the prayers of the people on his behalf. He suggests that the many who had prayed should now thank God for the answer—the gift of deliverance. This points out a weakness in many prayers. Too often our prayers are requests that are not followed by prayers of thanksgiving. All eternity will not suffice to thank Him for the gift of salvation which He provided through the suffering of Jesus Christ on the cross of Calvary. Thanking God for Paul's deliverance would help the Corinthians to look to God for deliverance from their trials which were largely the result of the work of the false teachers in their midst and of their own failure to follow the standard of conduct Christ had set for them.

Paul's defense of His Conduct and Writing

Scripture

1:12-14. For our glorying is this, the testimony of our conscience, that in holiness and sincerity of God, not in fleshly wisdom but in the grace of God, we behaved ourselves in the world, and more abundantly to you-ward. 13 For we write no other things unto you, than what ye read or even acknowledge, and I hope ye will acknowledge unto the end: 14 as also ye did acknowledge us in part, that we are your glorying, even as ye also are ours, in the day of our Lord Jesus.

Comments

For our glorying.—Paul had just written of his deliverance from death which clearly suggested God's approval upon him as an apostle of Jesus Christ through the will of God. The basis for his view was two-fold: (1) his own sincere conduct before the Corinthians and (2) the trustworthy letters which he had written to them. He called upon his own conscience, that is, his sense of right and wrong, to testify for him in this matter. He was confident before God that what he had done and what he had written was right.

holiness and sincerity of God.—His life of purity and sincerity had God's approval. He did not act upon the basis of fleshly wisdom. This may be a suggestion that those who were troubling the church at Corinth were acting from such a motive. He had reminded them in his first letter that he had not spoken to them in excellence of speech or of wisdom, that is, in the manner ordinarily used by men, for he depended upon that revelation that came directly to him through the Spirit of God. He made sure that his conduct was in harmony with God's revealed will, lest he himself should be disqualified after having preached the gospel to others. See I Cor. 9:25-27. Paul insisted that his conduct was in harmony with the gracious privilege that God had given him, first of all to be a follower of Jesus Christ and then to be an apostle of Christ. Christ lived in him, for he was living the life of faith, and by so doing he did not make void the grace of God. See Gal. 2:20-21.

in the world and more abundantly to you-ward.—Paul was always careful about his conduct. It was not one thing before the world and something else before the Corinthians. He was particularly careful to conduct himself in a Christlike manner in their presence because he was aware of the fact that the false apostles were searching for an excuse to discredit him before them. Note his attitude toward the subject of money. See II Cor. 8:21.

for we write no other things unto you.—He was aware that some had been saying that his letters were bold but he was weak. See 10:10. He knew that some were "puffed up" rejecting the promise that he had made to visit them. See I Cor. 4:18. He assured them that they could trust what they read in his letter. He meant exactly what he said. He wanted them to continue to understand this with reference to everything that he was writing. What they read and understood him to say in his letters corresponded exactly to what he was before God and in the world.

unto the end.—Since this has to do with his writing it seems to suggest that he wanted the Corinthians to have a clear understanding of all he was writing. The phrase "to the end" is also found in I Cor. 1:8. There, however, it is associated with the day of the coming of the Lord Jesus Christ, for Paul was concerned about their remaining stedfast in their faith until that day.

as also ye did acknowledge us in part.—Some, perhaps the majority, had clearly understood what he had written about his intended visit, but some had not submitted to his authority. He told them plainly that he would not spare such when he came again. They could depend on it. See II Cor. 13:2; I Cor. 4:21. Would they have him come with a rod of chastisement, or in love and a spirit of gentleness? How eager he was that it should be the latter! It was his fond hope that in the day of the Lord Jesus Christ they might be able to glory in the fact that they had accepted the message that had come to them through the apostle of Christ. Paul was also hoping that they would remain faithful so that he would be able to glory in their Christian conduct. They were to be the evidence of his faithful ministry as an apostle of Christ.

Explanation of His Deferred Visit

Scripture

1:15-24. And in this confidence I was minded to come first unto you, that ye might have a second benefit; 16 and by you to pass into Macedonia, and again from Macedonia to come unto you, and of you to be set forward on my journey unto Judaea. 17 When I therefore was thus minded, did I show fickleness? or the things that I purpose, do I purpose according to the flesh, that with me there should be the yea yea and the nay nay? 18 But as God is faithful, our word toward you is not yea and nay. 19 For the Son of God, Jesus Christ, who was preached among you by us even by me and Silvanus and Timothy, was not yea and nay, but in him is yea. 20 For how many soever be the promises of God, in him is the yea: wherefore also through him is the Amen, unto the glory of God through us. 21 Now he that establisheth us with you in Christ, and anointed us, is God; 22 who also sealed us, and gave us the earnest of the Spirit in our hearts.

23 But I call God for a witness upon my soul, that to spare you I forbare to come unto Corinth. 24 Not that we have lordship over your faith, but are helpers of your joy: for in faith ye stand fast.

Comments

And in this confidence.—Paul was confident that the Corinthians understood that he was their spiritual father and that they were his spiritual children. See I Cor. 4:14-16. With this in mind, he had planned at first to come to Corinth and after passing through their area to go on to Macedonia and then to come back from Macedonia to Corinth in order that he might visit them twice. In this way he would demonstrate his good toward them. This differed from the original only in that it would give the Corinthians a second benefit, that is, they would have the privilege of having the apostle with them on two occasions. It suggests a deeper concern for them than for the Macedonians. It was not to be understood as cancelling his original plan. See I Cor. 16:5-7. He wanted them to continue to understand that what he had written in the first letter about his intention to visit them would be fulfilled.

set forward on my journey.—This does not seem to suggest any financial aid, since Paul had made a rule in dealing with Corinth to accept no support from them, lest his motives be misunderstood or he should give occasion to the false teachers to justify their desire to be paid.

Luke tells of an occasion when Paul met with the brethren from Ephesus on his way to Jerusalem. He told how Paul spoke to them and then knelt down and prayed with them. All wept and fell on his neck and kissed him, sorrowing most of all for his word that they would not be able to see him again. See Acts 20:17-28. Paul probably had a meeting of this sort in mind when he suggested coming back to Corinth and have them send him on his way to Judea.

When I was thus minded.—The defense which Paul makes at this point is against anticipated objections. This is common in his writings because he knew the minds of those to whom he wrote. An example of it is given in Rom. 6:1-7:25 where he answered possible objections on the part of his readers.

There is no indication that the Corinthians had known anything about this plan to visit them twice until they read it in this letter. Timothy, of course, had been sent to Corinth and was with Paul as he was writing II Corinthians. See I Cor. 4:16-17 and 16:10. There is no indication, however, that he knew anything about the plan mentioned in the above verses while he was at Corinth.

Titus also had been sent to Corinth. This fact is mentioned in 2:13; 7:6-14; 8:6, 16, 23, and 12:18. There is no indication that Titus could have known that Paul was planning to make a trip first to Corinth and then to Macedonia. Paul had not been able to make contact with him until he found him in Macedonia, from which point he was writing this second Corinthian letter.

It seems best then to assume that Paul was anticipating possible criticism of the plan which he had not been able to put into effect. The Corinthians were being informed about it for the first time as they read this letter. He wanted them to know about it because he wanted them to understand his love for them as their father in the gospel. He also knew that there were some among them who assumed that he would not come at all. See I Cor. 4:18.

did I show fickleness?—The word translated "fickleness" means "lightness." Some assume that Paul was vacillating as if he had been saying one thing but was now saying something entirely different. Paul explained this word by using two other expressions: (1) "purpose according to flesh"; and (2) "the yea, yea, and the nay, nay."

"According to flesh" seems to suggest the manner in which men make plans without considering their relation to God, a thing that Paul never did. See v.12 on "fleshly wisdom." James mentions those who say "today or tomorrow we will go into the city and spend a year there and trade and get gain." (James 4:13). He adds that because a man doesn't know what the morrow will bring, he ought to say, "If the Lord will, we shall both live and do this or that" (4:15). When Paul wrote to the Corinthians about his proposed trip he said "I will come to you shortly if the Lord will" (I Cor. 4:19). Later, he spoke of his desire to spend some time with them and added, "If the Lord permit" (I Cor. 16:7).

James also throws light on the meaning of "the yes, yes." See James 5:12. It is in a different context, for James is reminding the brethren that they are not to swear by heaven or earth or anything else. That is to say, they could not bind heaven and earth to make up any deficiency in the truthfulness of their statement. Therefore their "yes" was to be "yes." This was to be a positive affirmation that what they are saying was true or that their "no" meant just "no." But Paul is talking about his plan that had to do with future events. He could not, as men might do, say "Yes" affirming by this "yes" that he did not need to consider the Lord's will. The defense that Paul is making in these somewhat difficult phrases (that is, difficult for us to understand, not for the Corinthians) seems to be against the possible charge that he made his plan lightly, not considering the will of God. That this is so, seems to be clear from the fact that he stated these questions in forms that required "No" for an answer. He wasn't treating the matter lightly, was he? The only answer that could be given was "No." He didn't make the plan according to men who disregard God, did he? The answer was "No." His "Yes" wasn't "Yes" without considering God's will, was it? Again, the only answer was "No."

But as God is faithful.—The questions which Paul had just asked required a negative answer. To make sure that the Corinthians understood it, he added, "Our word to you is not 'Yes and No'." This does not suggest vacillation, for it is based on the principle of the trustworthiness of God. The visit he planned to make to Corinth and had deferred was based on the principle of truthworthiness of God whom he served as an apostle of Jesus Christ through the will of God.

For the Son of God, Jesus Christ.—Having stated that his plan to visit Corinth had not been made lightly, he now proves his trustworthiness by a three-fold argument: (1) that based on his preaching; (2) that based on God's promises; and (3) that based on the evidence of God's approval on his ministry.

Paul and his companions, Silvanus and Timothy, had preached the Son of God, Jesus Christ, in the midst of the Corinthians. This was not a matter on their part of "Yes" and "No," for in Him— that is, in Christ—is the "Yes." The certainty—validity, trustworthiness—of the message of the apostle and his companions was not a matter of men's speech but of Christ Himself.

For how many soever be the promises of God.—God is trustworthy; the message concerning His Son, Jesus Christ, is trustworthy; the promises of God which are fulfilled in His Son are likewise trustworthy.

Paul and those associated with him could wholeheartedly say "Amen" to this.

Now he that establisheth us with you in Christ.—God is the One who established both Paul and the Corinthians in their relationship to Christ, and in the "day of our Lord Jesus" (verse 14).

The Corinthians had gotten their sins washed away by the blood of the Lamb, when they were baptized into Christ; they were separated from their sins; they were pardoned in the name of the Lord Jesus Christ and in the Spirit of our God. See I Cor. 6:11. They could depend on that relationship because they were instructed by the inspired apostle of Christ. Paul had obeyed the gospel which Ananias had preached to him when he said, "Now why do you delay? Arise and get yourself baptized and wash away your sins, because you called on the name of the Lord" (Acts 22:16). They could be sure about their relationship to Christ because of their obedience to the word that had come from Him.

anointed us.—Anointing had to do with one's installation in office. In the Old Testament times, both prophets, priests, and kings were anointed as they were installed in office. Christ Himself was anointed with the Holy Spirit as He began His ministry as Prophet, Priest, and King. See Luke 4:18; Acts 10:38. The apostles were baptized

in the Holy Spirit so that they might speak as the Spirit gave them
utterance and reveal the message from God. See I Cor. 2:6-16.

When Paul insists that God anointed "us," in all probability he
was referring to the whole apostolic group. When John wrote to
the church mentioning the anointing which they had from the Holy
One, he referred to this power that came to the apostles who were
baptized in the Holy Spirit and those upon whom they laid their
hands in order that they might bring the inspired teaching to all
who would hear. John affirms that the message thus spoken was true.
See I John 2:19-27. In the same way, the Corinthians could trust
what Paul said because he was an apostle of Christ through the will
of God.

who also sealed us.—Paul tells the Ephesians that they had been
sealed by the promised Holy Spirit. See Eph. 1:13. The Holy Spirit
through the apostles by the word which they preached had produced
in them the identifying marks of a Christian, that is, Christian
character and conduct. See Gal. 5:22-24; Rev. 7:3.

Paul was speaking of those things that marked him as a genuine
apostle of Jesus Christ. His word was trustworthy. See 12:12 where
he reminded them that the signs of an apostle were wrought among
them. They were the signs and wonders and mighty works which he
had done in the midst of them.

Since God's approval rested on him, they could trust his word
and be assured of the sincerity of his plan to come to them.

and gave us the earnest of the Spirit in our hearts.—Paul also refers
to "earnest" in 5:5 and Eph. 1:14. It ought not to be confused with
"firstfruits" (I Cor. 15:20) which suggest that Christ's resurrection
indicates that all the dead will be raised.

"Earnest" is usually defined as money paid down to guarantee the
full payment of a debt. An instance in which the word meant a pledge,
token or guarantee that one's word would be made good is mentioned in Gen. 38:17-18, 25. This meaning fits well each of its uses in
the New Testament in which it is used. It is something that guaran-
tees that God's promise will be fulfilled.

The earnest or the guarantee is the Spirit, that is, the Holy Spirit
is the One who gives the guarantee. In this instance, the guarantee
had to do with Paul's apostleship and truthworthiness of his word.
See I Cor. 2:6-16 where Paul argues for his inspiration as well as
that of the other apostles. He declared that the Spirit had revealed
the mind of God to them, and that they spoke that revelation in words
that were Spirit-taught. He affirmed that we—the apostles—have the

mind of Christ. He knew that Christ, by the Spirit, had guided him into all the truth (John 16:13-14). He was aware of the fact that the Corinthians could trust his word because it was guaranteed by the Holy Spirit, for it came from God through the Holy Spirit.

in our hearts.—that is, in the hearts of the inspired apostles. The inspired message was in their minds, for they had the mind of Christ. This is not intangible subjectivism, but an awareness on the part of the apostles that they were actually being used by the Holy Spirit to reveal the truth of God. The accompanying miracles gave objective testimony to this truth. See Heb. 2:3-4.

But I call God for a witness.—In this most solemn manner Paul assured the Corinthians that they could understand that he was telling the truth. The trip that he was planning had to be deferred because he had not learned of their reaction to the instruction given in First Corinthians. He had asked, "Shall I come to you with a rod of chastisement, or shall I come in love and a spirit of gentleness?" It was to spare them the embarrassment and sorrow of having to be reproved again, that he deferred the trip until he could hear from Titus and know about the situation at Corinth. See 2:12 and 7:6.

Not that we have lordship over your faith.—In First Corinthians, Paul had reminded them that he and Apollos were ministers—deacons—through whom they had believed. See I Cor. 3:5. They were responsible to the Lord, not Paul, for their belief. He challenges them in the closing words of this second letter to test out their ownselves to see if they were in the faith—faith, that is, in the Lord Jesus Christ. All that Paul could do was to work for their joy, by encouraging them to remain faithful to the Lord and instructing them in their privileges and responsibilities as Christians. He couldn't believe for them.

for in faith you stand.—They had taken that stand when Paul preached the word of Christ to them. They had demonstrated that faith is obedience to Christ. There was no other foundation on which to build.

This in no way suggests that Paul was unaware of the fact that some were ready to listen to the appeal of the false teachers who were disturbing them, as the closing chapters of the letter clearly indicate. It does show his concern that they remember that their relation to Christ, the Lord, depended on faith expressed in obedience to Him.

Summary

Paul began his second epistle in a manner that was intended to insure a favorable reception on the part of his readers. In his usual, gracious manner he addressed them as the church of God. The brethren at Corinth were made aware of the fact that what he said to them was intended for all the saints in the whole of Achaia.

While this letter was to be critical of many things that were going on in Corinth, Paul began by telling them how God had comforted him in his sufferings for Christ. The merciful Father had done this so that he might be able to help others in their trials. He had a sure hope for them because he knew that as they were sharers of the sufferings so also they would be of the comfort.

He mentioned the thing he had suffered in Asia. It had been beyond his ability to endure; he utterly despaired of life. This was like a death sentence to him. He dared not trust in himself, but in God who raises the dead. God delivered him from such a death. He was confident that God would do so again if he should face the same trial again. The Corinthians had prayed for his deliverance which made this gift from God a matter of thanksgiving on the part of many people.

Paul had been conscientious in his conduct everywhere, and especially at Corinth. He wanted them to know that he intended to keep his promise to visit them again just as he had written in his first epistle. A delay had become necessary, but he would come again to Corinth.

They, for the most part, had understood that this promise had been made by their spiritual father. They were his beloved children. They could be proud that he was their father in the gospel, and he could be proud of his relation to them in the Day of our Lord Jesus.

Confident that they understood this relationship, Paul had planned to visit them first, then go to Macedonia and again return to them. They would have the privilege of helping him on his journey to Judea. Such a visit would prove his kindly feeling for them. They would have no reason to be jealous over his attention to other churches.

Was such a plan mere words spoken lightly with no intention of carrying out the plan? Nothing in his preaching could lead them to suppose he had been so fickle. The promises of God which they had heard from him were trustworthy. Moreover, God had established him in his relationship to them as the apostle through whom they had learned about Christ. He had equipped him to speak the wisdom from God. God had given him the identifying marks of an apostle. As an inspired apostle, he had in his mind and heart the message which the Holy Spirit had revealed to him on which he based his confidence in God and His promises. No word of his was spoken lightly.

Why then had he delayed his coming? He called upon God to testify for him that it was to spare them from sorrow. The delay would give them time to examine their position and make sure about their faith in the Lord.

Questions

1. Why did Paul call attention to the fact that he was an apostle of Christ Jesus through the will of God?
2. Why did he mention Timothy in the salutation?
3. Why did he speak of the church as "the church of God"?
4. Why did he address the letter to all the saints in the whole of Achaia as well as to the church in Corinth?
5. Why did he speak of "saints" in this connection?
6. What significance did his greeting of grace and peace have to the Corinthians at this time?
7. How did Paul prepare his readers to accept the message of his epistle?
8. What are the three principal topics which Paul discussed in the epistle?
9. What was Paul's characteristic approach to the problem of suffering?
10. What had he done when he and Silas were imprisoned in Philippi?
11. In writing to the Colossians, what did he say about his attitude toward sufferings?
12. How do we know that Paul was not merely asking for sympathy when he told about his sufferings?
13. Why should Paul speak of "God our Father" and of "the God and Father of our Lord Jesus Christ"?
14. What significant difference is there in the two phrases?
15. What is the probable significance of "Lord" as Paul used it to refer to Jesus Christ?
16. What additional truths are suggested about Him in the names "Jesus" and "Christ"?
17. Why does he speak of God as the Father of mercies and God of all comfort?

18. What does the psalmist say about God's pity for his children?
19. How is all this demonstrated in the attitude of Jesus toward those who suffered?
20. How did God comfort Paul as he faced the possibility of death in Asia?
21. What was God's purpose in comforting Paul?
22. What did Paul mean by the sufferings of Christ? How did these sufferings sweep over him like a flood?
23. Why did Paul write about his hope for the Corinthians despite his knowledge of their sins?
24. Why did he mention the affliction that befell him in Asia?
25. Why did he mention the sentence of death?
26. How had the Corinthians cooperated in his deliverance?
27. What is taught in the Bible about the place of prayer in the providence of God? What is providence?
28. What clearly defined limitations of prayer are indicated in this matter?
29. What did Paul suggest that the Corinthians do since their prayers had helped in his deliverance? Why?
30. What had deliverance from death suggested as to God's attitude toward the apostle?
31. How did Paul view his conduct at Corinth and the letter he had written to them?
32. How could Paul make sure that his conduct had the approval of God?
33. In what other area was Paul concerned about his conduct?
34. How did Paul let the church know that he meant exactly what he had written in the first epistle about his intended visit?
35. How had the majority reacted to his letter?
36. What would happen to those who had not submitted to his authority as an apostle?
37. On what was Paul's confidence based when he planned to visit Corinth a second time?
38. What had he told them about the trip in the first epistle?
39. What was the second benefit that he had planned for them?
40. How did he expect the Corinthians to send him on his journey to Jerusalem?
41. When did the Corinthians first learn about this intended second visit?
42. What was his point in mentioning it here?

43. Why did he defend himself against the possible charge of fickleness?
44. What is his point in the question about "yes" and "no"?
45. What did he always take into consideration when he made his plans?
46. How did Paul defend himself against the possible charge of vacillation?
47. How did Paul prove his trustworthiness?
48. Why did Paul refer to the many promises of God?
49. How had the relationship of Paul to the Corinthians as the apostle who had preached Christ to them been established?
50. What did he mean by the fact that God had anointed him and also sealed him?
51. What is the earnest of the Spirit? What bearing does this have on the issue of Paul's relationship to the Corinthians?
52. Why did he call on God "for a witness"?
53. What is meant by "lordship over your faith"?
54. Why did he say, "For in your faith you stand"?

For Discussion

1. What may be learned from the manner in which Paul approached the Corinthians' problem that might help in presenting the gospel today?
2. What is the relation of reliability in personal obligations to the effective teaching of the Word of God?

CHAPTER TWO

Analysis

A. Paul continued the explanation of his deferred visit to Corinth (1-13).
   1. He explained his personal reason for the delay (1-4).
      a) He had decided not to come again in sorrow.
      b) He gave his reason: If I make you sorry, who is there to gladden me but the one I made sorry?
      c) He reminds them that he had written—in First Corinthians—this very thing:
         (1) He did so in order that he might not have sorrow from those who ought to make him rejoice.
         (2) He had done so because he was confident that his joy was their joy—his visit was to be enjoyed by all.
      d) He told them about the nature and purpose of his writing (First Corinthians).
         (1) He wrote it out of affliction, anguish of heart, and many tears.
         (2) He did so not to cause sorrow, but that they might know of his abundant love for them.
   2. He explained his attitude toward the one who had caused the sorrow (5-11).
      a) He explained his reasons for this attitude (5-7).
         (1) He had caused sorrow not to Paul alone but, in part, to all.
         (2) His punishment at the hand of the many was sufficient.
         (3) It was Paul's judgment that he should be forgiven lest he be overcome by his sorrow.
      b) He appealed to them to let the one who caused the sorrow know of their forgiveness (8-11).
         (1) He urged them to confirm their love for him.
         (2) He had written (in First Corinthians) to put them to the test, that is, to see whether or not they would obey him in all things.
         (3) He joined with them in forgiving this one for their sakes in the presence of Christ.

    (4) Such forgiveness would prevent Satan from gaining
    the advantage over them.

    (5) He gave his reasons for this appeal: We are not
    ignorant of Satan's thoughts.

3. He explained why he left Troas and went to Macedonia
(12-13).

  a) The move to Troas.

    (1) It was for the gospel of Christ.

    (2) There a door was opened for him in the Lord.

  b) The move to Macedonia.

    (1) He had found no relief for his anxiety over Corinth.

    (2) He had not found Titus.

B. Paul interrupted the account of his search for Titus with an
expression of thanks to God for Triumph in Christ (14-17).

  1. His thanksgiving: (14).

    a) For His continuous leading in triumph in Christ.

    b) For His making manifest through His messengers the
    savor of His knowledge in every place.

  2. His explanation: (15-16a).

    a) The messengers are a sweet savor of Christ unto God.

    b) The message is true with reference to those who are
    saved and those who perish.

    c) In one it is a message from death unto death, and the
    other from life unto life.

  3. His question: (16b-17).

    a) Who is adequate for these things?

    b) "We are," is his implied answer.

    c) The reason for this answer:

      (1) We are not as the many corrupting the Word of
      God.

      (2) We speak with sincerity in the sight of God in
      relation to Christ.

Further Explanation of the Deferred Visit

Scripture

2:1-4. But I determined this for myself, that I would not come
again to you with sorrow. 2 For if I make you sorry, who then is he
that maketh me glad but he that is made sorry by me? 3 And I
wrote this very thing, lest, when I came, I should have sorrow from
them of whom I ought to rejoice; having confidence in you all, that

my joy is the joy of you all. 4 For out of much affliction and anguish of heart I wrote unto you with many tears; not that ye should be made sorry, but that ye might know the love which I have more abundantly unto you.

Comments

But I determined this for myself.—Putting the Corinthians first in his consideration, Paul explained that he had deferred his visit for their sakes, that is, to spare them the embarrassment of his having to reprove them upon his arrival at Corinth. He had left the choice up to them when he wrote I Cor. 4:21. Would they have him come with a rod or in the spirit of gentleness and love? But he also had a personal reason: he did not want to come again with sorrow.

This raises the question about the number of visits Paul made to Corinth. Acts records only two: the first, when the church was established at Corinth, and a second which lasted three months before setting sail for Syria. See Acts 18:1, 20:1-3. But in II Cor. 12:14 and 13:1 he mentions a third coming. In 13:2 he speaks of the second time when he was present with them. In 2:1 he says that he was determined not to come again with sorrow.

Various attempts have been made to harmonize all these references. The consensus is that Paul actually made at least three visits to Corinth, one of which is not mentioned in the book of Acts. This is the supposed sorrowful visit which, according to the theory, he made after writing First Corinthians and before writing II Corinthians.

These problems are interesting, but they do not affect the doctrine of the epistles of Paul or the history which Luke records in Acts. The Corinthians to whom Paul wrote these letters were fully aware of the number of times he had visited them as well as the number of letters he had written to them. We must also remember that it was not Luke's purpose to give every detail of every event in the journies of Paul. It is possible, however, to harmonize all the known facts without assuming that Paul made three visits to Corinth. The problem is with the number two visit—the so-called sorrowful one. A possible solution is found in I Cor. 5:3-4. There Paul declares that although he was absent in body he was present in spirit when they were gathered together in the name of our Lord Jesus to deliver the offending brother to Satan for the destruction of the flesh that the spirit might be saved in the day of the Lord Jesus. That most certainly was a sorrowful experience for Paul, as much so as if he had actually been present in the flesh. He knew all the facts of the case;

he understood the seriousness of the situation; he was aware of the fact that the man might not repent; he was also certain that this action was the only thing that could possibly bring him to his senses and cause him to change his way before it was too late. The reference in II Cor. 13:2 to the second visit is very similar to his remarks in I Cor. 5:3-4. Although we must admit that he does not say that he was present the second time in spirit, the footnote in ASV which reads "as if I were present the second time, even though I am now absent," lends some support to the view.

if I make you sorry.—The gospel which Paul preached was not intended to make people sorry, except those who were guilty of sin. Paul, of course, did not hesitate to tell the truth about sin even though it might make some sorry. Such sorrow was intended to lead them to repentance which would bring salvation. See II Cor. 7:8-10.

The angel who announced the birth of Christ said, "Behold I bring you good tidings of great joy, which shall be unto all the people." When Philip preached Christ in Samaria there was much joy in the city. See Acts 8:4-12. Paul wrote to the Philippians calling them his joy and his crown. See Phil. 4:1. Jesus spoke of the joy in heaven over one sinner who repents. The Ethiopian went on his way rejoicing after Philip had preached Christ to him and had baptized him into Christ. See Acts 8:39. Paul was eager to have the Corinthians overcome their sinful practices through obedience to the instructions he had written to them that his next visit might be one of rejoicing.

who then is he that maketh me glad.—The Corinthian Christians who were his children in the gospel were a source of real joy to Paul. John held the same view toward those whom he had taught. He said, "Greater joy have I none than this, to hear of my children walking in the truth" (II John 4). If it should become necessary for Paul to reprove the Corinthians when he visited them again, it would mean that the one whose heart had been gladdened by them was causing them sorrow. He did not want this to happen, for he was looking forward to a joyful meeting with the saints of God.

And I wrote this very thing.—Paul had explained in his first epistle that he was not writing to shame them but rather to admonish them as his children. There was still another reason: The delay had given them time to think about their sinful ways and to correct them.

This raises the issue of the number of letters Paul wrote to the

Corinthian church. Opinions vary. Some assume that he had written a "lost epistle" before writing First Corinthians. See I Cor. 5:9. See comment on this issue in *Studies in First Corinthians*. Others assume that the section from II Cor. 6:14 to 7:1 was originally a part of a "harsh letter" which somehow became incorporated into this epistle. Still others assume that chapters ten through twelve of this epistle were originally part of some letter which Paul had written at another time to defend his apostleship.

A careful reading of Second Corinthians, however, reveals a very definite plan into which every part of this letter fits perfectly. Those who object to the sharp contrast between the expression of Paul's affection and his strong warning about being unequally yoked with unbelievers as seen in chapter six, fail to see that such contrasts are to be found frequently in Paul's writings. See Galatians five for the contrast between the works of the flesh and the fruit of the spirit. Second Corinthians is exactly what one would expect it to be in view of the deep concern Paul had for the church at Corinth. He expresses his heartfelt concern for those who were guilty of sin. But he turned to the opposite, expressing great hope and confidence and joy as he thought of the recovery—repentance—of God's people from those things that had disgraced them.

The absence of any manuscript evidence to the contrary leaves us with the conclusion that Paul wrote only two epistles to the Corinthians. The discovery, even at this late date, of another genuine epistle of Paul to the Corinthians would show that he wrote more than two epistles, but, since he always wrote under the direction of the Holy Spirit, we can rest assured that it would in no way affect the doctrinal issues of the two letters which we know he did write to them. While some may find it worthwhile to spend time in these speculative things, it would seem that for the most of us, it would be better to spend our time learning those all important lessons which are so clearly presented in these letters that by the providence of God have come down to us with their solutions for problems which we face in this very day.

of whom I ought to rejoice.—Paul's hope for rejoicing depended on their obedience to the word which he had written to them. More than that, he was confident that they would, for the most part, obey the message of Christ which he as the inspired apostle had written to them. That would mean not only joy for Paul but for all the brethren at Corinth.

I wrote unto you with many tears.—The distress and anguish of the apostle can be seen in his first letter. He was distressed that their sinful divisions were destroying the temple of God. It was with anguish of heart that he wrote to them to deliver to Satan the brother who was guilty of immoral conduct, the like of which was not even found among pagans. His tears stained the manuscript of First Corinthians—those stains were evident to all who had the privilege of seeing it—as he thought about the tragic divisions that made it impossible for them to keep the Lord's Supper. His deep concern for them caused him to show them the more excellent way of love to counteract their strife over spiritual gifts that had been given them for the purpose of building up the body of Christ. He was distressed that some of them were denying the very foundation of the faith by denying the fact of the resurrection.

that ye might know the love.—It was his love for them that caused his concern over the low state of affairs in the church at Corinth. As he considered the height to which they could rise by obeying the Word of Christ, he boldly declared his overflowing love for them.

The One Who Caused Sorrow

Scripture

2:5-11. But if any hath caused sorrow, he hath caused sorrow, not to me, but in part (that I press not too heavily) to you all. 6 Sufficient to such a one is this punishment which was inflicted by the many; 7 so that contrariwise ye should rather forgive him and comfort him, let by any means such a one should be swallowed up with his overmuch sorrow 8 Wherefore I beseech you to confirm your love toward him. 9 For to this end also did I write, that I might know the proof of you, whether ye are obedient in all things. 10 But to whom ye forgive anything, I forgive also: for what I also have forgiven, if I have forgiven anything, for your sakes have I forgiven it in the presence of Christ; 11 that no advantage may be gained over us by Satan: for we are not ignorant of his devices.

Comments

if any hath caused sorrow.—Paul does not name the offending one, but the Corinthians knew who he was, and that is all that really matters. Our concern, of course, is with the restoration of the erring one. Since Paul chose to leave his identity undisclosed, we may assume that the principles involved in the case may be applied to any individual in the church who may become involved in sin.

There has been a great deal of speculation as to the identity of the offending party as well as the one offended. The case of the guilty party mentioned in I Cor. 5:1 corresponds to all the issues mentioned in this chapter. The instruction which Paul gave in that case should be carefully reviewed as we undertake the study of what he says here. These points should be noted: (1) the man was guilty of sinful conduct the like of which would not be tolerated even by pagans; (2) the church had neglected to take action in correcting the matter; (3) Paul, though absent, had written to them instructions to be followed which were as binding as if he had actually been present in their assembly; (4) his decision as the inspired apostle of Christ was that such a one must be delivered to Satan for the destruction of the flesh in order that the spirit might be saved in the day of the Lord Jesus Christ; (5) when the church came together in the name of the Lord Jesus, they were to carry out this order.

While Paul's instruction was intended to bring about repentance on the part of the sinner, the present chapter indicates what should be done by the church when they discovered that the man had repented. The course to pursue in the case of the restoration of an erring brother is indicated in various places of the New Testament, for example, Paul's instruction to the Galations, "Brethren, even if a man be overtaken in any trespass, ye who are spiritual restore such a one in the spirit of gentleness, looking to thyself lest thou also be tempted" (Gal. 6:1). Simon the sorcerer is another example. He had believed Philip's preaching and had been baptized and continued with Philip. Subsequently when he saw that by the laying on of the apostles' hands the power to perform miracles was given, he offered them money that he might buy the power to do that very thing himself. "But Peter said unto him, thy silver perish with thee because thou hast thought to obtain the gift of God with money. Thou hast neither part nor lot in this matter for thy heart is not right before God. Repent therefore of this thy wickedness and pray the Lord if perhaps the thought of thy heart shall be forgiven thee" (Acts 8:20-22). James also has a word to say on the subject: "My brethren if any among you err from the truth and one convert him, let him know that he who converteth a sinner from the error of his way shall have a soul from death and shall cover a multitude of sins" (James 5:19-20). John indicates not only the procedure, but the means of accomplishing this desired end. "If we confess our sins, He is faithful and righteous to forgive our sins and to cleanse us from all unrighteousness" (I John 1:9). Then he proceeds to say: "My little children these things write I unto you that ye may not sin; and if any man sin we have an advocate with the Father, Jesus Christ the righteous; and he is the propitiation for our sins and not for ours only but also for the whole world" (I John 2:1-2). To sum up, the erring brother is to (1) repent, that is to make up his mind that he is not going to continue in the same sin. See Rom. 6:1-12; I John 3:9. If God's Word abides in a man, that is, becomes the ruling principle of his life, he cannot go on sinning for sin is the violation of the Word of God. (2) The erring sinner is called upon to make confession of his sin, not to man, but to God, for He alone can dictate the condition upon which the sin is to be removed. His Word makes it very clear that it is the blood of Christ that cleanses one's conscience from dead works to serve the living God. See Heb. 9:14.

not to me.—Paul had already indicated that the conditions in the church in Corinth had caused him distress and anguish of heart. The individual, however, of whom he now speaks had caused sorrow, not merely to Paul, but, in a measure, to the whole church. He said that the sorrow was caused "in part" that he might not press his charge too heavily on this man, for there were some who assumed the arrogant attitude that it was possible for one in the church to indulge in such conduct with impunity. The embarrassment and shame must have been felt by all with exception of a very few. Responsible leaders in the church who should have led in correcting the sin had become "puffed up" over their positions and had failed to take proper action in that tragic case.

sufficient to such a one is his punishment.—The punishment mentioned in I Cor. 5:3-5 was severe. The guilty one was to be delivered to Satan, that is, left entirely to the company of Satan. Paul explicitly stated that the church members were not to get mixed up with the brother who was guilty of such sinful conduct. They were to do nothing that in any way would give anybody the impression that the church approved what he was doing.

by the many.—It is very plain that there were some diehards in the church at Corinth that did not obey Paul's instruction. Many did obey and their action brought the desired result, that is, the sinner was brought to repentance. The negligent leaders of the church had been reminded of their responsibility and had acted to clear the church of this sinful situation.

forgive him and comfort him.—Jesus told about the case of the unforgiving servant. "And his lord called him unto him and said to him, Thou wicked servant, I forgave thee all that debt because thou besoughtest me. Shouldest not thou also have had mercy on thy fellow-servant even as I had mercy on thee? And his lord was wroth and delivered him to the tormentors until he should pay all that was due. So shall also my heavenly Father do unto you if ye forgive not everyone his brother from your hearts" (Matt. 18:32-35).

Paul wrote to the Ephesians saying, "be ye kind to one another, tenderhearted, forgiving each other, even as God also in Christ forgave you" (Eph. 4:32).

God Himself sets the standard of forgiveness, when He says, "And their sins I will remember no more" (Heb. 8:12).

swallowed up by his overmuch sorrow.—The failure on the part of the church to forgive the erring brother would ruin the whole purpose of the remedial action recommended by the apostle.

confirm your love toward him.—This unfeigned love of the brethren must proceed from the heart. See I Pet. 1:22. Remembering what some of them had been before becoming Christians, it should not have been hard for them to forgive and show love toward the brother who had repented. See I Cor. 6:9-11. For a definition of exactly what Paul means by love see I Cor. 13:4-8. Among other things "love is kind." This is exactly the attitude which he now suggests that they should take toward the man who had repented of his sin.

to this end also did I write.—He had given instructions in I Cor. 5:1-13 for dealing with a situation just like this. His closing word was, "Put away the wicked man from among yourselves." He wrote it putting them to the test whether or not they would obey the instruction given by the inspired apostle of Christ in all things. The man had been punished; he had responded to the corrective measures taken by the church; he was now to be forgiven. As they had joined with Paul in the punishment, so they were now urged to join with him in forgiving the one who had repented.

for your sakes, in the presence of Christ.—What had been done to cause Paul sorrow was inconsequential as compared to the sin against the body of Christ. What he now recommends was for the sake of the church as indicated by this: "that no advantage be gained over us by Satan." Forgiveness and reinstatement into the fellowship of the church was the only way to prevent Satan from recapturing this brother because of his sorrow in being cut off from the saints of God. How often has the failure to forgive on the part of the brethren given the advantage to Satan!

for we are not ignorant of his devices.—Many are the schemes by which Satan seeks to destroy the work of the church of God. Some of them are: (1) an unforgiving attitude which replaces brotherly love; (2) division over party loyalty of men that replaces the unity that should be expressed in loyalty to Christ; (3) worldliness that brings the church into disrepute that should be replaced by a life of purity and consecration to the Lord Jesus Christ; (4) the works of the flesh (Gal. 5:19-21) that should be replaced by the fruit of the spirit (Gal. 5:22-24); (5) the garments of sin which should be replaced by the garments of Christian character and conduct (Col. 3:5-17).

One of the most subtle of all of Satan's schemes is the substitution of human wisdom for the revealed wisdom of God in the Bible. "For seeing that in the wisdom of God, the world through its wisdom knew not God, it was God's good pleasure through the foolishness of preaching to save them that believe" (I Cor. 1:21).

Paul says "we are not ignorant of his devices." The only sure way for us not to fall victims to them is to study God's Word until we know what He says and with deep convictions seek to put it into practice in our daily lives. However alluring Satan's schemes may appear to be, we must be on guard against those systems which borrow the techniques and procedures from the very Word of God but fail to point sinners to the only One who can forgive them and to the only remedy that blots out sin, the blood of Christ.

Troas to Macedonia

Scripture

2:12-13. Now when I came to Troas for the gospel of Christ, and when a door was opened unto me in the Lord, 13 I had no relief for my spirit, because I found not Titus my brother: but taking my leave of them, I went forth into Macedonia.

Comments

when I came to Troas.—The record in Acts shows that Paul was in Troas on two different occasions, neither of which corresponds to the one he mentions here. According to Acts, he first came to Troas on his second missionary journey after having been forbidden by the Holy Spirit to speak the word in Asia. While at Troas he had a vision of the man of Macedonia who said "Come over into Macedonia and help us" (Acts 16:6-10). He stopped at Troas again on his third journey, spending about a week there in fellowship with the church. On the first day of the week they gathered together to break bread, and Paul preached to them. He continued his speech until midnight intending to leave the next day. Eutychus went to sleep and fell from the third story and was taken up dead. After the miracle of bringing him back to life, Paul took leave of the brethren and continued his journey to Jerusalem.

Paul reminded the Corinthians of another brief stopover at Troas not reported in Acts. In his eagerness to learn from Titus about conditions in Corinth, he had gone to Troas hoping to find Titus. Failing to do so, he went on to Macedonia where he did meet him and received his report.

for the gospel of Christ.—In all his travels, Paul's only purpose was to proclaim the gospel of Christ. His mission was to tell the good news concerning Christ.

when a door was opened.—Paul had reminded the Corinthians of his intention to remain at Ephesus until Pentecost for a great and effectual door was open to him for the preaching of the gospel, and there were many adversaries. Again at Troas, he found an opportunity to preach the gospel awaiting him.

I had no relief for my spirit.—Why did the Lord allow Paul to suffer anxiety over the situation at Corinth because of the lack of information? Why didn't He send an angel or give him direct revelation through the Holy Spirit? There are basic reasons why this was not done: Miraculous communication was used (1) to reveal the truth of the gospel (I Cor. 2:6-16), and (2) to give direction to the preachers of this inspired message in the apostolic period. For example, an angel spoke to Philip and told him to leave Samaria and go to the Gaza road where he met the Ethiopian. There the Spirit told him to join the chariot. He preached Jesus to the man who was reading from Isaiah. Paul himself had been under immediate direction of the Holy Spirit as he went through the country before coming to Troas the first time. Following his arrest in Jerusalem, while in prison, the Lord told him that as he had borne witness for Him in Jerusalem so he must also bear witness in Rome. See Acts 23:11. The Holy Spirit, of course, had directed him as he wrote to the Corinthians giving them instruction about their problems. But it was their responsibility to act upon that information and correct their problems. The principle is clear: Miraculous guidance and information was given in connection with the preaching of the gospel in the absence of the written Word. But communication between the apostle and established congregations followed this procedure: When the apostles directed their letters to the churches, the letters were written by the inspiration of the Holy Spirit. Information regarding the reception of the message depended on the presence of the apostle himself or someone such as Titus, in this case, or Timothy, on another occasion, to report to the apostle on the situation in the church. One of the burdens which Paul bore throughout his entire ministry was "anxiety for all the churches" (11:28).

I found not Titus, my brother.—Timothy probably figured more prominently in the ministry of Paul than Titus. But Paul's affection for Timothy seems also to have been shared by Titus, whom he calls "my true child after a common faith" (Titus 1:4). Paul had trusted him with a very important mission in Crete, where he was to set things in order and appoint elders in every city. See Titus 1:5.

Titus is mentioned in Paul's last letter to Timothy as having been associated with him in his imprisonment in Rome (II Tim. 4:10). Perhaps the greatest tribute paid to Titus is the mission on which he was sent to Corinth to learn of their reception of Paul's instruction regarding their many problems and to return with that news. This he ultimately did and gladdened Paul's heart with it. An important tribute is paid to him in connection with his role in gathering funds for the sufferers in Jerusalem. Of him Paul wrote "Whether any inquire about Titus, he is my partner and my fellow worker to youward" (II Cor. 8:23). See also Paul's tribute of the work of Titus in II Cor. 7:5-16. Titus figured in the solution of an important issue among the Galatian churches. Some had insisted that Gentile Christians be required to keep the Jewish custom of circumcision. Paul laid the matter before the brethren in Jerusalem but not even Titus who was a Greek was compelled to be circumcised. Gentiles did not have to become Jews in order to be Christians. The gospel was open to Jew or Gentile on the basis of faith expressed in obedience to the commands of the Lord Jesus Christ. See Gal. 2: 1-10.

I went forth into Macedonia.—Since there was an open door of opportunity to preach the gospel at Troas, the question comes: Why did Paul leave Troas and go into Macedonia to find Titus in order to learn what had happened in Corinth? There is no indication that the Lord had instructed him to do so. However, Paul did everything taking into consideration this principle: "If the Lord permit." This decision evidently had to be made on the basis of his own consecrated

Christian thinking with purpose in mind to serve the Lord in caring for "all the churches." His decision to leave Troas and go into Macedonia would easily lead the Corinthians to understand his deep concern and Christian love for them. To save that church, it seems, was the more important of the two issues that confronted him. This in no way suggests that Paul left Troas without doing something about the promotion of the cause of Christ in that city. That the opportunity was not ignored is indicated by the fact that when he came back to Troas on his third journey he met with the brethren, spending a week in their fellowship and preaching the Word.

Triumph In Christ

Scripture

2:14-17.   But thanks be unto God, who always leadeth us in triumph in Christ, and maketh manifest through us the savor of his knowledge in every place. 15 For we are a sweet savor of Christ unto God, in them that are saved, and in them that perish; 16 to the one a savor from death unto death; to the other a savor from life unto life. And who is sufficient for these things? 17 For we are not as the many, corrupting the word of God: but as of sincerity, but as of God, in the sight of God, speak we in Christ.

Comments

But thanks be unto God.—Paul began this letter with an expression of praise to God for His mercy and comfort which had been shown him in all his afflictions. Having reminded his readers that he had gone into Macedonia, he turned to the expression of thanks to God for his triumphant ministry in Christ. It is not until 7:5 that he tells about finding Titus in Macedonia and learning what had happened in Corinth. Some speak of this as a long digression. The digression, however, if there is one, is the brief reference to the fact that he had not found Titus, and that when he did meet him he had learned the truth about the Corinthians' situation.

leadeth us in triumph in Christ.—God who comforted him in Asia led him in triumph in Christ in Macedonia and everywhere he went in his ministry. The figure which Paul uses to describe this fact is that of the victorious general leading his army in triumphal procession before the people. Some assume that Paul is thinking of himself as a captive of Christ having been taken captive on the Damascus road. It is true that Paul refers to himself as the "prisoner of the Lord," but in a different context. See Eph. 4:1. Captives in the triumphal Roman march were being displayed to the people just before being put to death. The triumph which Paul referred to was the victory God gave him in the gospel as an apostle of Christ wherever he went—Asia, Troas, Macedonia, and Corinth. Regardless of his personal suffering, Paul thought only of victory for the gospel.

the savor of his knowledge in every place.—The gospel message was one of triumph over Satan. It told of God's power to save the believer (Rom. 1:16). It told of the whole armor of God that enabled the Christian to stand against the wiles of the devil. With the shield of faith they were able to quench all the fiery darts of the evil one. See Eph. 6:10-18. The knowledge about God, as revealed in Christ and preached by His apostles, was like the sweet smelling fragrance of incense offered with the sacrifices of the worshippers. This fragrance accompanied those marching with the triumphant general and his soldiers.

for we are a sweet savor of Christ.—The messengers as well as the message were acceptable in the sight of God. Their lives and their work were like the sweet smelling fragrance that accompanied the triumphal march.

in them that are saved and in them that perish.—The gospel message is one of salvation for those who accept it, but one of destruction, for those who reject it. Jesus said to the apostles, "Go ye into all the world and preach the gospel to the whole creation. He that believeth and is baptized shall be saved; but he that disbelieveth shall be condemned" (Mark 16:15-16).

a savor from death unto death.—This explains the fact that the gospel message is one of salvation to the believer and destruction to the one who rejects it. The expressions, "from death unto death" and "from life unto life" have been understood in various ways. It is quite possible that we do not have the exact meaning of these intensified forms. There can be no doubt about the fact that they refer to destruction on one hand and salvation on the other. "Death unto death" may suggest endless death, and "life unto life" eternal life. This lesson is clearly taught by Our Lord in these words, "and these shall go away into eternal punishment but the righteous into eternal life" (Matt. 25:46). The gospel deals with the death of Christ which also indicates the death—that is, eternal separation from God —of the one who remains in sin. It also deals with the life of Him who arose from the dead, and depicts the eternal life of the one who

48

dies to sin with Him and is buried with Him through baptism into death that he might arise to walk with Him in the new life.

and who is sufficient for these things?—Since the gospel deals with eternal life and eternal death, the conscientious apostle raises the question about the one who is adequate for the task of preaching this gospel. He leaves no doubt in the minds of the readers, for he immediately answers, "We are not as the many who corrupt the word." In this he clearly implies that the apostles of Christ were adequately equipped to preach this gospel message. It also suggests that those who were claiming to be apostles but actually were false apostles were not qualified. This was not idle boasting on the part of Paul for he had already written "I am the least of the apostles that am not meet to be called an apostle because I persecuted the church of God. But by the grace of God I am what I am and His grace which was bestowed upon me was not found vain; but I labored more abundantly than they all. Yet not I, but the grace of God which was with me" (I Cor. 15:9-10).

corrupting the word of God.—The footnote in the American Standard Version reads, "making merchandise of the word of God." The word actually refers to the corrupt practice of some merchants who diluted their wares or in some manner falsely displayed them. Paul says that some were handling the Word of God as if they were dishonest peddlers.

but as of sincerity, but as of God.—Paul who was an apostle through the will of God declares his absolute sincerity in dealing with this all important task of preaching the gospel of Christ. This was not arrogant boasting for he was speaking in Christ.

Summary

Paul was waiting to find out about the response of the Corinthians to his first letter before visiting them again. He had given them specific directions in it about many things, among them what to do with the man who had been living with his father's wife. A deferred visit did not mean cancellation. He would come, as he had said in his first letter, even if it meant using a rod of chastisement. But he had decided to delay the coming so that he might not cause them sorrow. They had gladdened his heart by their response to the gospel which he preached to them. He wanted to give them time to correct any disorder in their midst so that he might not cause them sorrow, for it would be a painful thing for him to be forced to punish them.

Paul was confident that they would be looking forward to his next visit with joy just as he was. It was true that he had written them out of affliction and anguish of heart. Perhaps the very manuscript was stained with his tears. But this was not intended to cause them grief. As their father in the gospel, Paul wanted them to know about his genuine love for them.

The brother who had done wrong had not caused sorrow to Paul alone, but, in part, to all of them. They had acted upon his instruction in the first letter—he had learned this from Titus—and had "delivered him to Satan." The remedy, though severe, was effective. The man had repented. The next move was up to them: they were to forgive him! Paul had, just as he had joined in administering the punishment to the one who had sinned. Forgiveness was necessary to defeat Satan's scheme to keep the brother in his clutches forever. An unforgiving attitude on their part would serve his purpose just as well as the temptation that had led the man to sin in the first place. Paul was not ignorant of Satan's schemes, nor did he want the brethren at Corinth to be.

Paul had gone to Troas, hoping to learn from Titus what the church had done about correcting their many sins. He was writing this second letter, of course, after he had met Titus in Macedonia, but he wanted the brethren to know of his deep concern over the situation at Corinth. That is why, even though he had a wonderful opportunity to further the gospel in Troas, he went to Macedonia. They could not fail to see his great anxiety over them that resulted from his sincere love for them.

The Corinthians were aware of the meeting with Titus in Macedonia, although Paul did not actually mention it until after he had written a somewhat lengthy explanation of the triumphant ministry in which the Lord had led him everywhere. No personal grief, no joy that ever came to him stirred him more deeply than the awareness that it was God who always led him in triumph in Christ. His thanksgiving knew no limits as he thought of the privilege that had been given to him to be a messenger of the gospel that had been accepted everywhere he had preached it.

The ministry of Paul was like a sweet smelling fragrance of Christ unto God. The message was also acceptable to God as it brought salvation to those who believed, even though some chose to perish because of disobedience. God's love was so great that He gave His Son to die for them that they might live through Him.

Who was adequate for the task of carrying such a message? Unflinchingly, Paul indicated, "We are." He gave two reasons for his response to the staggering task of preaching the gospel that brought salvation to those who obeyed it and destruction to those that rejected it. He was not guilty of diluting the message of God. With complete sincerity, knowing that God was watching every move he made, he was preaching the message of Christ.

Questions

1. How many times did Paul visit Corinth?
2. Why had he postponed his coming to see them?
3. How had he caused them sorrow?
4. How had they gladdened his heart?
5. What was his purpose in writing to them as indicated by I Cor. 4:14?
6. What are some of the ways in which the gospel message brings joy?
7. How many letters did Paul write to the Corinthians?
8. Instead of causing him tears, what did Paul have a right to expect from the brethren at Corinth?
9. What was it that had caused him such anguish of heart?
10. What was Paul's purpose in telling them about his sorrow?
11. Why didn't Paul name the one who had caused the sorrow?
12. How does the case of the one mentioned in the fifth chapter of First Corinthians fit this situation?
13. What do the Scriptures say about the responsibility of Christians toward an erring brother?
14. What do they say that the erring one should do?
15. To whom besides Paul had this one caused sorrow?
16. Was the church unanimous in believing that this one had caused them sorrow?
17. How had the majority reacted to the direction which Paul had given for punishing the guilty one?
18. What was that punishment? What was its purpose?
19. Since the guilty person had repented, what was the church to do?
20. What did Jesus say about those who fail to forgive?
21. What did Paul say might happen to him if the church failed to forgive?
22. How were they to show their love for the one who had repented?

23. What advantage would Satan gain through an unforgiving attitude on their part?
24. Why did Paul say, "We are not ignorant of his devices"?
25. What are some of the ways in which Satan destroys the work of the church of God?
26. Why did Paul go to Troas?
27. What opportunity for the gospel did he find there?
28. What indication is there that he did not overlook this, even though he left Troas and went to Macedonia to find Titus?
29. What did his going on to Macedonia reveal to the Corinthians about Paul's attitude toward them?
30. Why didn't Paul receive direct communication from God about the issues in Corinth instead of his having to wait until Titus reported to him?
31. What limit did God put on direct communication to the messengers of the gospel?
32. What did Paul think of Titus?
33. Why did Paul break off the description of his anxiety without saying whether or not he had met Titus in Macedonia?
34. What did he thank God for?
35. How could every effort of the apostle, even when the gospel was rejected by some, be thought of as triumph in Christ?
36. With what familiar custom did Paul describe his triumphant ministry for Christ?
37. To what did he liken the knowledge about Christ?
38. How did he indicate that Christ's messengers were also acceptable to God?
39. With what two issues does the gospel message deal?
40. What did Paul mean when he asked, "Who is sufficient for these things"?
41. What made him adequate for the task of preaching the gospel?
42. What may this have suggested as to the false apostles who were troubling the Corinthians?
43. What figure did Paul have in mind when he spoke of those who were corrupting the Word?
44. By contrast, what did Paul say of his own sincerity?

For Discussion

1. What are some of the subtle ways in which Satan may be destroying the effectiveness of the church today?
2. What can the church do today to avoid misrepresenting the message of the gospel?

CHAPTER THREE

Analysis

A. Paul answered the anticipated charge of self-commendation (1-11).
   1. He asked two questions (1).
      a) Are we beginning again to commend ourselves?
      b) Do we, as do some, need letters of commendation to you or from you?
   2. He gave two answers (2-11).
      a) As seen in his relation to the Corinthians (2-3).
         (1) They are his epistle of commendation (2).
             (a) This epistle is written in his heart.
             (b) It is known and read of all men.
         (2) They are also an epistle of Christ (3).
             (a) It is evident that they are an epistle of Christ.
             (b) The service of writing was done by Paul.
             (c) This involves a two-fold contrast.
                 i) It was written not with ink but with the Spirit of the living God.
                 ii) It was not in tables of stone but in tables that are hearts of flesh.
      b) As seen in his glorious ministry under the New Covenant in contrast to the glory of Moses' ministry under the Old Covenant (4-11).
         (1) The source of his sufficiency under the New Covenant is God (4-6).
             (a) His confidence toward God was in Christ.
             (b) He explained that in himself he was not adequate for the task (5a).
             (c) His fitness was from God who made him a minister of the New Covenant (5b-6a).
             (d) Characteristics of the New Covenant (6b).
                 i) Not of letter but of spirit.
                 ii) The letter kills; the spirit gives life.
         (2) The contrast between the glory of the Old and New Covenants justifies his glorious ministry (7-11).
             (a) Contrasted as a ministry of death and a ministry of spirit (7-8).
                 i) The ministry of death (Old Covenant)

written on stones was with glory so that Israel could not look upon the face of Moses.

    ii) The ministry of the spirit (New Covenant) is with glory, is it not?

  (b) Contrasted as a ministry of condemnation and of righteousness (9-10).

    i) The glory of the ministry of righteousness (the New Covenant) exceeds that of condemnation (Old Covenant).

    ii) The glory of condemnation (Old Covenant) is as nothing compared to the surpassing glory of the ministry of the New Covenant.

  (c) Conclusion from the contrast: If that which passes away (Old Covenant) was with glory, much more that which remains (New Covenant) is with glory.

B. Paul explained the reason for his great boldness of speech (12-18).

  1. As seen in the contrast between him and Moses (12-13).

    a) His hope in the abiding glory of the New Covenant was the basis of his great boldness of a speech (12).

    b) Moses, on the other hand, put a veil over his face to prevent Israel from seeing the end of the fading glory on his face (13).

  2. As seen in the contrast between those who were reading the Old Covenant and those who turned to the Lord (14-15).

    a) Their minds were hardened at the reading of the Old Covenant because they were unaware that the veil was taken away in Christ (14).

    b) Even in Paul's day wherever Moses was read the veil lay on their hearts (15).

  3. As seen in the result of turning to the Lord (16-18).

    a) The veil is taken away.

    b) The Lord is (identified with) the spirit-covenant (See verses 6 and 8 ASV).

    c) Where the spirit-covenant of the Lord is, there is liberty.

    d) Transformation results from looking into the glory of the Lord (as seen in the spirit-covenant).

      (1) This is to be done with unveiled face as we look

into the mirror—the New Covenant or spirit-covenant—where we see the glory of the Lord.

(2) The transformation is into the same image from glory to glory—from the Lord of the spirit-covenant.

Self-commendation

Scripture

3:1. Are we beginning again to commend ourselves? or need we, as do some, epistles of commendation to you or from you?

Comments

Are we beginning again to commend ourselves.—Paul had just written of the glorious triumph of the messengers of Christ and also of the message itself which had to do with eternal life and eternal death. He had indicated that he was adequate for this ministry. In his relationship to Christ as an inspired apostle, he spoke the Word of God with all sincerity. He did not make merchandise of it as some had done. The whole chapter is an explanation of his fitness for the task.

As he often does in his writings, Paul anticipated possible charges of self-commendation. He was well aware of the arrogance of some people at Corinth. See I Cor. 4:18. He knew of those who were bringing false charges against him. See II Cor. 10:10. The message of the Word of God was of such importance to the apostle Paul that he wanted to make sure that the Corinthians would not make the mistake of assuming that what he was writing was idle boasting about his own powers and abilities.

epistles of commendation.—There is certainly a place for letters of commendation. Paul had written many words of commendation about his fellow-workers, Timothy and Titus. In writing to the Philippians about Timothy, he had said, "for I have no man likeminded who will care truly for your state for they all seek their own and not the things of Jesus Christ" (Phil. 2:20-21). The closing words of First Corinthians contain words of commendation about some of the brethren who were also well known to the Corinthians. Paul wrote to the Romans commending Phoebe whom he calls, "our sister who is a servant of the church that is in Cenchrea." He urged them to treat her in a manner befitting the saints and to assist her in whatever matter she might have need" (Rom. 16:1-2). This faithful saint had been a helper of many including the apostle Paul. In the closing part of that epistle Paul mentioned a number of the brethren whom he commended in various ways because of their service in the Lord. His commendation of Luke, the beloved physician, is found in Col. 4:14. Mark, for some reason, had not completed the first missionary journey with Paul and Barnabas. This became a matter of sharp contention between them when they started on their second journey. Paul refused to take Mark with him. Long afterwards, he wrote to Timothy, saying, "Take Mark and bring him with thee for he is useful to me for ministering" (II Tim. 4:11).

to you from you?—Paul may have had in mind the many who were corrupting the Word of God and who may have brought epistles of commendation of themselves so that they might become established among the Corinthians. Paul knew about those who had caused so much trouble among the Galatian churches. They had come from James, but there is no good reason to assume that he had approved what they were doing. See Gal. 2:12. In the light of James' comments as reported in Acts 15 and Paul's investigation as given in Galatians two, one might readily assume that their claims were false.

Paul needed no letter of commendation to the church at Corinth, for he performed all the signs of an apostle in their midst. See II Cor. 12:12. Neither did Paul need a letter of commendation from them. He had written to them in First Corinthians saying, "If to others I am not an apostle, yet at least I am to you for the seal of mine apostleship are ye in the Lord" (I Cor. 9:2). This point is elaborated upon in the two-fold answer that follows.

Our Epistle

Scripture

3:2-3. Ye are our epistle, written in our hearts, known and read of all men; 3 being made manifest that ye are an epistle of Christ, ministered by us, written not with ink, but with the Spirit of the living God; not in tables of stone but in table that are hearts of flesh.

Comments

our epistle.—The reason he needed no letter from them is seen in the fact that they actually were such a letter. They were his beloved children in the gospel. See I Cor. 4:14-15. They had become Christians as a result of obedience to the gospel which Paul preached to them. Despite the fact that conditions at Corinth were far from what they should have been Paul was perfectly willing to risk his reputation as an apostle of Christ upon the testimony of the Christian character and conduct of those who were faithful to the Lord.

written in our hearts.—This letter was written in his mind, that is, his understanding and his affections. He knew about the establishment of the church for he was the first one to preach the gospel there, and he had kept in touch with them through the household of Chloe and through the letters which others had written asking questions about their own problems. Paul had just laid bare his own heart as he told them about his anguish and tears and sorrow over those who had failed to come up to the proper standard of Christian character and conduct. He also revealed his anticipated joy which all were to share when he came to them again. The Corinthians knew that he loved them and cared for them as a father for his beloved children.

known and read of all men.—While this epistle was written in the apostle's heart, he says that all men knew it and read it. This undoubtedly means that all who came in contact with the church in Corinth knew of their relationship to Christ. They were also aware of the fact that the apostle Paul had brought the gospel to them. Corinth was a strategic point in which to establish the church, for men from the known world came in and out of that city carrying on their commerce. As they did so they learned about the church of God which was at Corinth.

an epistle of Christ.—As men came to know the life of the church at Corinth, despite all the sordid things that were known about some of them, it became evident that they were an epistle of Christ. A comparison of what they were before and after conversion is given in I Cor. 6:9-11. To see such people after their sins had been washed away by the blood of the Lamb, and to hear them boldly tell of their forgiveness in the name of the Lord Jesus Christ must have made a profound impression on the minds of all who came in contact with them.

ministered by us.—Paul had likened his ministry among them to one who planted and that of Apollos to one who watered. He had served as the masterbuilder to lay the foundation, but another had built upon it. Now he says, "Ye are an epistle which Christ wrote." Paul was the servant of Christ through whom the writing had been

57

done. But this was said in humility, not self-commendation, for it was the grace of God that had made it possible for him to serve in this capacity. See I Cor. 15:10.

written not with ink but with the Spirit of the living God.—Paul now contrasts the letter which Christ had written—the New Covenant—with the Old Covenant. The epistle of Christ had not been written with ink, for it was not just a piece of parchment with words written upon it. It was written with the Spirit of the living God through the inspired apostle. It was the message of life unto life and death unto death. It could be read by all those who saw the changed character and conduct of the church at Corinth. In writing to the Corinthians, Paul had made it clear that his message had been the testimony of God about Jesus Christ and Him crucified. He had not spoken the wisdom of men, but the wisdom that had been revealed to him by the Holy Spirit. See I Cor. 2:1-2, 10-13.

not in tables of stone, but in tables that are hearts of flesh.—"Tables of stone" suggest the Old Covenant, that is, the Ten Commandments. See Ex. 34:28-29; Deut. 4:13. "Hearts of flesh" suggest the New Covenant. See Jer. 31:31-34 as quoted in Heb. 8:8-13. The essential difference in the two is indicated by the fact that the New Covenant became a living reality in the lives and hearts of those who became obedient to the gospel of Christ. This is the reason that the Corinthians were both an epistle of commendation of the apostle Paul and an epistle which Christ had written through the ministry of His inspired apostle.

Paul's Glorious Ministry Under the New Covenant

Scripture

3:4-11. And such confidence have we through Christ to God-ward: not that we are sufficient of ourselves, to account anything as from ourselves; but our sufficiency is from God; 6 who also made us sufficient as ministers of a new covenant; not of the letter, but of the spirit: for the letter killeth, but the spirit giveth life. 7 But if the ministration of death, written, and engraven on stones, came with glory, so that the children of Israel could not look stedfastly upon the face of Moses for the glory of his face; which glory was passing away: 8 how shall not rather the ministration of the spirit be with glory? 9 For if the ministration of condemnation hath glory, much rather doth the ministration of righteousness exceed in glory. 10 For verily that which hath been made glorious hath not been made glori-

ous in this respect, by reason of the glory that surpasseth. 11 For if
that which passeth away was with glory, much more that which remaineth is in glory.

Comments

And such confidence have we.—Despite the hardships which Paul
faced at Corinth, his ministry is characterized by confidence and
triumph. His confidence was through Christ, for he knew what
Christ had done for him. He knew of His resurrection which demonstrated that He had conquered Satan. He had surrendered to the risen
Christ on the Damascus road. He had committed himself wholeheartedly to the service of the Lord. He remembered that day when
Ananias told him to get himself baptized that his sins might be
washed away, because he had called upon the name of the Lord.
He had been summoned as an apostle of God. He was convinced
that the way of victory was through Jesus Christ. He was never
ashamed of Him nor of His gospel, for he was confident that it was
the power of God to save the believer, whether Jew or Greek.

our sufficiency is from God.—That is, it is God who made him adequate for the task of preaching the Word that dealt with eternal
life and eternal death. God had revealed the message through the
Holy Spirit to the apostles and thus equipped them for the glorious
ministry under the New Covenant. No one without that divinely
revealed message could possibly undertake such a ministry.

How unfortunate that many who undertake the work of the ministry today seem called upon to substitute the wisdom of man for this
divinely revealed message of God. Paul's confidence in this message
is expressed in his word to Timothy, "Every scripture inspired of
God is also profitable for teaching, for reproof, for correction, for
instruction which is in righteousness that the man of God may be
complete, furnished completely unto every good work" (II Tim.
3:16-17). He did not hesitate to urge Timothy to preach the Word;
to be urgent in season, out of season; to reprove, rebuke, exhort
with all longsuffering and teaching. See II Tim. 4:2. The same divine
Word which Paul preached will equip the consecrated minister of
today who has the courage to preach this message of eternal life and
everlasting death.

ministers of the new covenant.—A covenant is an agreement. When
that covenant is between God and man, God Himself dictates all the
conditions of the covenant as well as the blessings involved in it.
Man agrees to the terms of the covenant in order to enjoy its blessings.

In the case of the Old Covenant which was given at Mt. Sinai, God revealed the commandments to Moses. The people entered into the covenant relationship when they said all that the Lord has spoken, we will do. See Ex. 19:8. Subsequently, all who were born into the family of the Jews were parties to that Old Covenant. Under the New Covenant only those who are born of the water and of the Spirit are parties to the New Covenant—a spiritual birth in contrast to a physical birth.

The New Covenant is the gospel of Christ that promises remission of sins and eternal life to the believer whose faith is expressed through obedience to the commandments of Christ. Every individual who comes into this New Covenant relationship with Christ through the new birth, publically and in the sight of God as he makes the good confession, promises to be obedient to its terms and pledges his allegience to Christ. To say that I believe that Jesus is the Christ the Son of the Living God is to endorse all that is involved in ones total relationship to God through Jesus Christ. As Christ, He is our Prophet. Through His prophetic office the message of the Bible was revealed from heaven. See Heb. 1:1-2. As Priest He shed blood for the remission of sins. Significantly, in instituting the Lord's Supper, He blessed the cup and said, "This is my blood of the new covenant poured out for the many unto the remission of sins." As King, He is seated at the right hand of the throne of God in fulfillment of the promise of God made to David. See Acts 2:25-36. He exercises His authority as well as His watchcare over His people through the inspired Word spoken through the apostles. All of those who pledge themselves to keep the terms of the New Covenant must let the Word of Christ dwell in them richly in all wisdom and teaching. See Col. 3:16.

This New Covenant was given in promise to Abraham in the Scripture which says, "In thee shall all the nations be blessed." See Gal. 3:8. It was given to Abraham some four hundred and thirty years before the covenant at Sinai, but was not annulled by that covenant. See Gal. 3:16-17. It came to its fulness with the preaching of the gospel on the Day of Pentecost. All those who accept its terms become sons of God through faith in Jesus Christ. "for as many as are baptized into Christ have put on Christ" (Gal. 3:26-27). Furthermore, "if you are Christ's, then are you Abraham's offspring and heirs according to the promise" (Gal. 3:29).

God was a party to two covenants at the same time, but they were not in conflict because they served different purposes. One was with Abraham and Christ; the other, the Ten Commandments, was with Israel. It was added, Paul says, because of transgression. There was a time limit on it, for it was to last until the promised seed of Abraham should come—that is, Christ. It served in the capacity of a trusted slave who watched over a child until his majority, and as such held sin in check until Christ came. But since it was a law that could not make alive one who had died in sin, it was necessary that the promise to Abraham be fulfilled in Christ and be put into effect through the preaching of the apostles. On the Day of Pentecost, the apostles told those who were guilty of crucifying the Son of God to repent and be baptized for the remission of their sins, for the promise—that is, the promise God made to Abraham—was to them and to their children and all that were far off, as many as the Lord God should call unto Himself. See Gal. 3:19-22; Acts 2:38-39.

not of letter but of spirit.—This expression is found three times in Paul's writings: once in this epistle and twice in Romans. The first instance in Romans is found in 2:29. There he uses "letter" as a symbol of outward conformity to the Law that had been written on the tables of stone. On the other hand, he uses "spirit" as a symbol of the inward life of the individual, Jew or Gentile, who actually carried out the provisions of the Law. Moses had written that the one who actually carried out the righteousness which is of the Law lived thereby. See Romans 10:5. Paul had said that not the hearers of the Law but the doers of the Law shall be justified. See Rom. 2:13. Such persons showed the works of the Law written on their hearts, that is, they understood what was right in God's sight and willingly complied with it. This was not, as some have contended, an impossible thing. Moses wrote, "This commandment which I command you this day is not too hard for you, neither is it far off. It is not in heaven that you should say, 'Who will go up for us to heaven that we may hear it and do it?' Neither is it beyond the sea that you should say, 'Who will go over the sea for us and bring it to us that we may hear it and do it?' But the word is very near to you, it is in your mouth and in your heart so that you can do it" (Deut. 30:11-14). John says, "This is the love of God that we keep this commandment: and his commandments are not grievous" (I John 5:3).

The second instance in Romans is found in 7:6. The same basic idea is seen in this context. Newness of spirit refers to the new life in Christ which was characterized by intelligent, willing, loving obedience to Him. Oldness of letter, on the other hand, referred to the life under the jurisdiction of the Law. Because of violation of the Law, life was characterized by sinful passions that brought forth fruit unto death. In II Cor. 3:6, Paul uses "letter" as a symbol of the Old Covenant just as he had done in Romans, and "spirit" as a symbol of the life under the New Covenant. Keeping in mind Paul's use of these terms will aid in interpreting 3:17-18.

Two further observations need to be made: (1) "letter" is not contrasted with the Holy Spirit. Verse three plainly indicates that the epistle of Christ had been written with the Holy Spirit, but in verse six "spirit" (spelled with a small "s") is used as a symbol of the New Covenant; (2) There is no justification whatever for the assumption that letter and spirit refer to a literal interpretation of the Word of God as opposed to a so-called "spiritual" interpretation. All of God's Word is "spirit and life" (John 6:63).

The Word is directed to intelligence of man and it appeals to his heart. It shows the way to forgiveness and purity in Christ. It is life, for obedience to it brings the gift of life eternal.

for the letter killeth but the spirit giveth life.—This unfortunately has led some to assume that an attempt to actually obey God's Word results in death. How can such a view be harmonized with what James plainly says? "Wherefore putting away all filthiness and overflowing of wickedness receive with meekness the implanted word which is able to save your souls. But be ye doers of the word and not hearers only deluding your own selves" (James 1:21-22). Why then did Paul say that the "letter killeth"? Remembering that letter stands as a symbol of the Old Covenant, we may read "the Old Covenant killeth." The answer to the problem is clearly indicated in the Scriptures for Hebrews says that the Old Covenant gave place to the New because God found fault with those under the Old Covenant. He found fault with them because they continued not in His covenant. See Heb. 8:7. Paul shows that by the works of the Law no human being is pardoned in God's sight. See Rom. 3:20. By works of the Law he has in mind those ceremonies such as the animal sacrifices which only served to remind the one who had broken God's law that ultimately Christ would come providing the sacrifice that would actually blot out sin. See Rom. 3:25. He further states that if there had been a law given which would make alive then righteousness (pardon) would have been of the law. See Gal. 3:21. He also states that the law is not a matter of faith but "he that doeth them shall live in them" (Gal. 3:12). "Spirit" which stands for the New

Covenant gives life. Under this covenant the blood of Christ, who through the eternal Spirit offered Himself without blemish to God, actually cleanses the conscience from dead works to serve the living God. See Heb. 9:14. The testimony of the Holy Spirit is given in Jer. 31:31-34 and in Heb. 10:16 in these words: "This is the covenant that I will make with them after those days, saith the Lord. I will put my laws on their hearts and upon their minds also will I write them and their sins and their iniquities I will remember no more." As sin reigned in death, even so grace reigns through righteousness unto eternal through Jesus Christ our Lord" (Rom. 5:21).

The Glory of the Old and New Covenants

Scripture

3:7-11. But if the ministration of death, written, and engraven on stones, came with glory, so that the children of Israel could not look stedfastly upon the face of Moses for the glory of his face; which glory was passing away: 8 how shall not rather the ministration of the spirit be with glory? 9 For if the ministration of condemnation hath glory, much rather doth the ministration of righteousness exceed in glory. 10 For verily that which hath been made glorious hath not been made glorious in this respect, by reason of the glory that surpasseth. 11 For if that which passeth away was with glory, much more that which remaineth is in glory.

Comments

But if the ministration of death.—Paul had just spoken of the Old Covenant under the figure of the letter that kills. Now for the same reasons he speaks of it as a ministry that produced death. Nevertheless, he declares that the ministry that produced death—a letter which was engraved on stones—came with glory. Paul was not one to criticize the Law of God. Although he had violated it and as a result had died, he insisted that the law was holy and the commandment was holy and righteous and good. See Rom. 7:9-12. He is now about to contrast the glory of the Old Covenant with the glory of the New that brought him life in Christ. When Moses came down from the mountain after he had talked with God his face shone with a brilliance that made it impossible for the children of Israel to look intently at it. They were aware of the fact that Moses had been in the presence of God and that the word he was speaking was from God. When he finished speaking to them, he put a veil on his face. When he went again to speak to the Lord he took the veil off and came back to deliver the message to the people of Israel and then put the veil on his face again. See Ex. 34:29-35.

which glory was passing away.—The veil kept the people from seeing that the shining brilliance on the face of Moses was gradually fading away. It kept them from assuming that what he had said as the Word of God was only a temporary thing. But see verse fifteen for the distorted view that some continued to hold regarding this matter.

the ministration of the spirit.—Some assume that this is a reference to the ministry of the Holy Spirit and therefore capitalize the word. Let it again be emphasized that Paul has already indicated that the New Covenant came into existence through the work of the Holy Spirit as He spoke through the inspired apostle. The word "spirit" in this verse however is to be taken, as it is in verse six, as a symbol of the New Covenant. As such it is contrasted with the ministry of death which is a symbol of the Old Covenant. The apostles' question was, "If the ministry of the Old Covenant, which was a ministry that brought death, came with glory as indicated by the shining face of Moses, how shall not also the ministry of the spirit-covenant (New Covenant) which brings eternal life be with glory?" The verses that follow indicate the surpassing glory of this spirit-covenant.

for if the ministration of condemnation.—The New Covenant which was symbolized by "spirit" gave life and was called a ministry of righteousness. Paul explained this righteousness as something apart from the Law, as a righteousness of God to which the Law and Prophets had borne witness. It was the righteousness of God through faith in Jesus Christ for all those who believe. It provided pardon from sin for all who fall short of the glory of God—that is, of His approval. That pardon is freely given because of God's grace through the redemption that is in Jesus Christ. He is the One who through His blood blots out sins of those who believe in Him and expresses that belief in obedience to His commands. See Romans 3:21-26; Acts 2:38; 22:16. Righteousness is used in a three-fold way in Paul's writings. First, referring to the fact that God is right or just in word and deed. Second, it refers to the standard of conduct which God requires of His people. Third, it is the status of one whose sins have been pardoned by the grace of God through faith in Christ. Is there any wonder that Paul insists that the glory of this ministry of righteousness exceeds the glory of the ministration that brought death? The glory of the New Covenant so outshines the glory of the Old as to cause it to appear as if it had not been at all.

For that which passeth away.—Paul explained in Galatians that the Law was to serve until Christ. But since faith in Christ has come, we are no longer under the Law. See Gal. 3:23-25. He also explained that Christ was born under the Law that He might redeem those who were under the Law. See Gal. 4:4-5. In the allegory of Abraham's two sons he again clearly points out that the possession of eternal life was not possible under the Old Covenant, for it belongs to those who enjoy the freedom under the New Covenant. Hager, the mother of Ishmael, represented the Old Covenant. She and her son were cast out—did not inherit the blessing of Abraham. Sarah and Isaac represent those who are under the New Covenant. Paul adds, "Now we brethren, as Isaac was, are the children of promise." He cited the Scripture that said, "Cast out the handmaiden and her son, for the son of the handmaid shall not inherit with the son of the free woman." Christians are children of the free woman—that is, the New Covenant—and are heirs of the promise of eternal life through Christ. See Gal. 4:21-31. This position is reinforced by the writer of Hebrews for he says, "In that he said a new covenant, he hath made the first old, but that which is becoming old and waxeth aged is nigh unto vanishing away" (Heb. 8:13).

It should be noted that verse eleven refers to the Old Covenant which was passing away. This had been symbolized by the fact that the glory that shone from Moses' face was also passing away. See verse 7.

that which remaineth is in glory—The New Covenant is the abiding covenant. Under it the perfect sacrifice has been made, and no further sacrifice is necessary since the blood of Christ actually cleanses the conscience of the worshipper. See Heb. 10:1-18. The glory of this covenant remains. Its glory is to be found in the fact that it came from God through Jesus Christ as He revealed it by the Holy Spirit through the inspired apostles. See John 16:13-14.

Paul's Great Boldness of Speech

Scripture

3:12-13. Having therefore such a hope, we use great boldness of speech, 13 and are not as Moses, who put a veil upon his face, that the children of Israel should not look stedfastly on the end of that which was passing away:

Comments

such a hope.—Paul's hope was based upon the abiding nature of the New Covenant. The blessings of the New Covenant were remission of sins, eternal life in Christ, and the hope of the glory of God. See Rom. 5:1-2.

great boldness of speech.—This is said in justification of his claim that he was adequately fitted for the task of preaching the message of the gospel which dealt with eternal death and eternal life.

not as Moses.—The fact that God spoke to Moses was symbolized by the shining brilliance on the face of Moses when he came down from the mountain, but that message was temporary. Since it was to act as a guardian over God's people until Christ should come, the temporary nature of that message is suggested by the fact that the shining brilliance of Moses faded away. Moses had put the veil on his face to keep the children of Israel from seeing when this happened. It was in direct contrast to the great boldness of speech which characterized Paul's message under the New Covenant which is permanent.

the end of that which was passing away.—Moses did not want the children of Israel to see that the glory had left his face. So long as they were under the Old Covenant, he wanted them to remember that it was God's Word. As Moses prepared the children of Israel to go over into the promised land, he said, "You shall not add to the word which I command you nor take from it that you may keep the commandments of the Lord your God which I commanded you" (Deut. 4:2). No other nation had a God like the Lord God of Israel; no other nation had a law like the law God had given them. See Deut. 4:7-8. The Lord spoke to Joshua as he was preparing to lead the children of Israel in their conquest of Canaan. "Be strong and very courageous being careful to do according to all that Moses my servant commanded you. Turn not from it to the right hand or to the left that you may have good success wherever you go" (Joshua 1:7). Paul reminds us that the law was holy, and the commandment was holy and righteous and good. See Rom. 7:12. All this, however, cannot compare with the surpassing glory of the permanent New Covenant with its blessings of remission of sins and eternal life through Jesus Christ Our Lord.

Some have suggested that "end" may refer to the purpose of the Law of Moses. But certainly Moses was not interested in obscuring that purpose, for he himself had said, "The Lord your God will raise up for you a prophet like unto me from among you" (Deut. 18:15). Peter quoted Moses and showed that this prophecy was fulfilled in Christ. See Acts 3:20-23. Moses simply did not want Israel to see that the brilliance had left his face for it was a symbol that God had spoken to him.

Hardened Minds

Scripture

3:14-15. But their minds were hardened: for until this very day at the reading of the old covenant the same veil remaineth, it not being revealed to them that it is done away in Christ. 15 But unto this day, whensoever Moses is read, a veil lieth upon their heart.

Comments

minds were hardened.—This hardness was a subject of the prophecy of Isaiah which was quoted by Jesus in connection with the failure of some to understand the parable of the sower. "By hearing ye shall hear and shall in no wise understand; and seeing ye shall see and shall in no wise perceive. This people's heart is waxed gross and their ears are dull of hearing, their eyes they have closed lest haply they should perceive with their eyes and hear with their ears and understand with their heart and should turn again and I should hear them" (Matt. 13:14-15). Paul warned his Jewish hearers about the same thing when he spoke to them in Antioch of Pisidia. He said, "Beware therefore lest there come upon you which is spoken in the prophets: Behold ye despisers and wonder, and perish; for I work a work in your days which ye shall in no wise believe, if one declare it unto you" (Acts 13:40-41). He also quoted Isaiah's prophecy to the Jews who met with him in Rome. See Acts 28:26-28.

at the reading of the old covenant.—Tragically many of the Jews failed to anticipate the coming of Christ and the New Covenant although these matters had been clearly set forth in their Scriptures. They became satisfied that they were the chosen people of God. Their religion had become largely a matter of external conformity to ritual and form. They were interested in the ceremonies and the keeping of feasts and sabbaths. But Jesus asked them on one occasion, "Why do you also transgress the commandment of God because of your traditions" (Matt. 15:3)? Now Paul charges them with spiritual blindness and stubbornness, for even in his day they still clung to the Old Covenant as if it were a permanent thing. They refused to admit that although God had spoken to the fathers in the prophets, that in the end of those days of revelation He had spoken with finality, completeness and authority in the exalted One who bears the name Son. See Heb. 1:1-2.

it is done away in Christ.—Moses removed the veil when he went back into the mountain to talk with God but the veil remained on the hearts of those who heard the reading of the Law of Moses for they were not aware that it is removed in Christ. What God said in the completed revelation of His will in the New Covenant is like speaking to Him face to face. See I Cor. 13:12. The examination of the facts concerning the life, death, and resurrection of Christ should convince one that God's approval rested upon Him. See Acts 2:22-36. The apostle Peter, recalling his experience in the holy mountain when God said this is my Son in whom I am well pleased, said, "We have the word of prophecy made more sure where unto you do well that ye take heed as unto a lamp shining in a dark place until the day dawn and the day star arise in your hearts, knowing this first that no prophecy of scripture is of private interpretation for no prophecy ever came by the will of man but men spake from God being moved by the Holy Spirit" (II Pet. 1:19-21). Paul indicates that God's gospel, which concerns His Son and the pardon that was made possible through His shed blood, is in accord with the testimony of the law and the prophets. See Rom. 1:1-4; 3:21-26.

whenever Moses is read.—Paul had had many experiences with the stubbornness of the Jews who steadfastly refused to accept Jesus as the Messiah. Disobedient Jews had rejected his message of Christ at Antioch. They led persecutions against him in Iconium and Lystra. They stirred up trouble for him in Thessalonica. Their hatred for him finally led to his arrest in the city of Jerusalem. Throughout his long imprisonment they pressed their charges with the hope of having him put to death. Only his appeal to Caesar prevented his falling into their murderous hands. Their stubborn hearts were veiled so that the light of the glory of the gospel of Christ did not penetrate that veil.

Transformed

Scripture

3:16-18.   But whensoever it shall turn to the Lord the veil is taken away. 17 Now the Lord is the Spirit: and where the Spirit of the Lord is, there is liberty. 18 But we all, with unveiled face beholding as in a mirror the glory of the Lord, are transformed into the same image from glory to glory, even as from the Lord the Spirit.

Comments

turn to the Lord.—The only way to remove that veil is to make an honest investigation of the claims of Christ as set forth in the gospel which was preached by the inspired apostles. When it, the veiled heart, turns to the Lord the veil is taken away. Then one can see that God has spoken with finality through the Son in the New Covenant. The veil kept the Jews from seeing that the Law of Moses was supplanted by the gospel. They did not know that God was speaking through Christ, not Moses. See Deut. 18:15. The veil, which Moses removed when he was in the presence of God or speaking to the children of Israel, is taken out of the way when one realizes that God did speak with finality through Christ.

Now the Lord is the Spirit.—The word "spirit" in this verse is rendered "Spirit," assuming that Paul was referring to the Holy Spirit. The Lord is Jesus Christ. See 4:5. See also comment on 1:3. But this is to identify the Lord with the Holy Spirit. We are well aware of the fact that Scripture makes it clear that there is an intimate unity between the Father and the Son and the Holy Spirit. But why should Paul refer to this unity at this point? He had already made it clear that the New Covenant came into being through the instrumentality of the Holy Spirit as he directed the minds of those who wrote down the message of the New Covenant. He had also indicated that "spirit" stood as a symbol of the New Covenant. Since in this context he is contrasting the reading of Moses, that is the Old Coveant, with the boldness of Paul's speech in connection with the New Covenant, it is possible that he is speaking about the Lord who is identified with that spirit-covenant. It is to the Lord that the veiled heart was to turn. And that was to be done by the reading of the New Covenant which was symbolized by "spirit" rather than "letter." The New Covenant is the fulfillment of the Old.

where the Spirit of the Lord is.—While this could refer to the Holy Spirit through whom the New Covenant came into being, consistency would suggest that the reference is still to "spirit" as the symbol of the New Covenant. Where the spirit-covenant of the Lord is, there is liberty.

there is liberty.—This is the very issue that Paul discussed with the Galatians in chapters four and five. The New Covenant is represented by Sarah, and the Christian by Isaac. Paul concludes, "Wherefore brethren we are not children of the handmaid but of the free woman" (Gal. 4:31). Again Paul says, "For freedom, did Christ set us free. Stand fast therefore and be not entangled again in the yoke of bondage" (Gal. 5:1). This freedom in Christ is within the regulation of the Law of Christ. "Bear ye one another's burdens and so fulfill the law of Christ" (Gal. 6:2). See also Rom. 8:1-4.

But we all, with unveiled face.—The reading of the Old Covenant is here contrasted with the reading of the New Covenant. While the Jew read with a veil upon his heart, the Christian—the one who turned to the Lord—is aware that the New Covenant is the abiding message of Christ.

beholding as in a mirror the glory of the Lord.—See James' use of the mirror as a symbol of the perfect law of liberty, that is, the gospel or the New Covenant. James 1:23-24. It is the glorious, abiding New Covenant that reveals the glory of the Lord. It reveals His deity, His majesty, His power and His authority. It reveals His work as Prophet, Priest, and King. It reveals Him as our example, in whose footsteps we should follow. See I Pet. 2:21. It reveals Him as the Shepherd and Bishop of our souls. See I Pet. 1:25. It reveals Him as the One coming again for those who wait for Him unto salvation. God's children will be like Him for they will see Him as He is. See I John 3:2.

transformed into the same image.—The tragic failure of the Jews under the Old Covenant is indicated by the fact that they were not transformed into God's children. Though they claimed God as their Father, the simple truth was that they were filled with hatred for His Son and disregard for His Word. Therefore Jesus called them children of their father, the devil. See John 8:39-44.

Will Christ tolerate anything less than genuine transformation into Christlikeness under the New Covenant? Paul wrote to the Romans and said, "Be not fashioned according to this world, but be ye transformed by the renewing of your minds so that ye may approve the will of God, the thing that is good, and acceptable in His sight, and complete" (Rom. 12:2). How tragic that many of the Corinthians had failed to see this. Their sin of division was destroying the temple of the Holy Spirit, their immoral conduct defiled the body which is the temple of the Holy Spirit, and their unChristian conduct made it impossible to keep the memorial feast of the Lord's Supper.

from glory to glory.—The image into which those who turn to the Lord are to be transformed is that of the glorious Person of the Lord Jesus Christ. Nothing short of Christlikeness in character and conduct meets this demand. Paul had written to the Corinthians to say, "Imitate me as I am also an imitator of Christ" (I Cor. 11:1). Guidelines to follow in this matter may be found in I Cor. 13:4-8. Christ demonstrated in His life the meaning of every one of these characteristics of love. Love is the crowning virtue of the Christian life. So the glory of Christ is to be seen in the glorious life of His church. He "cleansed it by the washing of the water with the Word that He might present the church into Himself a glorious church not having spot or wrinkle of any such thing, but that it should be holy and without blemish" (Eph. 5:26-27).

even as from the Lord the Spirit.—This glorious transformation comes from the Lord of the spirit-covenant. Again some assume that "Spirit" is in apposition to "Lord" thus identifying the Lord with the Holy Spirit. The point that Paul is making is that the Lord has spoken through the New Covenant in contrast with the fact that Moses spoke through the Old Covenant as God revealed it to him.

Summary

Following the claim to be equal to the task of proclaiming the message of the gospel which was a message of life and death, Paul asked two questions: (1) Is this self-commendation? and (2) We do not need, as some do, letters of commendation to you or from you, do we?

He began his answers by saying, "You are our epistle." Others might need letters of commendation, but Paul didn't. He knew that they had become Christians through his preaching. He had an abiding love for them. They, then, were like a letter written on his heart, known and read by everyone. They knew of his love for them and that they had become new creatures in Christ. Indeed, they were like a letter that Christ had written through his ministers who had preached the gospel to them. It was written on living hearts—the understanding and affections—not stone tablets as if it affected external conduct only. It was not an ordinary letter written with ink, but one written by the Spirit of the living God. Paul was confident of all this because he knew that it had God's approval. God alone had made him equal to the task of being a minister of the New Covenant. This led to a contrast between the Old Covenant—the Ten Commandments given at Mt. Sinai—and the New Covenant—the gospel covenant given in fullness on the Day of Pentecost. He spoke of the Old Covenant as a "letter" covenant, and the New Covenant as a "spirit" covenant.

To many, the letter-covenant was not obeyed out of love for God. It became a thing that killed, because death was the penalty for breaking it. The spirit-covenant, because it was intelligently, willingly, and lovingly obeyed, was a thing that made alive those who were dead in sin. The spirit-covenant was revealed by the Holy Spirit, but for that matter, so was the letter-covenant, and in some respects it too was spiritual. See Rom. 7:12-14. The expression, "the letter killeth but the spirit giveth life" has nothing to do with the literal interpretation of the Scriptures as opposed to a spiritual interpretation.

Paul contrasted the glory of these two covenants, that is, the Old Covenant which kills and the New that brings life. The Old brought condemnation to the disobedient, but the New brings forgiveness to those who willingly obey it. The glory of the Old was such that the sons of Israel could not look steadfastly at the face of Moses which shone with a brilliant light because he had talked with God who had given him the covenant for Israel. But the glory of the New Covenant excells the Old just as forgiveness excells condemnation. The glory of the Old could not equal the surpassing glory of the New. Even the glory on Moses' face faded away, a symbol of the fact that the Old Covenant was to be replaced by the New which is permanent. As a minister of the New Covenant, Paul spoke with great boldness.

Moses put a veil on his face to keep the people from seeing the end of the glory with which it shone. Moses wanted them to remember the glory as a symbol of the fact that God had spoken to them through Him. This kept them from seeing that the Old Covenant had been done away. Even in Paul's time, a mental picture of that veil remained in the minds of readers of the Law because they were not aware that the veil had been done away by the New Covenant of Christ. It was done away whenever the veiled heart turned to the Lord through whom God spoke with finality, completeness, and authority. See Heb. 1:1-2. The Lord is the Lord of the spirit-covenant. The message of the New Covenant is forever fresh just as if one were speaking to God "face to face." Where the spirit-covenant of the Lord is, there is liberty. With unveiled faces because we are talking to the Lord, we look as into a mirror when we read the New Covenant and see the glory of the Lord.

As we behold this glorious image of the Lord, we are transformed into the glorious likeness of the Lord of the spirit-covenant.

Questions

1. What is the connection between the content of this chapter and that of the preceding one?
2. Why did Paul anticipate charges of self-commendation?
3. What is the purpose of letters of commendation? How had Paul made use of them?
4. Why didn't he need such a letter to the Corinthians or from them.
5. How had signs and wonders served to commend him to them?
6. How did their lives as Christians commend him to others?
7. In what sense was this letter written on his heart?
8. How could all men know and read it?
9. Why does Paul also call it an epistle of Christ?
10. What did Paul have to do with writing it?
11. Why did he say that it was not written with ink, but with the Spirit of the living God?
12. What message had been written on tablets of stone?
13. Why did Paul suggest that the gospel message which he preached had been written on hearts of flesh?
14. Why did Paul speak with such confidence about this letter?
15. What was the source of his adequacy for his ministry?
16. What are some of the contrasts between the Old and New covenants?
17. To whom was the New Covenant first given as a promise?
18. How did Paul show that there was no conflict between the Old and New Covenants?
19. What does "letter and spirit" mean in its various contexts?
20. To what does "letter" refer in this chapter?
21. To what does "spirit" refer in this chapter?
22. What indicates that "letter" is not contrasted with "Holy Spirit" in this context?
23. What is meant by the statement that "the letter killeth but the spirit giveth life"?
24. What popular notion cannot possibly be supported by these words?
25. What did James say about actually doing what the Word says?
26. Why, then, was the Old Covenant spoken as the ministration of death?
27. In what way was the Old Covenant glorious?
28. What is the difference between its glory and that of the New?

29. When and why did Moses put the veil on his face?
30. What is the ministration of the spirit?
31. Why was the Old Covenant spoken of as a ministration of condemnation?
32. Why was the New Covenant called the ministration of righteousness?
33. What does righteousness mean in this context?
34. In what way does the glory of the New Covenant outshine that of the Old?
35. How does the allegory of Abraham's two wives explain the relation between the Old and New Covenants?
36. Why is the New Covenant spoken of as the one that remains?
37. On what was Paul's hope based?
38. Why could he speak with such boldness about the hope of the New Covenant?
39. Why did Moses put a veil on his face? When did he remove it?
40. What is meant by "the end of that which was passing away"?
41. What caused the minds of the Jews to become hardened?
42. What was their attitude toward the reading of the Old Covenant in Paul's day?
43. What happens when the veiled heart turns to the Lord?
44. With what covenant is the Lord associated in this context?
45. Where is liberty to be found?
46. Why is the Christian's face spoken of as unveiled?
47. What is the mirror in which we behold the glory of the Lord?
48. What happens when we do?
49. What did Paul mean by the expression "from glory to glory"?
50. What did he mean by "even as from the Lord the Spirit"?

For Discussion

1. What can be done through Christian living to promote the work of Christ?
2. What can be done to help church people speak with conviction about the Word of God?

CHAPTER FOUR

Analysis

A. Paul explained the nature of his ministry under the glorious New Covenant (1-6).

  1. His attitude toward his ministry (1-2).

    a) Since he had received it through the mercy that had been shown him by the Lord, he did not lose heart (1).

    b) He did, however, reject things that were unbecoming to such a ministry (2a).

      (1) He renounced the hidden things of shame.

      (2) He did not carry on his ministry by craftiness.

      (3) He did not handle the Word of God deceitfully.

    c) He conducted himself in such a manner as to commend himself to every man's conscience (b).

      (1) He did so by making the truth clear.

      (2) It was done openly as in the sight of God.

  2. His attitude toward the gospel which he preached (3-6).

    a) He assumed that his gospel might become veiled in some (3-4a).

      (1) This could happen in the minds of those who were perishing.

      (2) It was done by the god of this world.

      (3) It was the result of their being blinded by unbelief.

    b) He pointed out the result of this blindness: Those who are perishing do not see the light of the glory of the gospel of Christ who is the image of God (4b).

    c) He gave his reasons for this view of the veiled gospel (5-6).

      (1) Based on the message he preached:

        (a) He didn't preach himself but Christ Jesus as Lord.

        (b) He was their servant for Jesus' sake.

      (2) Based on what God said:

        (a) Let light shine out of darkness.

        (b) God caused light to shine in his heart by revealing His truth.

        (c) This caused him to see the light of the knowledge of the glory of God in the face of Christ.

B. Paul explained the secret of his ability to endure the trials of his ministry (7-15).

    1. He was but an earthen vessel in which this treasure was carried that it might be evident that the power of his ministry was of God, not of himself (7).

    2. Death was working in his case that they might have life (8-12).

       a) He described the trials which he endured in his ministry (8-9).

          (1) Pressed but not straightened.

          (2) Perplexed but not unto despair.

          (3) Pursued but not forsaken.

          (4) Smitten down but not destroyed.

       b) He explained the nature of these trials (10-12).

          (1) They were like bearing about the dying of Jesus that the life of Jesus might be manifested in his body.

          (2) He explained that he was delivered to death for Jesus' sake that the life of Jesus might be manifested in his mortal flesh.

          (3) This meant that death was working in him, but life in the Corinthians.

    3. His ministry was carried on in the spirit of faith (13-15).

       a) His faith was like that of the Psalmist who said, "I believed, therefore I spoke" (13).

       b) His faith was in God who raised up Christ and would raise him also (14).

       c) His ministry of faith was for their sakes that the multiplied grace of the many might cause thanksgiving to abound unto the glory of God.

C. Paul explained his view of temporal suffering (16-18).

    1. He did not lose courage in face of such suffering.

    2. He thought of them in contrast to things eternal.

       a) They were as light afflictions compared to the weight of eternal glory.

       b) Things that are seen are temporal; things that are unseen are eternal.

Paul's Response To The Ministry Under
The Glorious New Covenant

Scripture

4:1-6. Therefore seeing we have this ministry, even as we obtained mercy, we faint not: 2 but we have renounced the hidden things of shame, not walking in craftiness, nor handling the word of God deceitfully; but by the manifestation of the truth commending ourselves to every man's conscience in the sight of God. 3 And even if our gospel is veiled, it is veiled in them that perish: 4 in whom the god of this world hath blinded the minds of the unbelieving, that the light of the gospel of the glory of Christ, who is the image of God, should not dawn upon them. 5 For we preach not ourselves, but Christ Jesus as Lord, and ourselves as your servants for Jesus' sake. 6 Seeing it is God, that said, Light shall shine out of darkness, who shined in our hearts, to give the light of the knowledge of the glory of God in the face of Jesus Christ.

Comments

Therefore seeing we have this ministry.—Paul had just explained his great boldness of speech in connection with his ministry under the New Covenant. This is a continuation of his answer to those who might criticize him for his claim to be adequate for such a ministry. *even as we obtained mercy.*—Paul had already made it clear that his sufficiency for this ministry was from God. He did not hesitate to admit that in himself he had no right to make such claims, for he remembered his former attitude toward Christ and his church. As he wrote to Timothy about the gospel of the glory of the blessed God which had been committed to his trust, he reminded him that Christ had counted him faithful and had appointed him to His service. This was in spite of the fact that once he had been a blasphemer and a persecutor and an injurious person. He had readily admitted to the Corinthians that he was the least of the apostles, not even worthy to be called an apostle because he had persecuted the church of God. See I Cor. 15:9. But he obtained mercy because he did it ignorantly in unbelief. See I Tim. 1:11-14. God's mercy had brought him pardon; his sins had been washed away by the blood of Christ at the time of his baptism. See Acts 22:16. Although Paul had been a Pharisee, his humility as a Christian reminds us of the publican who prayed, "Be merciful to me the sinner" (Luke 18:13). Paul may have had in mind those arrogant false teachers who were troubling the church at Corinth, suggesting that they, too, should have called upon God for mercy.

we faint not.—Paul's humility is matched by his courageous faith and confidence in the Lord. He was like David who, after he had slain the lion and the bear, fearlessly faced the giant Philistine who had been defying the army of Israel. Like David, Paul also came in the name of the Lord. He refused to act the part of a coward as he faced the hardships of this glorious ministry. Neither was he frightened by the derogatory slander of the false teachers at Corinth.

we have renounced the hidden things of shame.—While "renounce" may have the sense of "give up," it is doubtful that this would be true in Paul's case.

As to the righteousness which is in the Law, Paul declared that he had been found blameless. See Phil. 3:6. This reminds us of the Rich Young Ruler who said to Jesus that he had observed all the commandments from his youth. See Luke 18:21. But he had failed to keep the first commandment which said, "Thou shalt have no other gods before me." Paul freely admitted, however, that before he had become a Christian he had been guilty of covetousness. Sin had dwelt in him, dominating his life and leading him to do many things he hated. See Rom. 7:7-20. But he had been released from the tyranny of that master when he became obedient to Christ the Lord. See Rom. 6:17-18.

"Renounce" also means to refuse. Even as a Pharisee, it is doubtful if Paul ever resorted to the shameful practices which he condemns in this context. But certain Judaizing teachers who had been disturbing the churches were guilty of them. Paul categorized the corrupt teachers who had been disrupting the Galatian churches as "false brethren, privily brought in, who came in privily to spy out our liberty which we have in Jesus Christ, that they might bring us into bondage" (Gal. 2:4).

It is true also that Paul had persecuted the church of God and had tried to destroy it, because he was convinced that it was wrong. See Gal. 1:13. "Breathing threatening and slaughter against the disciples of the Lord" he had traveled even to Damascus hunting them down. He had obtained letters from the high priest giving him authority to arrest any whom he might find that were of the Way, men or women, and bring them bound to Jerusalem. See Acts 9:1-2.

Whatever these hidden things of shame were, as an apostle of the Lord Jesus Christ, Paul refused to become involved in them. He gave full notice to all that he would not stoop to such practices in order to gain power over his fellowmen.

not working in craftiness.—This is a reference to the methods of those who indulged in the hidden things of shame. See Eph. 5:12. Some of them would do anything to accomplish their own selfish ends, even if it meant handling the Word of God deceitfully. Paul had already mentioned those who were making merchandise of the Word of God. As a fisherman uses a lure to attract the unsuspecting fish, so the false teacher used deceit in order to capture his victim. Paul, however, had said to the Ephesian elders: "I am pure from the blood of all men, for I shrank not from declaring unto you the whole counsel of God" (Acts 20:26-27).

There are various ways to use the Word of God deceitfully. Using a Bible text to preach a "sermon" that has little or nothing to do with the Bible is one of the common ways of doing it. Teaching it accurately, but refusing to live by it is equally deceitful. Jesus condemned the scribes and Pharisees for this very thing. See Matt. 23:1-2. Paul wrote about some of the Jews who were doing the same thing, saying, "for this reason the name of God is blasphemed among the Gentiles because of you" (Rom. 2:23).

Both Jesus and Paul demonstrated the proper use of the Scriptures. In the synagogue at Nazareth, Jesus read from the prophecy of Isaiah concerning Himself. When He had finished reading He explained the meaning of the prophecy to the people. They wondered at the gracious words which He spoke. See Luke 4:16-21. Paul told Timothy that the inspired Scriptures were profitable for teaching, correction, instruction in righteousness, and that they completely equip the man of God for every good work. See II Tim. 3:16-17. Paul insisted on proclaiming the truth of God's Word and letting that truth be seen in his life. See Gal. 2:20 and I Cor. 11:1.

commending ourselves to every man's conscience in the sight of God. —Paul's ministry was out in the open so that every man could see and know the truth for which he stood. And this is the thing that commended him to them. He was aware of the fact that as a servant of the Lord Jesus Christ all that he said and did was done in the sight of God.

even if our gospel is veiled.—He was, no doubt, anticipating the reaction to his remarks about the veil that lies upon those who hear the Law of Moses read. He frankly admitted that the gospel is veiled in the case of those who were perishing. They were perishing because they had failed to turn to the Lord who is revealed in the glorious New Covenant. The message of the gospel is about eternal life and also about eternal death. To reject the message of the Lord is to perish.

in whom the god of this world.—Satan is properly called the god of this age because he is worshipped by those who are perishing. Of course, there is only one true God, the Father, and one true Lord, the Lord Jesus Christ. See I Cor. 8:6. When Gentile sacrificed to idols, Paul said that they were sacrificing to demons and not to God. Idolatry was demon worship. Satan is known as the prince of demons. See Matt. 12:44. Satan even dared to challenge the Son of God to fall down and worship him, offering to give Him all the kingdoms of the world if He would do so. See Matt. 4:8. Jesus made it clear that no one can serve two masters. He said, "You cannot serve God and mammon" (Luke 16:13). Satan can be called the god of this age because of the time limit that is imposed upon his activities. At the close of this age, the devil will be cast into the lake that burns with fire and brimstone where are also the beast and the false prophet, and they shall be tormented day and night for ever and ever. See Rev. 20:10.

Christ conquered Satan at the cross and provided the means whereby His followers may also overcome him, that is, by the blood of the Lamb, the Word of their testimony, and their dedication to the Lord that is indicated by the fact that they love not their lives even unto death. See Rev. 12:11 and Heb. 2:14.

blinded the minds of the unbelieving.—Belief in Christ rests solidly on the evidence of His resurrection. See Rom. 10:9-10. The sheer weight of that evidence compelled the apostles who had investigated every phase of it to believe that God had raised Jesus from the dead. The inspired writers have left us a reliable record of the evidence of that greatest fact of history.

Paul knew that many were blind because they did not want to believe. They were satisfied with the Old Covenant and proud of their own righteousness.

Jesus had found this same blindness among the people of His day. They did not understand what He said because they did not hear what He was really saying. Why? Because they were intent on doing the evil which their father, the devil, was suggesting to them. He was a liar and the father of liars. His offspring were not interested in the truth which the Son of God spoke. See John 8:42-46.

that the light of the gospel of the glory of Christ.—Unbelief had closed the minds of those who were perishing. They would not permit the knowledge of the gospel which tells of the glory of the Lord Jesus Christ to enlighten their darkened minds. They "loved the darkness rather than the light" (John 3:19).

who is the image of God.—Paul pointed out the seriousness of this blindness. To reject Christ is to reject God, for He is the image of God, that is, "the image of the invisible God" (Col. 1:15). John, also, says that "No man hath seen God at any time; the only begotten Son, who is in the bosom of the Father, he hath declared him" (John 1:18). Thus both John and Paul emphatically state their belief in the deity of Jesus. John says that "the Word was God" (John 1:1), and that "the Word became flesh and dwelt among us (and we beheld his glory, glory as of the only begotten from the Father full of grace and truth" (John 1:14).

The Gospel of John unfolds the story of the Father as He is seen in the Person of Jesus Christ. Jesus declared, "I and the Father are one" (John 10:30). He also said "no one cometh unto the Father but by me" (John 14:6). When Philip said, "Lord, show us the Father and it sufficeth us," Jesus answered, "Have I been so long time with you, and do you not know me, Philip? He that hath seen me hath seen the Father" (John 14:8-9). Indeed, if they had recognized Him, they would have known the Father. See John 14:7. The writer of Hebrews indicates that the Son is the exact representation of God. See Heb. 1:3. The veil of unbelief prevented many from seeing this truth.

Paul declared that in Christ "dwelleth all the fulness of the Godhead bodily" (Col. 2:9). The most complete explanation of this profound truth of Christianity is found in Phil. 2:5-11. His deity and humanity are presented by Paul in terms similar to those used by John in his Gospel and his first epistle. See John 1:1-8 and I John 1:1-4.

for we preach not ourselves.—In no way did Paul preach himself. He always preached Christ Jesus as Lord. He was merely the agent through whom the knowledge of Christ had been made known in every place. He had no lordship over their faith; his task was to help them in their joyous relationship to the Lord.

Of himself he could say, "I am your servant for Jesus' sake." In so doing he was following the standard which the Lord had set for all who would serve Him. "Whosoever would be first among you," He said, "let him be servant of all." The Son of Man did not come to be ministered unto, but to minister and to give His life a ransom for the many. See Mark 10:44-45.

This attitude was the opposite of that of the false teachers who were troubling the Corinthians, for they were commending themselves and measuring themselves by their own standards. See II Cor. 10:12.

Seeing that it is God.—This is Paul's reason for preaching Christ. In contrast to what he had said about the god of this world who had blinded the minds of the unbelieving, Paul declared that it was God who caused light to shine out of darkness and who had shined in his heart to give the enlightenment that comes from the knowledge about the glory of God as it is seen in the face of Jesus. He wrote to the Galatians to say that God had revealed His Son in him that he might preach Him among the Gentiles. See Gal. 1:16.

Several contrasts are seen in these verses: (1) The god of this age is contrasted with God who created the world. (2) The blinded minds of the unbelievers are contrasted with the enlightened heart of Paul as a believer in Christ. (3) Unbelief which prevented the light of the gospel of the glory of Christ from dawning on the darkened minds is contrasted with the faith of the opened heart that allows the enlightenment that comes from the knowledge of the glory of God which is seen in the face of Christ to shine.

The shining brilliance on the face of Moses suggests the thought of the glory of God in the face of Jesus Christ. Moses' face shone as he spoke to Israel the message which God had given him. Christ is the One through whom God revealed His gospel to the apostles, and they preached Christ Jesus as Lord for the salvation of the believer.

Paul had been permitted to see the brilliant light and to hear the voice of Christ when He commissioned him to preach the gospel to the Gentiles. See Acts 26:12-18. Jesus told him that through his preaching the Gentiles were to "open their eyes, that they might turn from darkness to light and from the power of Satan unto God, that they might receive remission of sins and an inheritance among them that are sanctified by faith in Christ."

Since Paul has been discussing the Old Covenant in contrast to the New, it might be well to recall what the writer of Hebrews said about the mountain from which God spoke to Israel. That mountain "burned with fire and unto blackness and darkness, and tempest and the sound of a trumpet, and the voice of words; which they that heard entreated that no more should be spoken unto them" (Heb. 12:18-19). The message that came from Mount Zion, however, brought the good news of remission of sins that had been promised to all believers from the time of Abraham. See Gal. 3:6-14; Isa. 2:1-4.

John wrote of Christ saying "In him was life; and the life was the light of men. And the light shineth in the darkness; and the darkness apprehended it not" (John 1:4-5). Jesus said, "I am the light of the world: he that followeth me shall not walk in the darkness, but shall have the light of life" (John 8:12). All this seems to say the same thing that Paul did when he spoke of "the enlightenment of the knowledge of the glory of God in the face of Jesus Christ."

Paul's View Of His Ministry

Scripture

4:7-18.   But we have this treasure in earthen vessels, that the exceeding greatness of the power may be of God, and not from ourselves; 8 we are pressed on every side, yet not straitened; perplexed, yet not unto despair; 9 pursued, yet not forsaken; smitten down, yet not destroyed; 10 always bearing about in the body the dying of Jesus, that the life also of Jesus may be manifested in our body. 11 For we who live are always delivered unto death for Jesus' sake, that the life also of Jesus may be manifested in our mortal flesh. 12 So then death worketh in us, but life in you. 13 But having the same spirit of faith, according to that which is written, I believed, and therefore did I speak; we also believe, and therefore also we speak; 14 knowing that he that raised up the Lord Jesus shall raise up us also with Jesus, and shall present us with you. 15 For all things are for your sakes, that the grace, being multiplied through the many, may cause the thanksgiving to abound unto the glory of God.

16 Wherefore we faint not; but though our outward man is decaying, yet our inward man is renewed day by day. 17 For our light affliction, which is for the moment, worketh for us more and more exceedingly an eternal weight of glory; 18 while we look not at the things which are seen, but at the things which are not seen: for the things which are seen are temporal; but the things which are not seen are eternal.

Comments

But we have this treasure.—Paul's ministry as an apostle in connection with the New Covenant had been obtained through the mercy of God. He, therefore, did not hesitate to declare that he was in no way shrinking from the responsibilities involved in it. To him, it was a privilege to proclaim the gospel of the glory of Christ, for it is this gospel that gives enlightenment to the believer as he comes to know about the glory of God as it is seen in the Person of Christ. This gospel message is the treasure in such earthen vessels as the apostles. God had committed it to them as a trust. See I Tim. 1:11.

Paul wrote to Timothy telling him to guard that which had been committed to him—the gospel which was the precious treasure which had been given to him in trust for safe keeping—urging him to "turn away from profane bablings and oppositions of the knowledge which is falsely so called, which some professing have erred concerning the faith" (I Tim. 6:20-21). The human being is indeed a fragile vessel in which to entrust the precious message of eternal life, but such is the confidence that God had in Paul and others who dedicate themselves to the service of the Lord Jesus Christ. Paul said to Timothy, "The things which thou hast heard from me among many witnesses, the same commit thou to faithful men, who shall be able to teach others also" (II Tim. 2:2).

the power may be of God and not from ourselves.—This is the secret of Paul's ministry. The power of his message was not in himself but in God. He had written to the Corinthians in the first letter saying, "I was with you in weakness, and in fear, and in much trembling: And my speech and my preaching were not in persuasive words of men's wisdom but in demonstration of the Spirit and of power" (I Cor. 2:4). To the Romans he wrote, "For I am not ashamed of the gospel for it is the power of God unto salvation to everyone that believeth; to the Jew first, and also to the Greek" (Rom. 1:16).

Paul's enemies at Corinth were evidently proud of their personal appearance, their ability as orators, and their power to persuade the Corinthians to believe them rather than the gospel which Paul had preached. Paul did not bother to defend himself against their insinuations that his bodily presence was weak. He took it as an occasion to point out that his power was from God, not from himself. This power could be seen in the miracles which the apostles performed. The miracles demonstrated that their message came from God. Its effect had been seen in the transformed lives of those whose sins had been washed away by the blood of Christ. They were living a life of separation from sin and dedication to the service of God. They had been pardoned in the name of the Lord Jesus Christ and in the Spirit of God. See I Cor. 5:11.

There was another side to this ministry that had to do with life and death. It was that of human frailty facing the hardships of this ministry, facing them in such a manner that the power of God might be seen in His servants. Paul pointed out five examples of this human weakness. In none of them was he preaching about himself, for his faith and hope were in God throughout all his trials. The first four examples present contrasts between the hardships he faced and the relief that always came. The last explains his attitude toward all the hardships which he suffered in preaching the gospel.

pressed on every side, yet not straitened.—This begins the list of physical hardships which Paul suffered in his ministry. He had been in tight places, but always found the way out. The riot at Ephesus is a good example. See Acts 19:23-41. The town clerk quieted the mob that would have destroyed Paul and made it possible for him, after having exhorted the disciples, to go on to Macedonia. The arrest in Jerusalem was another tight spot in which Paul was saved from the violence of the angry crowd by the Roman soldiers that policed the temple area. See Acts 21:35. The pressures of his ministry finally resulted in his imprisonment. On the night following his arrest in Jerusalem, the Lord stood by him and said, "Be of good cheer, for as thou hast testified concerning me at Jerusalem, so must thou bear witness also at Rome" (Acts 23:11).

perplexed, yet not unto despair.—The difficulties involved in communication between himself and the Corinthian church left him at his wits end. He was eager to help them and to prevent the false teachers from making havoc of the church of God. But he did not despair; he took the necessary action that finally led him to Macedonia where he found Titus and learned about the situation at Corinth.

pursued, yet not forsaken.—Paul's enemies pursued him wherever he went; but he was never left in the lurch, for the Lord was always with him. His enemies pursued him until they succeeded in having him arrested, but this led to his being sent to Rome where he presented his case—actually, the case for the gospel—before Caesar. In the stormy crossing of the sea that threatened the lives of all on board the ship, an angel of God said to Paul, "Fear not, Paul, thou must stand before Caesar. And lo, God hath granted thee all them that sail with thee" (Acts 27:23-24). In the trial that followed, when all other had forsaken him, the Lord stood by Paul. See II Tim. 4:17. Out of confidence of victory, Paul wrote this message to Timothy, "Be thou sober in all things, suffer hardship, do the work of an evangelist, fulfill thy ministry. For I am already being offered, and the time of my departure is come. I have fought the good fight, I have finished the course, I have kept the faith: henceforth there is laid up for me the crown of righteousness, which the Lord, the righteous judge, shall give to me at the last day; and not to me only, but to all that have loved the Lord's appearing" (II Tim. 4:5-8).

smitten down, yet not destroyed.—Paul knew what it meant to be struck down like a soldier on the battle field. At Lystra the enemy stoned him and dragged him out of the city thinking that he was dead. But as the disciples stood around him he rose up and entered into the city, and on the next day went on to Derbe. See Acts 14: 19-20.

always bearing about in the body the dying of Jesus.—The Jews were constantly seeking to kill Jesus. See John 5:18; 7:1. When they could not meet the logic of His wisdom in open debate, they took up stones to cast at Him. See John 8:59; 10:31. They would have done it too, except for the fact that it was not His hour to die. He had the right to lay down His life and the right to take it again. See John 10:18; 7:30. But they were determined to put Him to death; their only problem was how to get it done. Judas gave them the opportunity they had been looking for when he offered to betray Him into their hands. Their charge of blasphemy on which they agreed that He was worthy of death meant nothing to Pilate, and they knew it. Therefore they brought such charges as insurrection against Caesar that they might force the governor to sentence Jesus to die on the Roman cross. But He arose in triumph from the dead and "ever lives to make intercession for us" (Heb. 7:25). As an apostle of Christ, Paul was always facing death at the hands of his persecutors. They finally succeeded; but for Paul, death simply meant being absent from the body and at home with the Lord. See also Col. 1:24 for further information on Paul's attitude toward suffering for Christ.

that the life of Jesus also may be manifested in our mortal flesh.— The life of Jesus is His life which survived the experience of death, for God raised Him up.

So then death worketh in us, but life in you.—The earthen vessel was subject to death and persecution. But it held the glorious message of eternal life for the believers in the Lord Jesus Christ. Paul was their servant for the sake of Jesus Christ.

the same spirit of faith.—Defending his courage to speak even in face of death, Paul turned to the message of Psalms 116:8-11 to show that he had the same attitude of faith as the Psalmist who faced the threat of death. Paul's confidence was in God and in the power of the gospel to save. He knew that God had raised Jesus Christ from the dead, for he had seen the risen Lord. He was also certain that God would raise him up from the dead and present him to Christ along with the saints at Corinth. See Eph. 5-25-27.

For all things are for your sakes.—All that God had done through the Lord Jesus Christ was for the sake of the believer. All that Paul had suffered in order to bring the gospel to them was for their sakes. God's grace multiplied by the many who were brought to life in Jesus Christ caused thanks to abound unto the glory of God.

Wherefore we faint not.—Paul declared again his courage to carry on the ministry of the gospel of Christ. He had faced hardships, even death itself, in fulfilling his ministry. He courageously continued on his course knowing death would overtake him some day. He develops this thought beginning in 4:16 and continuing through 5:10.

our outward man is decaying.—By "outward man" Paul meant the physical body in which he had endured so many hardships. See the list in 11:24-28. It leaves us wondering how any man could have endured all this. But it was a different story with the man who lived in that body, that is, "the inward man." While the body was subject to death, the inward man was being renewed day by day. Paul said, "For which cause I suffer also these things: yet I am not ashamed; for I know him whom I have believed, and am persuaded that he is able to guard that which I have committed unto him against that day" (II Tim. 1:12).

our light affliction.—As we think of the affliction suffered by Paul, we wonder how he could have called it light. It was light as compared to the eternal weight of glory which he anticipated at the close of his faithful ministry. The affliction was for the moment, but the glory will be forever, eternal in the heavens. The afflictions could be seen, but the glory cannot be seen with the physical eye. The things that are not seen, however, are eternal. Paul discusses these things in 5:1-10.

Summary

Explaining his attitude toward the ministry of the New Covenant, Paul showed why he preached Christ, even though his gospel was obscured in the minds of some.

He had obtained this ministry through God's mercy, not by any merit of his own. He was determined not to act like a fainthearted coward in discharging his obligations to it. He renounced methods and motives not in harmony with the gospel and rested his case on the presentation of the truth. He refused to resort to the secret things that belonged to the shameful practices of false teachers. He did not resort to craftiness, nor did he deceitfully use the gospel. By making the truth clear to his hearers, he commended himself to the consciences of men before God.

Paul had said that some were blind to the true nature of the Old Covenant, and he readily admitted that the gospel might be obscured in the minds of those who were blinded by the god of this age. The sin of unbelief kept the glorious light of the gospel from dawning on them. Even so, Paul was determined not to preach himself, but Christ Jesus as Lord. He was their servant for Jesus' sake. God caused the light of the knowledge of His glory to shine through the preaching of the apostle that it might bring enlightenment to the believer.

This gospel was like a precious treasure which God kept in earthen vessels—his apostles and preachers of the Word. Paul trusted, not in himself, but in God for strength to endure the hardships of his ministry. He was hard pressed, but not to the extent that he could not move. He was perplexed, but never gave up. He was pursued by men, but never forsaken by God. He was struck down, but never left to die until his time to go home to be with the Lord. Paul, just as Jesus had done, faced death constantly at the hands of his persecutors. But he was delivered from death that he might continue to tell of the risen Lord, for this meant life for the Corinthians who believed.

As the Psalmist believed in God who delivered him from death, so Paul also believed that God would deliver him. He spoke with boldness and confidence about his hope that God who raised up Jesus would raise him also from the dead and present him in the resurrection with the faithful Corinthians. He reminded them that he had endured all these things for their sakes in order that God's grace which was multiplied by the many trials through which the faithful go might abound in thanksgiving on their part to the glory of God.

Paul was not afraid to face the hardships of his ministry, even the constant danger of death. He knew, of course, that his physical body was wearing out. But this was more than offset by the fact that his inward man was being renewed constantly. These afflictions were a momentary light load as compared to the eternal weight of glory to which he looked after patiently enduring the trials of this life. He did not look at these perils as one who keeps his eyes on things which can be seen, for he was thinking of things that cannot be seen with the physical eye, that is, the things that are eternal in the heavens.

Questions

1. Why did Paul again refer to his ministry at this point?
2. What merciful thing had God done for Paul in connection with his ministry?
3. In what way had Paul's conversion changed his Pharisaical views?
4. What might this suggest as to the teachers who were disturbing the church at Corinth?
5. What was Paul's attitude toward the hardships which he faced?
6. What were the hidden things of shame which Paul renounced?
7. What kind of a life had he lived as a Pharisee?
8. How do the practices of the false teachers in Galatia show what Paul meant by "hidden things of shame"?
9. What were some of the crafty, deceitful practices of some of the false teachers in Paul's day?
10. What did Paul say to the Ephesian elders about his own relation to the whole counsel of God?
11. How did Paul seek to commend his ministry?
12. Why did he speak of the possibility of the gospel being veiled?
13. Who is the god of this age?
14. How does he blind the minds of some to the truth of the gospel?
15. What will ultimately happen to the god of this age and to all who worship him?
16. On what does belief in Christ rest?
17. What experience did Jesus have with this kind of blindness?
18. What is the light of the gospel?
19. What did Paul mean when he spoke of Christ as the image of God?
20. What did Jesus say about His relation to the Father?
21. What did Paul mean when he said, "We preach not ourselves, but Christ Jesus as Lord"?
22. Why did he speak of himself as their servant?
23. Why did Paul refer to the fact that God said, "Light shall shine out of darkness"?
24. How had God enlightened the heart of Paul? How does he enlighten hearts of others?

25. What contrasts may be seen between the god of this world and God who sheds light on our minds through the gospel?
26. What did Paul mean by "the glory of God in the face of Jesus Christ"?
27. What is the connection between this thought and that of the glory on the face of Moses?
28. What contrast may this suggest between the message that went forth from Sinai and the gospel that was preached on the Day of Pentecost?
29. What was the treasure in earthen vessels?
30. What were the earthen vessels?
31. What important view of Paul's ministry does this give?
32. Why did Paul mention the frailty of the human body at this point?
33. What experience of Paul had caused him to be pressed on every side, yet not straitened?
34. How did the failure to find Titus cause him to be perplexed, yet not unto despair?
35. How did Paul show that the Lord had never forsaken him?
36. When had he been smitten down, but not destroyed?
37. In what way was he always bearing about in the body the dying of Jesus?
38. What was the purpose of this?
39. What did he mean by saying, "Death works in us, but life in you"?
40. To what spirit of faith did Paul refer? Why?
41. Why was Paul cheerful even though he knew that his physical body was wearing out?
42. With what did he compare his "light affliction"?
43. What is "the eternal weight of glory"?

For Discussion

1. What can be done to exalt the gospel today when so many are preoccupied with human systems of thought?
2. How can the unseen glories of heaven be made real to us?

CHAPTER FIVE

Analysis

A. Paul contrasted the earthly and heavenly dwelling places as he continued the explanation of his courageous outlook for the future (1-10).

　1. He pointed out that we know that we will have a building from God (1).

　　a) This will be when the earthly, temporary dwelling—our physical body—is folded up like a tent when it is no longer needed (1a).

　　b) We have waiting for us a permanent dwelling place from God (b).

　　　(1) It will be a permanent dwelling in contrast to the earthly, mortal body.

　　　(2) It is eternal in contrast to the temporary body of this life.

　　　(3) It is to be in heaven in contrast to the one that is for earth.

　2. He spoke of his longing to be in that heavenly dwelling place (2-5).

　　a) In this earthly body we have pain and distress which cause us to be deeply disturbed.

　　b) This makes us long for the heavenly dwelling.

　　c) The heavenly dwelling will replace the earthly one so that we will not be without a body.

　　d) He explained that we do not want to be without a body; rather, we want one that will take the place of this mortal body.

　　e) He who provided this very thing for us is God, and He guaranteed it through what is revealed by the Holy Spirit (5).

　3. He explained why he faced the future with such courage (6-10).

　　a) He was aware of the fact that as long as we make our home in this physical body we are away from home, that is, away from the Lord (6).

　　b) In this state we walk by faith, not by sight; we put our trust in the Lord because of the knowledge we have through the revelation by the Spirit (7).

    c) Because we are confident of this, we wish to be away from this earthly home, the physical body, that we might be at home with the Lord. (8).

    d) Consequently, Paul made it his aim to be well-pleasing to the Lord (9-10).

        (1) This was his aim whether at home in the body or absent from it.

        (2) This was true because he faced the time when all will appear before the judgment-seat of Christ. There each one will receive the verdict, based on what he has done in the body, whether good or bad.

B. Because he knew the meaning of reverence for God, Paul explained his ministry of reconciliation (11-21).

    1. He explained the motivating forces of this ministry (11-17).

        a) Since he was aware of the Judgment, he was endeavoring to persuade men to obey God so that they might be prepared for it (7-13).

            (1) This was evident to God, and he hoped that they were aware of it too (11).

            (2) He was not commending himself as he told about this ministry (12-13).

                (a) He was giving them an opportunity to boast on his behalf.

                (b) This gave them an answer to the ones who were boasting about appearance and not reality.

        b) He told them of the love of Christ which was the compelling force in his ministry of reconciliation (14-17).

            (1) He was held on this course by the force of Christ's Christ's love for him (14-15).

                (a) It was the fact that Christ died for all sinners that made him aware of this love (14a).

                (b) It is evident, then, that all sinners have died (14b).

                (c) It is also true that Christ died for all sinners—that included Paul—so that they might no longer live for themselves but for Him who died and rose for their sakes.

            (2) He explained the view he held because he had

come to understand the love of Christ for him (16-17).

    (a) He no longer considered any man as a mere human being, although he had once thought of Messiah from this point of view (16).

    (b) He looked upon any man who was in Christ as a new creature; old thing had passed away; behold, they have become new.

2. He explained that he had received this ministry from God (18-19).

    a) God had reconcilled Paul to Himself through Christ and had given him this ministry of reconciliation (18).

    b) Paul explained what this meant (19).

        (1) It meant that God was, in Christ, reconciling the world unto Himself.

        (2) It meant that He was not reckoning their trespasses against them, but through His ambassador He was offering them the way of reconciliation.

3. He explained what he was doing as an ambassador of Christ (20-21).

    a) God was pleading with them through the ambassador of Christ that they reconcile themselves to Him (20).

    b) God had made this reconciliation possible through Christ (21).

        (1) God made Christ, who was sinless, to represent sin when He died on the cross.

        (2) This was done that we might become the representatives of the righteousness of God in Him.

The Building From God

Scripture

5:1-10 For we know that if the earthly house of our tabernacle be dissolved, we have a building from God, a house not made with hands, eternal, in the heavens. 2 For verily in this we groan, longing to be clothed upon with our habitation which is from heaven: 3 if so be that being clothed we shall not be found naked. 4 For indeed we that are in this tabernacle do groan, being burdened; not for that we would be unclothed, but that we would be clothed upon, that what is mortal may be swallowed up of life. 5 Now he that wrought us for this very thing is God, who gave unto us the earnest of the Spirit.

6 Being therefore always of good courage, and knowing that, whilst we are at home in the body, we are absent from the Lord 7 (for we walk by faith, not by sight); 8 we are of good courage, I say, and are willing rather to be absent from the body, and to be at home with the Lord. 9 Wherefore also we make it our aim, whether at home or absent, to be well-pleasing unto him. 10 For we must all be made manifest before the judgment-seat of Christ; that each one may receive the things done in the body, according to what he hath done, whether it be good or bad.

Comments

For we know.—Paul continued to explain his courageous effort to preach the gospel of Christ. He had told of his awareness of the fact that this precious treasure was in earthen vessels. He was constantly aware of the weakness of the vessel. He did not despair, however, for he knew what lay ahead for the faithful servant of Christ. He knew that this life was only temporary, but beyond it there was eternal life with God. This information had been revealed to him through the Holy Spirit. See I Cor. 2:6-16. More than that, he had actually seen the risen Lord. This fact confirmed the testimony that had been made known to him and, through him, to all who are willing to accept the Word of God. The hope of heaven is based solidly upon the testimony of the Scriptures.

Two factors influence the interpreters of this chapter: (1) the assumption that Paul was anticipating the return of Christ in his own lifetime; and (2) the assumption that he had in mind the intermediate state of the dead as he discussed the issues of this chapter. But we raise the question: "Did Paul expect the return of Christ in his lifetime?" Jesus had made it clear to His disciples that no one knew the time of His coming, "not even the angels of heaven, nor the Son himself, but only the Father" (Matt. 24:36). The information given orally to the apostles by Jesus was recalled to their minds by the Holy Spirit. See John 14:26. Paul, who was also an inspired apostle of Christ, surely had all the information that was given to the other apostles. In writing to the Thessalonians, he used the very expression that Jesus had used about the second coming: "For yourselves know perfectly well that the day of the Lord so cometh as a thief in the night" (I Thes. 5:2). In his second epistle to them, he corrected the false notion that was held by some of them that the day of the Lord was just at hand. He reminded them of certain things, such as the apostasy, that were to come before that day. See II Thes.

2:12. In I Cor. 15:51, Paul wrote "Behold, I tell you a mystery: We all shall not sleep, but we shall be changed." Some have understood this to mean that Paul was expecting the return of Christ before his death. It seems more likely that he was making a general statement in agreement with what he had said in I Thes. 4:13-18. Some will be alive at the time of the return of Christ, but there is no indication that Paul expected to be one of that number.

Paul did say to the Philippians, "For to me to live is Christ—magnified by my ministry of preaching His gospel—and for me to die is gain" (Phil. 1:21). Although he had a strong desire to be with Christ—what faithful Christian doesn't?—he added, "I know that I shall abide, yea and abide with you all for your progress and joy in the faith" (Phil. 1:25). But Paul, of course, was well aware of the fact that his physical body which was subject to death was wearing out. As he faced that eventuality, he wrote to Timothy saying, "I am already being offered and the time of my departure is come" (II Tim. 4:6). It seems idle, therefore, to speculate over the apostle's supposed expectation of being alive when Christ comes.

The saints of all ages should remember the words of Christ when He said, "Watch and be ready!" Paul made it his aim whether in this life or the heavenly state to be well-pleasing to God.

As to the matter of the intermediate state, there is a question whether or not Paul even hints at it in this context. For a discussion of the intermediate state of the dead, see *Studies in Luke,* pages 278-279.

if the earthly house.—This does not indicate that Paul had any doubt as to whether or not he might die before the coming of Christ. The only uncertain thing in his mind was the time of his death. The statement may be more properly rendered as follows. "For we know that whenever the earthly house of our tabernacle shall be dissolved, we have a building from God, a house not made with hands, eternal, in the heavens." We have a similar statement in I John 3:2: "We know that if he shall be manifested, we shall be like him." But there is no doubt in the mind of John about the fact that He will be manifested. It would, therefore, be better to translate—and correct, too—as follows: "We know that whenever he shall be manifested, we shall be like him."

For an illustration of the fact that "if" should sometimes be rendered "when," see Heb. 3:7. The American Standard has "if" but R S V has "when" and correctly so.

we have a building from God.—The contrast is between the physical body and the resurrection body. The one is earthly and temporal; the other is eternal and heavenly. Some in Corinth had been doubting the fact of the resurrection. They had asked about the kind of body in which the dead were to be raised. See I Cor. 15:35. Paul said there is a natural body—one that is suited to this life—and there is also a spiritual body. See I Cor. 15:44. He described it as follows: "For our citizenship is in heaven: whence also we wait for a savior, the Lord Jesus Christ: who shall fashion anew the body of our humiliation, that it may be conformed to the body of his glory, according to the working whereby he is able to subject all things unto himself" (Phil. 3:20-21). This agrees with John that the saints shall be like Him when they see Him as He is.

It is doubtful that the thought of a tabernacle that will give place to a permanent building in heaven was derived from the Tabernacle in the Wilderness that gave place to the permanent Temple in Jerusalem. People in Paul's day were thoroughly familiar with tents as well as permanent structures. It was natural for Paul to use the figure for he was a tentmaker. Peter uses the same figure referring to his physical body when he referred to his approaching death as "the putting off of his tabernacle" (II Pet. 1:14 and John 21:18-19). The reference in John is to the manner of Peter's death and not necessarily to the time of it. Paul spoke of "the time of his departure," using a phrase in common use. It referred among other things to the soldier who folded his tent as he prepared to leave for home.

a building from God.—This does not suggest that the body we have is not from God, for we are His creatures. Paul's thought was of the permanent abode of the saints of God as a creation of God, not a house that man makes. Abraham "looked for the city that has foundations whose builder and maker is God" (Heb. 11:10). Peter describes it as "an inheritance that is incorruptible, and undefiled, and that fadeth not away, reserved in heaven for you, who by the power of God are guarded through faith unto the salvation ready to be revealed at the last time" (I Pet. 1:3-5). This is the Father's house in which, according to Jesus, there are many mansions. See John 14:2.

Paul spoke of the spiritual body and the permanent building in which the saints will dwell in heaven. Both concepts describe the contrast between heaven and the earthly, temporal, perishing body in which we live in this life. The terms do not contradict each other; neither do they necessarily refer to different phases of the life beyond the grave.

For verily in this we groan.—Whatever that suffering was that brought Paul near death in Asia, it was an experience that left a vivid impression on his mind. As he thought of it, he sighed the relief that heaven would bring. Like a soldier who longs for victory and the time to go home, Paul was eager for the battle to be over so that he might lay aside the temporary physical body and be clothed with the habitation which is from heaven.

not be found naked.—Those who assume that Paul had in mind the intermediate state of the dead—the Scriptures clearly teach that there is such a state—assume that he is speaking about it in this passage. But it seems more likely that he was only contrasting this life with the heavenly state. Then what does "not be found naked" mean? The Corinthians were thoroughly familiar with the philosophical view that taught that absence from the body meant freedom from trial and hardship. The goal was to have no body at all. But this was not Paul's idea. Rather than this being a discussion of the intermediate state of the dead, it seems to be Paul's answer to those who might have held false views of the resurrection. Some of the Corinthians had been denying the resurrection. Paul's desire to be free from the body was based on what he knew by revelation concerning the resurrection body. No one with this knowledge would look forward to a time when he would be without a body that is, be found naked. The resurrection body will be like the glorious body of Christ. This explains why Paul said, "We that are in this tabernacle groan, being burdened." The afflictions, distresses, imprisonments, and hardships which he suffered were heaven burdens. But to Paul they were light when compared to the eternal weight of glory that awaits the faithful follower of Christ. He explained the expression, "not be found naked" by saying, "not that we would be unclothed but that we would be clothed upon, that what is mortal may be swallowed up with life."

the earnest of the Spirit.—See comment on 1:22. The earnest of the Spirit is the guarantee or pledge that God will provide a spiritual body for the saints in heaven. When we say that the Holy Spirit is the guarantee, we are using the well known figure of speech, metonymy, which puts the person for the thing he does. The Holy Spirit is the Person who gives the guarantee or reveals the pledge. It was revealed directly to the apostle, but written in the sacred Scriptures for us. It is proper, then, to say that the saints of God have a written guarantee that there is a building from God, a house not made with hands, eternal, in the heavens.

97

for we walk by faith.—As to the heavenly home, we must depend on the information God has made known by His Spirit through the inspired apostles. We do not see heaven, but we hope for it because God says it is waiting for His people. This is the basis of Paul's undaunted courage in face of hardship. He was willing, of course, to be absent from the body that he might be at home with the Lord.

There are two thoughts expressed here: (1) At home in the body means absence from the Lord; and (2) absence from the body—death—means at home with the Lord. Since Paul, apparently, did not choose to discuss the intermediate state at this point but concentrate upon the goal of heaven, it seems unnecessary to consider it in the explanation of his remarks. When Christ comes at the end of the age, the dead will be raised and those that are alive will together with them be caught up to meet the Lord in the air, and so shall they ever be with Him. See I Thes. 4:13-18.

That the righteous dead will be with the Lord in the intermediate state seems to be indicated by the words of Jesus to the dying thief: "Today shalt thou be with me in Paradise. See comment on this passage in *Studies in Luke,* page 380.

Wherefore we make it our aim.—Paul's constant concern was that he be well-pleasing to the Lord. He seemed quite content to leave the matter of the time when he would be absent from the body and present with the Lord in His hands. This is in accord with what Jesus said about the unknown time of His coming. The faithful need to watch and be ready! Paul did not want to be like that unfaithful servant who, because his master had delayed his coming, began to mistreat his fellow-servants. See Matt. 24:45-51. Jesus said that the unfaithful servant would be cut asunder and have his portion appointed with the hypocrits. Paul knew of the judgment which all will face. His mission was to help others prepare for that Day.

For we must all be made manifest before the judgment-seat of Christ.
—Paul uses the figure of a military tribunal to describe the Judgment. The judgment-seat is the elevated platform on which the judge sits. All will be gathered before the Judge.

Jesus used the figure of a royal throne to describe the same Judgment scene. "When the Son of man shall come in his glory and all his angels with him, then shall he sit on the throne of his glory: and before him shall be gathered all the nations; and he shall separate them one from another, as the shepherd separateth the sheep from the goats" (Matt. 25:31-32). John describes the Judgment Day by using the figure of the great white throne: "And I saw a great white throne, and him that sat upon it, from whose face the earth and the heaven fled away; and there was found no place for them. And I saw the dead, the great and the small, before the throne; and the books were opened: and another book was opened which is the book of life: and the dead were judged out of the things which were written in the books according to their works" (Rev. 20:11-12).

Some assume that these are three different judgments. Since all of them refer to the end of the world and the coming of Christ, it is clear that all of them describe the same Judgment Day.

God through Christ is the Judge. "He hath appointed a day in which he will judge the world in righteousness by the man whom he hath ordained whereof he hath given assurance unto all men in that he hath raised him from the dead" (Acts 17:30). Ecclesiastes closes with the same thought: "This is the end of the matter. Fear God, and keep his commandments; for this is the whole duty of man. For God will bring every work into judgment, with every secret thing whether it be good or evil" (Eccl. 12:13). Revelation indicates that the books will be opened on that day. One of them is the record of the deeds of men whether they be good or bad. Another of the books is the Book of Life. If any man's name is not found written in that book, he will be cast into the lake of fire which is the second death. Still another book is the gospel which Paul preached: "God shall judge the secrets of men, according to my gospel by Jesus Christ" (Rom. 2:16). The Judgment Day is a strong motivating force leading to repentance.

Jesus said, "Marvel not at this for the hour cometh, when all that are in the tombs shall hear his voice and shall come forth; they that have done good, unto the resurrection of life; and they that have done evil, unto the resurrection of judgment" (John 5:28-29). Paul's ambition was to be well-pleasing to God so that in the Judgment Day he might be among those who have done good.

Motivating Forces

Scripture

5:11-17 Knowing therefore the fear of the Lord, we persuade men, but we are made manifest unto God; and I hope that we are made manifest also in your consciences. 12 We are not again commending ourselves unto you, but speak as giving you occasion of glorying on our behalf, that ye may have wherewith to answer them that glory in appearance, and not in heart. 13 For whether we are beside ourselves, it is unto God; or whether we are of sober mind, it is unto you. 14 For the love of Christ constraineth us; because we thus judge, that one died for all, therefore all died; 15 and he died for all, that they that live should no longer live unto themselves, but unto him who for their sakes died and rose again. 16 Wherefore we henceforth know no man after the flesh: even though we have known Christ after the flesh, yet now we know *him so* no more. 17 Wherefore if any man is in Christ, he is a new cerature: the old things are passed away; behold, they are become new.

Comments

Knowing therefore the fear of the Lord.—Paul turns from the thought of man's responsibility to God and the fact that all shall be made manifest before the judgment-seat of Christ to the responsibility that lay upon him in relation to his ministry of reconciliation. He discussed two basic motivating forces of that ministry: (1) the fear of the Lord and (2) the love of Christ.

A sense of reverence and awe arises from the fact that all must appear before the Judge of the universe to give account of the things done in the body. The guilty fear the punishment that is associated with wrong doing. The sincere servant of the Lord has a dread of doing that which is not pleasing to God. Paul wrote to the Ephesians and said, "Grieve not the Holy Spirit of God, in whom ye were sealed unto the day of redemption" (Eph. 4:30). David prayed, "Keep back thy servant also from presumptuous sins" (Psa. 19:13). Paul mentioned his fear and trembling on coming to Corinth. See *Studies in First Corinthians*, page 34. Since children are to be like their fathers, Peter writes, "If ye call on him as father, who without respect of persons judgeth according to each man's work, pass the time of your sojourning in fear: knowing that ye were redeemed, not with corruptible things, with silver or gold, from your vain manner of life handed down from your fathers: but with precious blood, as of a lamb without blemish and without spot, even the blood of Christ" (I Pet. 1:17-18). John explained the fear of the disobedient in contrast to the love of those who do the will of God. See I John 4:17-19. The disobedient fear punishment, but perfect love—love that is expressed in obedience to the commandments of God—casts out fear. Our love for God springs from the fact that He first loved us.

Adam was afraid of God because he knew that he was guilty of transgressing His command. Anxiety caused the guilty one to attempt to cover his own sin. Adam used the fig leaf in a vain attempt to hide his disobedience from God. Ever since that day, man has been trying through his own schemes to blot out the effect of his sins, but the fact remains that only God can forgive sins.

The divine plan is to blot out sin by the blood of Christ. Paul was suddenly stopped in his mad effort to destroy the church of God when he accepted the mercy of God and got his sins washed away by submitting to baptism at the hand of Ananias. From that time forward, the love of Christ for him kept him aware of the need to obey His Lord as a faithful servant.

we persuade men.—Opinions differ over the meaning of this statement. Some assume that Paul was attempting to persuade men of his own sincerity. He had been reminding the Corinthians that he was not indulging in self-glory. As to the charge of the false teachers on this issue, he rested his case on the truth of the gospel message which he proclaimed and the evidence of Christian character which his converts displayed.

It seems more likely, then, that Paul was referring to his ministry in which he was persuading men to be reconcilled to God. His converts at Corinth were proof of his effectiveness. He was persuading men to obey Christ that they might be prepared to stand before the judgment-seat of Christ. At Corinth, Paul had "reasoned in the synagogue every sabbath and persuaded Jews and Greeks" (Acts 18:4). At Thessalonica, he had gone into the synagogue of the Jews and "for three sabbath days reasoned with them from the scriptures, opening and alleging that it behooved Christ to suffer, and to arise from the dead; and that this Jesus, whom, said he, I proclaim unto you is the Christ" (Acts 17:2-3).

Paul consistently presented the facts about Jesus in persuading men to believe that He was the Christ. He told them of the goodness of God that was leading them to repentance. He told them of the love of God who gave His Son to die for us while we were sinners. He told them about the judgment that all face and appealed to them to repent in preparation for that day. He told of the command to be baptized for the remission of sins as he urged men to obey God.

Paul's own conversion had followed this same persuasive pattern. Stephen's message profoundly affected the young man named Saul. He knew well the history of his people, the Jews, as Stephen related it. He knew of their stubborn disobedience that led some to attempt to go back to Egypt. He knew that the temple had taken the place of the tabernacle in the wilderness, and he was fully aware of the fact that God does not dwell in houses made with hands. He knew also that the fathers had persecuted the prophets and killed those who had showed beforehand the coming of the Righteous One. Stephen had burned this truth into the minds of his audience when he said, "You have now become murderers of that One." But Stephen also presented the evidence of the resurrection of Christ when he said, "Behold, I see the heavens opened, and the Son of man standing on the right hand of God" (Acts 7:55).

When Saul met the Lord on the Damascus Road, his question was: "What shall I do?" Stephen had impressed him with the mercy and love of God, for Saul had heard him when he prayed, "Lord, lay not this sin to their charge" (Acts 7:60). See Paul's own comment in Acts 22:16-21 and I Tim. 1:12-14. The person who believes in the Lord Jesus and understands his love and mercy readily responds to the reasonable command to be baptized for the remission of sins. See Acts 9:17-19 and 22:16.

Immediately upon his conversion, Paul began to preach Christ, for he was not disobedient to the heavenly vision. See Acts 26: 19-23. He urged Gentiles as well as Jews to repent and turn to God, doing works worthy of repentance.

we are made manifest unto God.—On the Judgment Day, God will judge the secrets of men according to the gospel, by Jesus Christ. See Rom. 2:16. Paul was aware of the fact that God knew his heart at all times and that no motive of his was hidden from Him. In this frame of mind he had carried on his ministry as an apostle of Christ. He had dealt frankly and sincerely with the Corinthians and believed that he had a right to hope that they were aware of his attitude. He had already called their attention to his sincerity in dealing with them in contrast to those who were corrupting the Word of God.

we are not again commending ourselves unto you.—It seemed necessary for Paul to defend his sincerity because of false charges that were being made against him continually. See 10:8-9. He was not commending himself by what he said about his ministry of persuading men, but giving the Corinthians a reason for being proud of the fact that the gospel had been brought to them by the apostle of Jesus Christ. This gave them a substantial answer to the claims of false apostles who were really deceitful workers of Satan. See 11:12-13. Such deceitful workers were proud of their external appearance, but Paul gloried in the fact that the secrets of his heart were known to God.

for whether we are beside ourselves.—If Paul were out of his mind, it would be evident to God, for God had placed His approval upon him in appointing him to the apostleship. Festus, listening to the defense that Paul made of the gospel before King Agrippa, cried out: "Paul, thou art mad; thy much learning is turning thee mad" (Acts 26:24). But Paul assured him that he was speaking only words of truth and soberness. He was sure that the king knew this too. The Corinthians had ample opportunity to know the mind of Paul for he had determined not to know anything among them except Jesus Christ and Him crucified. His appeal to them had been made on the basis of known facts of the gospel which were in accord with the Scriptures. See I Cor. 15:1-4. He had sincerely proclaimed the message of Christ to them. As one sent from God to do this task, he was aware that what he did was done in the sight of God.

for the love of Christ constraineth us.—Paul's reverence for God led him to a life of sincerity in his ministry of preaching the gospel. Christ's love for him became an irresistible force that held him on the true course. See Rom. 5:6-8.

that one died for all.—The doctrine of the vicarious or substitutionary atonement is based on the theory of a limited atonement. This doctrine of limited atonement springs from the doctrine of predestination which asumes that God predetermined that certain individuals would be saved and that others would be the objects of His wrath with no hope of salvation. According to the theory, those predetermined to be saved cannot resist the grace of God. They will persevere unto the final salvation of their souls—no chance of being lost! The doctrine of a limited atonement teaches that Christ died for these only, that is, He died in their stead and they will, therefore, be saved. The theory assumes that Paul's words, "He died for all," means for all who were predetermined to be saved. The argument, among other things, is based upon the translation of the preposition that is rendered "for," assuming that it means "instead of." But the same preposition is rendered "for their sake" in the last clause of verse fifteen. Christ "died and rose again for their sakes." This would seem to suggest that if He died instead of them, He also rose instead of them, which, of course, doesn't make sense. Since Paul uses the same preposition in the two phrases, consistency suggests that they be translated by the same words in each case. This leads to the conclusion that Christ's death and resurrection were *for the benefit* of all who believe on Him. In I Cor. 15:3, Paul says, "Christ died for—this is the same word which he used in II Cor. 5:14-15—our sins according to the Scriptures." His death concerned our sins. It was for the benefit of all sinners, "for God so loved the world that He gave His only begotten Son that whosoever believeth on Him might not perish but have everlasting life." No limited atonement here! "And the Spirit and the bride say, Come. And he that heareth, let him say, Come. And he that is athirst, let him come: he that will, let him take the water of life freely" (Rev. 22:17). Rather than a limited and substitutionary atonement, the Scriptures indicate that Christ's death was for all sinners, that they might hear the gospel and repent and be baptized for the remission of their sins. Mark 16: 15-16; Acts 2:38.

The standard by which Paul evaluated the death of Christ was the Scriptures. See I Cor. 15:3. But through the centuries men have been influenced by the doctrines of predestination and total depravity which have led them to the theories of limited atonement, irresistible grace, and perseverance of saints.

The Scriptures clearly indicate that God predetermined that believers would be saved, whether Jews or Gentiles. See Rom. 9:24, 30; Rom. 5:8; John 3:16. The Scriptures teach that as a result of Adam's sin physical death passed to all men. See Rom. 5:12; I Cor. 15:22 and Heb. 9:27. Spiritual death, on the other hand, is the result of one's own personal sins. See John 8:21, 34; Eph. 2:1-6; Rom. 6:23. To assume that the human being, as a result of Adam's sin, is in a state of depravity which renders him incapable of doing or thinking anything good in the spiritual realm is to make the preaching of the gospel for the salvation of the lost a meaningless gesture. But Paul declared that it was the good pleasure of God through the foolishness of what was preached to save those who believe. See I Cor. 1:21. If it requires a regenerating act of the Holy Spirit before man can believe, then the Word of the Cross truly is in vain. But Jesus clearly indicated that sinners for whom He died were to hear the Word through the inspired apostles and believe. See John 17:20-21.

Some assume that the doctrine of substitutionary atonement is taught in Matt. 20:28 and Mark 10:45. Jesus gave His life as a ransom for, or on behalf of, the many. Some would translate, "instead of many" which is possible except for the fact that it does not harmonize with the whole teaching of Scripture on the subject. Paul's comment in I Tim. 2:6 explains the meaning of Matt. 20:28, for he says that "Christ gave himself a ransom for all."

Out of the references to ransom, two more closely related theories of the atonement have come: (1) The ransom theory, and (2) the commercial theory. Based on the thought that we are redeemed by the blood of Christ (Eph. 1:7) or "bought with a price" (I Cor. 6:20) some have taught that God paid the price of the blood of Christ to the devil to buy the release of the sinner. But the Scriptures simply state that we were bought with a price, the blood of Christ, without any assumption that it was paid to Satan. The commercial theory assumes that the death of Christ was exactly equal to the punishment that God would have inflicted on sinners, and that because of Christ's death He is just in forgiving them. The theory assumes that God in His purity and holiness was offended by the sinner and that only the death of Christ could change His attitude. The Scriptures state, however, that while we were yet sinners, God commended His own love toward us through the death of Christ. See Rom. 5:8.

The Scriptures present the death of Christ in various relationships: (1) In relation to God, it shows His love and His justice in passing over the sins done under the first covenant. See I John 4:9-10; Heb. 9:15; Rom. 3:35-36. (2) As to Christ, it was to destroy the works of the devil. See I John 3:8; Heb. 2:14. (3) As to the sinner, it was to save him from the wrath of God—punishment in the Day of Judgment—and restore him to fellowship with God. See Rom. 2:5-11; 5:9-11. (4) As to sin, it is the means of blotting out sin. Propitiation or expiation has to do with sin. The only way to escape the wrath of God is to obey the gospel. Under the New Covenant the blood of Christ cleanses the conscience from dead works to serve the living God. See Heb. 9:14. God promises those who accept the terms of the New Covenant that He will be merciful to their iniquities and their sins He will remember no more. See Heb. 8:12.

This brief glimpse of the teaching of the Scriptures about the death of Christ enables us to see something of the motivating power of love in the life of Paul.

therefore all died.—In I Cor. 15:22, Paul says: "As in Adam all die so in Christ shall all be made alive." But this is a reference to the resurrection of the body which is to follow physical death. All who die physically will be raised from the dead, some to the resurrection of condemnation and some to the resurrection of life. See John 5:28-29. But in II Cor. 5:14, Paul is dealing with spiritual death. Since he says that Christ died for all—that is, for all sinners—

it is evident that all who have sinned have died spiritually. See Rom.
5:16-18.

and he died for all.—This does not teach universal salvation. It does
indicate that an opportunity to be saved is provided for all men.
See I Tim. 2:3-4. Paul speaks of God who is the Savior of all men,
especially those who believe. See I Tim. 4:10. God has made it
possible for all men to be saved through the death of Christ; those
who accept His offer through belief expressed in obedience to His
commands are saved. Those who are saved are no longer to live in
selfishness; they are to commit themselves to Christ who for their
sakes died and rose again.

no man after the flesh.—The standard by which Paul recognized the
value of a man was his relation to Christ. If any man is in Christ,
he is a new creature. Paul said, "For as many of you as were baptized
into Christ did put on Christ. There can be neither Jew nor Greek,
there can be neither bond nor free, there can be no male and female;
for ye are all one in Christ Jesus" (Gal. 3:27-28).

have known Christ after the flesh.—Paul, speaking of his kinsmen
according to the flesh, recognized the fact that Christ was of the
Jews according to flesh. See Rom. 9:3-5. He may have in mind the
same concept here. In common with most Jews, he had probably
expected Messiah to set up a political kingdom. He, as most Jews, had
been unable to reconcile this view with the claims of Jesus of Nazareth who said He was Son of God. See John 10:34-35; Luke 22:66-
71. When the apostles, however, on the Day of Pentecost preached
the fact of the resurrection of Christ and His exaltation to the right
hand of God, three thousand Jews were convinced and got themselves
baptized in the name of Jesus Christ for the remission of their sins.
See Acts 2:36-40. After Paul had seen the risen Lord, he argued with
the Jews on the basis of the Scriptures that it was necessary for
Christ to suffer and rise from the dead and that this Jesus whom he
proclaimed was the Christ. See Acts 17:3.

There is no way of knowing whether or not Paul had seen Jesus
before He appeared to him on the Damascus Road. Paul's relation
to Christ was based on the gospel which he heard from Stephen and
Ananias and the fact that he had actually seen the risen Lord.

The Ministry of Reconciliation
Scripture

5:18-21. But all things are of God, who reconciled us to himself
through Christ, and gave unto us the ministry of reconciliation; 19

to wit, that God was in Christ reconciling the world unto himself, not reckoning unto them their trespasses, and having committed unto us the word of reconciliation.

20 We are ambassadors therefore on behalf of Christ, as though God were entreating by us: we beseech you on behalf of Christ, be ye reconciled to God. 21 Him who knew no sin he made to be sin on our behalf; that we might become the righteousness of God in him.

Comments

But all things are of God.—For Paul, the old things had passed away. He had suffered the loss of all things that he might gain Christ. See Phil. 3:1-16. Once he had thought that he ought to do many things contrary to the name of Jesus of Nazareth. See Acts 26:9. He had actually tried to destroy the church of God. See Gal. 1:13. But God reconciled him unto Himself and gave him the ministry of reconciliation. He had become a new creature in Christ. *God was in Christ reconciling the world unto himself.*—This sentence should, in all probability be punctuated as follows: "God was, in Christ, reconciling the world unto himself." It was through Christ that God created the world; it was through Him that God was reconciling the world unto Himself. Paul was the ambassador of Christ working together with God. This in no way contradicts the plain teaching of Scripture as to the deity of Jesus. His mission was to reveal the Father and save the lost. See Col. 2:9; John 1:1-2, 14; 14:7-8. Paul said that Jesus existed in the form of God on an equality with God. See Phil. 2:5-11. The Gospel of John was written to show how Christ revealed the Father. See John 1:18. At the height of His ministry, Philip said to Jesus, "Show us the Father, and it will suffice us." Jesus answered, "Believest thou not that I am in the Father and the Father in me? The words that I say unto you I speak not of myself: but the Father abiding in me doeth his works. Believe me that I am in the Father, and the Father in me: or else believe me for my very works sake" (John 14:10-11). If they had only recognized Him, they would have known the Father. See John 14:7. The ministry of Christ shows the Father's effort to bring men into fellowship with Himself again. Sin which caused the separation is blotted out by the blood of Christ. Paul had accepted this profound truth and had gotten himself baptized by Ananias that his sins might be washed away. *not reckoning unto them their trespasses.*—See Paul's comment in Rom. 4:6-8. The blood of Christ covers the sin of the one who believes in Christ; for that reason, the Lord will not reckon his sin against him. As an apostle of Christ, Paul told sinners how to be saved that they might be reconciled to God.

we are ambassadors.—This term refers to the apostles of Christ whom He equipped by the baptism in the Holy Spirit to speak for Him. See John 16:8-14; I Cor. 2:6-16. The wisdom of God had been revealed to them through the Spirit of God. They were ambassadors on behalf of Christ, that is, they were acting on His authority when they revealed the terms on which sinners could be reconciled to God. Instead of reckoning their trespasses against them, God was urging sinners to accept His terms and be brought into fellowship with Him again.

Him who knew no sin.—The sinlessness of Jesus is determined by the fact that He was tempted in all points like as we are yet without sin. See Heb. 4:15. God made Him represent sin when He died on the cross for our sakes. This made it possible for us to become representatives of the righteous standard of conduct which God approves. The words of Christ on the cross, "My God, my God, why hast thou forsaken me?" show what it meant to represent sin. The cross shows what it means to be lost. The life of dedication to Christ shows what it means to become a representative of the kind of life God approves. Paul put it this way: "I have been crucified with Christ; Christ lives in me." See Gal. 2:20. What was true of Paul is also true of those who belong to Christ, for they have crucified the flesh with the passions and lusts thereof. See Gal. 5:24.

The sin offering under the Old Covenant sheds light on the meaning of the cross. The sacrificial animal had to be physically perfect. After the priest had confessed the sins of the people, the animal was slain to symbolize the fact that death is the penalty for sin. The perfection of the sacrifice symbolized the purity of the worshipper whose sins had been covered by the blood.

the righteousness of God in him.—With his sins washed away in the blood of the Lamb, the believer becomes the representative of the kind of life God expects His people to live. Christ set the perfect example of this righteous conduct, for He did not sin. Peter, commenting on this, said, "Christ also suffered for you, leaving you an example, that ye should follow in his steps: who did no sin" (I Pet. 2:21-22).

Paul, speaking of the grace of God which reigns through righteousness unto eternal life through Jesus Christ, asks: "What shall we say then? Shall we continue in sin, that grace may abound? God forbid.

We who died to sin, how shall we any longer live therein?" (Rom. 5:21-6:2). To those who have been buried with Christ through baptism into death and have been raised together with Him to walk in the new life, Paul adds, "Even so reckon yourselves to be dead unto sin, but alive unto God in Christ Jesus. Let not sin therefore reign in your mortal bodies that ye should obey the lusts thereof: neither present your members unto sin as instruments of unrighteousness; but present yourselves unto God, as alive from the dead, and your members as instruments of righteousness unto God! (Rom. 6:11-13).

Summary

Paul faced the future with undaunted courage because he knew that although his body was growing weak under the load he was carrying there was a home for him in heaven. His physical body was like a tent in which he was living temporarily, but the heavenly building would be a permanent dwelling place with the Lord.

Pain and hardship made Paul long for the time when he would be in that heavenly house not made with hands. He was not anticipating a condition without a body. Pagan philosophers thought such a state would be heavenly, because they would then be free from pain and suffering associated with the physical body. Paul looked to the time when the Lord would fashion anew this mortal body that it might conform to the body of His glory. We shall be like Him, for we shall see Him in His glorious body.

Paul was sure of this because of the guarantee God had given through the revelation from God by the Holy Spirit. We can read about it in the Bible. In this confidence, Paul longed for the time when he would be able to leave this earthly home and be at home with the Lord in that permanent, heavenly dwelling.

Therefore, Paul made it his aim to be well-pleasing to the Lord in this life and in the heavenly state. The verdict that will be rendered on the Judgment Day will depend on what we have done in the body in this life, whether it is good or evil.

Because of this solemn thought, Paul had committed himself to the ministry of reconciliation which he had received from God. He was endeavoring to persuade men to obey God and be prepared for the Judgment Day. He knew that this was evident to God and he hoped that the Corinthians were aware of it too. Their own response to this message of reconciliation would allow them to boast of the fact that they had received it from God's apostle. This differs from the situation of those who were boasting in false hopes instead of the real hope that comes from obedience to the gospel.

Christ's love for him was the compelling force that kept Paul on this true course. He knew that Christ had died for him, for He died for all sinners. Paul knew that he had died through his trespasses and sins; the greatest of these was his attempt to destroy the church of God. But Christ died for sinners so that they might no longer live for themselves but for Him who for their sakes died and rose again.

Since he had come to understand what the love of Christ had done for him, he no longer looked at any man as a mere human being but as one who could become a new creature through obedience to Christ. Once he had looked upon Messiah—indeed, most Jews had done the same thing—as a human Christ. But His death and resurrection changed all this for Paul. Old things had passed away, behold, they had become new!

Thus God had reconciled Paul to Himself through Christ and had given him the ministry of reconciliation. God was, in Christ, reconciling the world unto Himself. He was not entering their trespasses in the record against them, but through His ambassador He was pleading that they reconcile themselves to Him. This was possible because He made the sinless Christ to represent sin as He died on the cross that they might become the representatives of righteousness which God approves by their relation to Christ.

Questions

1. Why did Paul speak of his confidence in the future?
2. On what did he base his confidence?
3. What is to be said in the light of Scripture about the assumption that Paul was anticipating the return of Christ in his own lifetime?
4. What had Jesus said to the apostles about the time of His second coming?
5. What bearing does this problem have on the fact that Paul wrote as an inspired apostle?
6. What had he written to the Thessalonians about this issue?
7. What did Paul mean when he wrote: "We all shall not sleep, but we shall be changed"?
8. What did he write to the Philippians about the necessity of carrying on his ministry for their sakes?
9. As he faced death, what did he write to Timothy about it?

10. What warning did Christ give in connection with His coming?
11. What is taught in the Scriptures about the intermediate state.
12. Did Paul discuss the intermediate state of the dead, or did he have in mind the permanent dwelling with the Lord in heaven?
13. How did Paul contrast the physical body with the permanent home in heaven?
14. How does he describe the building from God?
15. What had been the attitude of some toward the resurrection?
16. What had Paul written to the Corinthians in his first epistle about the kind of body they were to have in the resurrection?
17. How had he described the resurrection body to the Philippians?
18. What did the apostle John say about it?
19. What did Paul have in mind when he spoke of the physical body as a tabernacle or tent?
20. How had Peter referred to his physical body as he anticipated death?
21. Why did Paul say that the building from God is not made with hands?
22. What kind of a city was Abraham looking for?
23. How did Peter describe the salvation which will be revealed at the close of this age?
24. How explain Paul's deep emotions arising from the things he suffered in the body?
25. What does "not be found naked" mean?
26. What was the attitude of the Greeks about being free from the body?
27. How did Paul expect that which is mortal to be swallowed by life?
28. What did he mean by the earnest of the Spirit? Why did he mention it here? Where may we read about it?
29. What does it mean to walk by faith?
30. Why did he speak of being at home with the Lord?
31. What did Paul write to the Thessalonians about the things that will happen when Christ comes again?
32. Why did Paul make it his aim to be well-pleasing to God?
32. Why was he trying to persuade men to obey God?
34. What is the judgment-seat of Christ? By what other figures is the Judgment described?
35. What did Paul tell the men of Athens about the Judgment?
36. What did the writer of Ecclesiastes say about it?

37. What does the Book of Revelation say about it?
38. What did Paul write to the Romans about it?
39. What did Jesus say about the Judgment?
40. What were the controlling forces in Paul's ministry?
41. What place does fear—reverence for God—have in the life of the Christian?
42. What was Paul persuading men to do?
43. How is this illustrated by his efforts at Thessalonica?
44. What pattern did Paul follow in his work of persuading men?
45. How had Paul been influenced by the effort of Stephen to persuade men of the truth of the gospel?
46. Why did Paul say, "We are made manifest to God"?
47. Why did he again raise the issue of self-commendation?
48. What answer was given to those who insinuated that Paul was out of his mind?
49. What caused Paul to realize the compelling force of the love of Christ?
50. What is meant by "one died for all"?
51. On what is the doctrine of "substitutionary atonement" based?
52. On what is the doctrine of "limited atonement" based?
53. How does Paul's statement about the death of Christ in I Cor. 15:3 help to understand what he wrote about it in II Cor. 5:14-15?
54. What is the doctrine of "irresistible grace"?
55. What is its bearing on the doctrine of the "perseverance of the saints"?
56. What are some of the things involved in the doctrine of predestination?
57. What is the "commercial theory" of the atonement?
58. What do the Scriptures teach about the death of Christ in its various relationships?
59. What did Paul mean by, "therefore all died"?
60. Why did Christ die for all sinners?
61. Why did the death of Christ change Paul's views about men and Christ?
62. Why does Paul speak of the fact that God gave him the ministry of reconciliation?
63. What is meant by: "God was in Christ reconciling the world unto Himself"?
64. What do the Scriptures teach about the deity of Jesus? About the unity of the Father and the Son?

65. Why is it stated that God did not reckon their trespasses unto men?
66. What is an ambassador? How does this describe Paul's ministry?
67. What do the Scriptures say about the sinlessness of Jesus?
68. What do the words, "he made sin on our behalf" mean?
69. What is meant by: "that we might become the righteousness of God in him"?

For Discussion

1. What is the place of punishment as a motivating force to obedience in the home? the school? the state? to God?
2. How does it compare with love in these areas?

CHAPTER SIX

Analysis

A. Paul told how he had endeavored to keep his ministry of reconciliation blameless (1-10).
   1. He gave some additional information about the ministry of reconciliation (1-2).
      a) He was working together with God (1a).
      b) He strongly urged the Corinthians not to receive the gracious favor of God in vain (b).
      c) He gave his reasons for this exhortation (2).
         (1) It was based on the Scripture that told how the Lord had listened to the cry of His people and had helped them when they needed salvation.
         (2) He explained that the acceptable time, the day of salvation, is now.
   2. He explained how he had kept his ministry blameless (3-4a).
      a) He gave no occasion for anyone to stumble because of him.
      b) He followed this course that his ministry might be blameless.
   3. He listed the areas in which his ministry was blameless (4b-7a).
      a) He had patiently endured in (1) afflictions, (2) necessities (3) distresses, (4) stripes, (5) imprisonments, (6) tumults, (7) labors, (8) watchings, and (9) fastings.
      b) He listed eight more areas in which his ministry was blameless. They were in (1) pureness, (2) knowledge, (3) longsuffering, (4) kindness, (5) holy spirit, (6) love unfeigned, (7) word of truth, and (8) power of God.
   4. He told of the means by which he had carried on his blameless ministry (7b-8a). They were (1) weapons of righteousness, (2) glory and dishonor, and (3) evil report and good report.
   5. He explained the manner in which he had served (8b-10). He had done so (1) as unknown, yet well known; (2) as dying, and behold we live; (3) as chastened, and not

killed; (4) as sorrowful, yet always rejoicing; and (5) as having nothing, yet possessing all things.

B. Based on his blameless ministry, Paul made a strong appeal to be accepted by the Corinthians (11-18).

   1. He plead for reciprocal affections (11-13).

      a) In doing so, he spoke openly to them.

      b) He reminded them of his enlarged affection, for there was room in his heart for all of them.

      c) The only limit was on their part, not his.

      d) He urged them to enlarge their hearts for him, for they were his children in the Lord.

   2. He plead for complete separation from unbelievers and their contaminating practices (14-18).

      a) What this meant to their lives (14-16a).

         (1) They were not to be unequally yoked with unbelievers.

         (2) Righteousness and iniquity cannot be partners.

         (3) Light and darkness cannot mix.

         (4) Christ and Belial cannot be in agreement.

         (5) Faith has no part with unbelief.

         (6) The temple of God cannot be based on the same foundation as an idol's temple.

      b) Why he plead for this separation (16b-17a).

         (1) God said, "I will dwell in them and walk in their midst."

         (2) He also said, "I will be their God and they my people."

         (3) The Lord also said, "Come out from among them and be ye separate; touch no unclean thing."

      c) The promise of the Lord God Almighty to those who respond (17b-18).

         (1) I will receive you.

         (2) I will be your Father.

         (3) You will be My sons and daughters.

The Blameless Ministry

Scripture

6:1-10. And working together with him we entreat also that ye receive not the grace of God in vain 2 (for he saith,

At an acceptable time I hearkened unto thee,
And in a day of salvation did I succor thee:
behold, now is the acceptable time; behold, now is the day of salvation): 3 giving no occasion of stumbling in anything, that our ministration be not blamed; 4 but in everything commending ourselves, as ministers of God, in much patience, in afflictions, in necessities, in distresses, 5 in stripes, in imprisonments, in tumults, in labors, in watchings, in fastings; 6 in pureness, in knowledge, in long suffering, in kindness, in the Holy Spirit, in love unfeigned, 7 in the word of truth, in the power of God; by the armor of righteousness on the right hand and on the left, 8 by glory and dishonor, by evil report and good report; as deceivers, and yet true; 9 as unknown, and yet well known; as dying, and behold, we live; as chastened, and not killed; 10 as sorrowful, yet always rejoicing; as poor, yet making many rich; as having nothing, and yet possessing all things.

Comments

And working together with him.—While the words "with him" do not appear in the Greek, the context makes it clear that Paul as an ambassador on behalf of Christ was working together with God. He had spoken of himself and Apollos as God's fellow-workers in his first epistle. See I Cor. 3:9. Each of them had his own work to do, but God gave the increase. Paul and Apollos were fellow-workers who belonged to God.

Those who teach and preach the gospel must work together to present the message of reconciliation effectively. But they should also remember that they are privileged to work with God in this ministry, for God through this means is reconciling the world unto Himself.

receive not the grace of God in vain.—This was no idle warning. The Corinthians were in constant danger of forsaking the truth which Paul had delivered to them because of the presence of false teachers in their midst.

This was also true of almost every church that had been taught the gospel by Paul. False teachers came to Antioch and caused even Peter and Barnabas to be influenced by their claims. They went so far as to refuse to eat with Gentile Christians. Paul had to set the matter straight and resist Peter to the face. Paul showed him that he had been crucified with Christ and that Christ was living in him. Therefore he was not making the grace of God a meaningless thing. See Gal. 2:11-21.

116

There is a serious question about much of the program of the church today: Does it make the grace of God meaningless? Is the Word of the Cross foolishness to those who should count it, as Paul did, the very power to save the believer? Too often the church resembles a club composed of nice people, but with little to remind one of the body of Christ. Is the first business of the church being neglected? Is the church actually seeking to save the lost?

The chrurch, in altogether too many cases, has become a tree without fruit. It should be called upon to repent and do its first work, just as Jesus called on Ephesus to do. It needs to be like the disciples in Jerusalem who "went everywhere preaching the Word" (Acts 8:4).

The grace of God is made meaningless when we fail to live in such a manner that it becomes evident that Christ lives in us. It is made meaningless when we fail to share the gospel of His grace with others. The driving force in the life of Paul was this: "Christ Jesus came into the world to save sinners" (I Tim. 1:15).

for he saith.—The pronoun is inferred from the context and suggests that God is speaking through the Scriptures. The quotation is from Isa. 49:8 where it is introduced with the phrase, "Thus saith the Lord."

In the absence of the pronoun in our text, it would be equally correct to say, "The Scripture says," for God is the Author of the sacred writings. See Heb. 3:7-11 where the quotation from Psalm 95:8-11 is introduced with the statement, "The Holy Spirit saith." These statements all say one thing: The Bible is the Word of God. It is His message of reconciliation, for He heard the cry of His people and came to their rescue in "the day of salvation."

behold, now is the acceptable time.—The whole gospel age is the time of salvation. It began on Pentecost and will end when Christ comes again. It is the time during which God welcomes home sinners who repent.

Men should welcome the opportunity to be saved while it is here. They should be like prisoners who welcome release; like the blind who welcome sight; like the lost who welcome the Savior. See Luke 4:16-22.

No one knows when the longsuffering of God will end and the day of salvation will be over. See II Pet. 3:8-13; Matt. 25: 10-13. We do know that death closes the door for every man. See Luke 16:31; John 8:21. But now is the day of salvation!

giving no occasion of stumbling.—Since God was entreating men through Paul, the apostle carried out his ministry in a blameless manner. This involved two things: (1) preaching the Word, and (2) living the Christlike life. He was not ashamed of the gospel of Christ. To him, the Word of the Cross was not an empty thing. He determined not to know anything except Jesus Christ and Him crucified. He knew that God saves the believer through the foolishness of the thing preached by His inspired apostles. He lived so that he could say, "Christ lives in me." (Gal. 2:20).

Paul was not like the Jewish religionists who had caused the name of God to be blasphemed among the Gentiles. See Rom. 2:24. They failed to practice what they taught. They abhorred idols, but robbed pagan temples for the gold and precious stones of which their idols were made. They gloried in the law, but dishonored it by their transgressions. See Rom. 2:17-24.

The way of salvation is strewn with stumbling blocks left by those who fail to preach the truth and live by its standard. The preacher should be able to say with Paul, "Be imitators of me as I am of Christ."

False teachers were real stumbling blocks in the pathway of the Corinthians. Paul had good reason to warn against them. See 6:14-7:1. Such protruding rocks in the pathway of salvation can cause many to be lost.

There were, of course, those who without cause found fault with Paul's ministry. They criticized his message because they preferred the wisdom of men to the wisdom that came down from above. They impugned his motives, implying that he preached for the sake of money. See II Cor. 11:6-15.

Every faithful gospel minister is subject to the same attacks. When they come, he should remember the word of Paul to Timothy, "Suffer hardship with me as a good soldier of Jesus Christ" (II Tim. 2:3).

in much patience.—Paul developed the thought of his blameless ministry, he told of the areas in which he served God. He listed nine of them.

Patience is the first of these areas. It is the ability to endure trials. It is represented by the soldier who withstands the attack of the enemy and remains in his position after the wave of battle has rolled on. It is genuine faith in the Lord Jesus Christ that produces this ability to stand up under the trials of this life. Such patient endurance leads to God's approval which is represented by the crown of life. See James 1:2-4, 12.

Paul wrote to the Romans saying, "We also rejoice in our tribulations: knowing that tribulation worketh steadfastness, and steadfastness approvedness; and approvedness, hope: and hope putteth not to shame; because the love of God has been shed abroad in our hearts through the Holy Spirit which was given to us" (Rom. 5:3-5).

in afflictions.—Trials, distresses, and afflictions beset the way of those who journey toward the heavenly home. The writer of Hebrews listed some of the trials through which men of faith have passed. See Heb. 11:32-12:2. Those who run the race set before them find encouragement in the example of those who have endured the trials.

Jesus reminded His disciples that in this world they were to expect tribulation. But He said, "Be of good cheer, I have overcome the world" (John 16:33). Paul told the churches of Lystra, Iconium and Antioch that through many tribulations they must enter into the kingdom of God. See Acts 14:21-22. Peter wrote to the early Christians saying, "Beloved, think it not strange concerning the fiery trials among you which cometh upon you to prove you: but insomuch as ye are partakers of Christ's sufferings, rejoice: that at the revelation of his glory ye may rejoice with exceeding joy" (I Pet. 4:12-13). John wrote to the seven churches of Asia reminding them that he was a partaker in the tribulation and kingdom and patience which are in Christ Jesus. See Rev. 1:9.

in necessities.—Paul wrote to the Corinthians in his first epistle using this word to describe the distress, whatever it was, that they were facing at that time. Depressions, wars, and the like are all accompanied with distress. Paul said, "I take pleasure in weakness, in injuries, in necessities in persecutions, in distresses, for Christ's sake: when I am weak, then I am strong" (II Cor. 12:10).

In this context, necessities seem to be those circumstances in which the Christian may be compelled to undergo various hardships. Patience would certainly be needed in necessities. Paul needed it in his blameless ministry.

in distresses.—The term suggests narrow confinement produced by pressures. Paul had experienced it while waiting to learn about the situation at Corinth. That pressure had prevented his carrying on an evangelistic effort at Troas. But his patience in the distress brought ultimate triumph.

in stripes.—This is a reference to the many beating which Paul endured for the sake of Christ. He had been beaten at Philippi and barely escaped one at Corinth. See Acts 16:23, 37. The Jews had dragged him before Gallio, the proconsul, and charged him with the guilt of persuading men to worship God contrary to the law. Gallio dismissed the matter for he was not minded to be a judge of such things. Thwarted in their attempt to have Paul punished, the Jews seized Sosthenes, the ruler of the synagogue, and gave him the beating. See Acts 18:12-17. Paul ran into mob violence at Jerusalem at the close of his third missionary journey. Roman soldiers came to his rescue and prevented the mob from killing him. See Acts 21:30-32. Looking back upon such experiences, Paul wrote of his being in "stripes above measure" (II Cor. 12:23). As the servant of God he endured them and fulfilled his ministry blamelessly.

in imprisonments.—On his second journey, even before he reached Corinth, Paul had been unjustly imprisoned. See Acts 16:37. At the close of his third journey as he was about to be torn in pieces by a confused mob, Paul was arrested and put in jail. See Acts 23:10. But "the night following, the Lord stood by him, and said, Be of good cheer; for as thou hast testified concerning me at Jerusalem, so must thou bear witness also at Rome" (Acts 23:11). Paul was taken to Caesarea where he remained in prison for about two years while awaiting settlement of his case before Felix. Festus succeeded Felix and, desiring to keep favor with the Jews, asked Paul if he would be willing to go back to Jerusalem and be tried there. But Paul appealed his case to Caesar, taking advantage of his Roman citizenship and was sent to Rome. Although he entered Rome in chains, he was given certain freedoms which allowed him to continue his ministry of reconciliation. Luke closes the account in these words: "And he abode two whole years in his own hired dwelling, and received all men that went in unto him, preaching the kingdom of God, and teaching things concerning the Lord Jesus Christ with all boldness, none forbidding him" (Acts 28:30-31). During that imprisonment the whole praetorian guard came to know Christ whom Paul preached. See Phil. 1:13. What an example of patient endurance that was!

in tumults.—Riotous mobs set upon Paul on his very first missionary journey. They convinced the people that Paul should be put to death. At Lystra, they stoned him and dragged him out of the city, supposing that he was dead. See Acts 14:19. It is significant that out of Lystra, there came one of Paul's most trusted and best loved fellow-workers, Timothy. On his second missionary journey, this young man joined Paul to suffer hardship with him as a good soldier of Jesus Christ. See Acts 16:1-5.

in labors.—Not just ordinary work, but toil that meant pain and suffering. Those who suppose that the ministry is an easy life should read the story of Paul's activities in his blameless ministry.

Paul listed the hardships he suffered without so much as a hint of complaint. He patiently endured them as a servant of God. See Col. 1:24-29.

in watchings.—This may have been one of those occasions when Paul had stood guard over one who was wrestling with his problems that involved his being reconciled to God.

in fastings.—Paul and Barnabas had been set aside to this ministry after the church at Antioch, acting upon the instructions from the Holy Spirit, had fasted and prayed and laid their hands on them. See Acts 13:1-3. Fasting was not merely depriving one's self of food; it was abstaining from food in order to give one's entire thought to his relationship to God. This exercise, also, required patience on the part of the servant of God.

in pureness.—Pureness like patience was an area in which Paul was blameless. Purity in mind and heart characterized his ministry.

in knowledge.—Paul's knowledge was based solidly on the divinely revealed wisdom of God rather than on the speculative theories of men. Jesus said, "If ye had recognized me, ye would have known the Father also" (John 14:7). Paul's knowledge centered in Christ. He said, "I know him whom I have believed, and am persuaded that he is able to guard that which I have committed unto him against that day" (II Tim. 1:12). Such knowledge is necessary if the servant of God is to have a blameless ministry.

in longsuffering.—This term emphasizes the long periods of time during which one is able to hold up under trials. Paul said, "Love suffers long and is kind" (I Cor. 13:4). Longsuffering is a mark of those who belong to Jesus Christ. See Gal. 5:22-24.

in kindness.—Love expresses itself in kindness. Paul said, "Be ye kind one to another, tenderhearted, forgiving each other, even as God also in Christ forgave you" (Eph. 4:32). Unkind words or deeds have no place in a blameless ministry.

in the Holy Spirit.—As an apostle, Paul was under the control of the Holy Spirit when he spoke and wrote. The Spirit directed him in specific instances as he went about his work for the Lord. He had all the powers of an apostle. He performed miracles, even raising the dead. He spoke in foreign languages under the power of the Holy Spirit. He and the other apostles were, of course, responsible for their response to the revealed truth of God just as any Christian is. See Gal. 2:11-21.

Since this is one of the areas in which Paul carried on a blameless ministry, it is quite possible that he was referring to his own spirit which was holy, for he had separated himself from all defilement of flesh and spirit when he became a Christian.

in love unfeigned.—Writing to the Romans, Paul said, "Let love be without hypocrisy" (Rom. 12:9). John writes, "My little children, let us not love in word, neither with the tongue; but in deed and in truth" (I John 3:18).

in word of truth.—This is the message of reconciliation that told the truth about God's love and grace that made it possible for sinners to be saved.

in the power of God.—Paul, of course, was fully aware of the fact that the message which had been revealed to him was the gospel. He was convinced that the gospel was the power of God to save the believer. Paul prayed for the Ephesians that they might be strengthened with power through the Spirit in the inward man. This was the same power that the Lord used in the wilderness temptation as He defeated the devil with the Word of God. In each temptation, He answered the challenge of Satan with a "Thus it is written." The Christian can also defeat Satan by following the example of Christ. See Eph. 3:16-17; 6:10-18.

This is the armor which is on the right hand and on the left, suggesting both the offensive and defensive aspects of the whole armor of God. For example, the sword of the Spirit would be in the right hand, but the shield of faith on the left.

by glory and dishonor.—There were those who sought to discredit every work of Paul and bring dishonor upon him. But there were many who approved his efforts to proclaim the gospel to save them. The converts to Christ at Corinth were like a monument to his faithfulness in teaching them the truth that had reconciled them to God.

Our Lord faced a similar situation in His ministry. Many glorified Him as they listened to the gracious words that fell from His lips. Many even of the rulers believed on Him, but they did not acknowledge Him openly because they loved the glory—approval—of men more than the glory of God. See John 12:43. But there were some who sought constantly for an excuse to discredit Him in the eyes of the people and finally succeeded on having Him crucified.

by evil report and good report.—Paul carried on this ministry in a blameless manner despite the fact that his enemies sought to destroy it by evil reports. See II Cor. 10:10-12. Paul's defense against all such reports was this: "He that glorieth, let him glory in the Lord. For not he that commendeth himself is approved, but whom the Lord commendeth" (II Cor. 10:17).

There are those who attempt to vilify preachers of the gospel by vicious gossip. Paul pointed out the only protection in such cases: His message and his life were blameless in the sight of the Lord.

as deceivers, and yet true.—This is the beginning of a series of clauses by which Paul shows the manner in which he conducted himself as a servant of God. Some said that he was leading men astray. Some believed he opposed the Law of Moses. But this was not true, for he "had done nothing but what the prophets and Moses did say should come" (Acts 26:22). The Jews had made similar charges against Jesus. The chief priests and Pharisees, appearing before Pilate after the crucifixion, referred to Him as "that deceiver." His resurrection showed how wrong they were.

as unknown, and yet well known.—At one time Paul had been well known as a persecutor of the church. He had actually tried to destroy the church of God. See Gal. 1:13-14; Acts 9:1-2. At Athens, however, Greek philosophers thought of him as an unknown babbler. He was preaching Jesus and the resurrection, but they thought he was speaking about some foreign god. Nothing he said resembled any system of philosophy worthy of their attention. See Acts 17:18. He had no standing among the professional of that day. See II Cor. 11:6. He was like Peter and John who were called ignorant and unlearned. See Acts 4:13. But Paul's credentials which the Lord furnished him established him as an ambassador of Christ working with God in his blameless ministry of reconciliation.

as dying, and behold, we live.—As the servant of God he was "always bearing about in the body the dying of Jesus, that the life also of Jesus might be manifest in his own body" (II Cor. 4:10). They thought he was dead at Lystra, but as sorrowing disciples stood about him he rose up and went into the city and on the next day proceeded on his journey. See Acts 14:20.

as chastened, and not killed.—Some assume that this is chastening from the Lord and cite such passages as Psa. 118:17-18 and Prov. 3:11-12 (quoted in Heb. 12:3-5) to support their view.

It is hard to see how "chastened, and not killed" could refer to

God's treatment of His apostle. But because he was a servant of God, he was punished by men on many occasions. Although men sought to kill him, the providence of God watched over him and prevented them from doing so.

as sorrowful, yet always rejoicing.—The Corinthians knew very well the sorrow they had caused him. See 2:1-11. Despite that sorrow he was able to rejoice over those who were faithful. See also Phil. 4:1; I Pet. 1:8; James 1:2-3.

as poor, yet making many rich.—When Paul wrote to the Philippians to thank them for the many times they had helped him, he said "I have learned, in whatsoever state I am in, therein to be content. I know how to be abased, and I know how to abound: in everything and in all things have I learned the secret both to be filled and to be hungry, both to abound and to be in want" (Phil. 4:11-12). Then he told his secret: "I can do all things in him that strengtheneth me" (Phil. 4:13). Paul had come to Corinth in want and for a time had supported himself by working as a tentmaker. See II Cor. 11:9; Acts 18:1-4. But the Corinthians knew how rich they had been made in spiritual things through the gospel ministry of Paul. See I Cor. 9:11; II Cor. 8:9.

as having nothing, yet possessing all things.—In connection with the incident of the rich young ruler who came to Jesus, Peter said, "Lo, we have left our own, and followed thee. And he said to them, Verily I say unto you, There is no man that hath left house, or wife, or brethren, or parents, or children, for the kingdom of God's sake who shall not receive manifold more in this time, and in the world to come eternal life" (Luke 18: 28-30). And to the Philippians Paul wrote, "I have all things, and abound: I am filled, having received from Epaphroditus the things that came from you, an odor of a sweet smell, a sacrifice acceptable, well-pleasing to God, and my God will supply every need of yours according to his riches in glory in Christ Jesus" (Phil. 4:18-19). Jesus told about the man who filled his barns to bursting. When he had done so, God said to him, "Thou foolish one, this night is thy soul required of thee; and the things which thou hast prepared, whose shall they be? So is he that layeth up treasure for himself, and is not rich toward God" Luke 12:20-21).

All the issues which Paul mentioned in this list can be illustrated from his own ministry, and many of them from the ministry of Christ. In a very real sense Christ lived in him.

Scripture

The Plea For Acceptance

6:11-18   Our mouth is open unto you, O Corinthians, our heart is enlarged. 12 Ye are not straitened in us, but ye are straitened in your own affections. 13 Now for a recompense in like kind (I speak as unto my children), be ye also enlarged.

14 Be not unequally yoked with unbelievers: for what fellowship have righteousness and iniquity? or what communion hath light with darkness? 15 And what concord hath Christ with Belial? or what portion hath a believer with an unbeliever? 16 And what agreement hath a temple of God with idols? for we are a temple of the living God; even as God said, I will dwell in them, and walk in them; and I will be their God, and they shall be my people. 17 Wherefore

> Come ye out from among
>   them, and be ye separate,

saith the Lord,

> And touch no unclean thing;
> And I will receive you,
> 18 And will be to you a Father,
> And ye shall be to me sons and daughters,

Comments

Our mouth is open unto you.—Paul had urged the Corinthians not to receive the grace of God in vain. He continued the appeal by urging them to accept him as the servant of God through whom the message of grace and reconciliation had been preached to them. With a clear message, a pure heart, and sincere motives he urged them to understand his great love for them.

Ye are not straitened in us.—The place the Corinthians occupied in the affections of Paul was not limited. His deep concern for them had led him to do more for them than for any other congregation among the many he had established. If there was any limitation, it was in their love for him. Some of them had come under the influence of false teachers and were failing to show proper respect for him as the one who had taught them to love the Lord. See I Cor. 4:14-21.

Now for a recompense in like kind.—Since Paul had boldly declared his love for them, he appealed to them as his children in Christ to demonstrate the same love for him.

Be not unequally yoked with unbelievers.—Some have assumed that it would have been impossible for Paul to have written these words immediately after the fervent declaration of his deep love for them. They seem to think that the contrast is too great and that he could not have changed from the expression of love to one of criticism which they assume characterizes this passage. See 6:14-7:1.

On these assumptions they build still another: That this section must have been taken from some other letter which he had written at another time. The absence of manuscript evidence to support the theory argues strongly against it. It also fails on two other counts: (1) This section, rather than being a rebuke is a continuation of Paul's earnest appeal for the Corinthians to rid themselves of whatever thing that had caused them to limit their love for the one who had led them to Christ and whose love for them was like that of a father. (2) Paul's writings abound in such sharp contrasts. For example, see his condemnation of the works of the flesh in contrast to his praise of the fruit of the spirit in Gal. 5:16-24. He did not hesitate to speak freely about his deep sorrow over someone who had fallen away from Christ and in the next moment tell of his joy as he contemplated the victory through Christ for all those who remain faithful to Him.

with unbelievers.—This passage is invariably interpreted as having to do with marriage. But there is no evidence in the context to show that Paul had this subject in mind at all. He had discussed that subject at length in the first epistle. See I Cor. 7:1-40. There, he indicated that marriage should be within the regulation of the Lord. He also gave instruction for the believer who was married to an unbeliever. The life of the believer was to be such that the unbelieving partner might be led to salvation in Christ. See also I Pet. 3:1-2. There is no question, of course, that it would be better for both husband and wife to be believers in the Lord Jesus Christ.

In this context, Paul seems to be referring to those unbelievers who were disturbing the church and keeping them from the proper attitude of Christian love toward him. The series of questions that follow shows the utter incompatibility of belief and unbelief.

what fellowship have righteousness and iniquity?—Can righteousness and lawlessness be partners? Some at Corinth seemed to think that these opposites could be yoked together. See I Cor. 5:1-13 for an attempt to do so.

The Corinthians were not the only ones who have tried to do this. Some church people today excuse their "bent to sinning" by blaming Adam for their "sinful nature" and insist that John said that "we sin every day." They miss the message of I John 1:8 by failing to read what he wrote in I John 3:1-10. They miss Paul's point in Rom. 7:17 by failing to read Rom. 6:16-18.

light with darkness?—These opposites cannot be yoked together as one team. John says, "God is light and in him is no darkness at all" (I John 1:5). Then he adds, "If we say that we have fellowship with him and walk in the darkness, we lie, and do not the truth: but if we walk in the light as he is in the light, we have fellowship one with another and the blood of Jesus Christ his Son cleanseth us from all sin" (I John 1:6-7).

Still some argue that there are "no such absolutes" in the Christian life. They insist that there must be some mixing of light and darkness, for "we all sin; nobody is perfect." Nobody is perfect in the sense that he cannot commit an act of sin. See I John 2:1-2. But the fact remains that the Bible allows no such mixing of light and darkness. James says that God is the "Father of lights, with whom there can be no variation, neither shadow that is cast by turning" (James 1:17). Then he adds, "wherefore putting away all filthiness and overflowing of wickedness receive with meekness the implanted word, which is able to save your souls. But be ye doers of the word, not hearers only, deluding your own selves" (James 1:21-22).

Christ with Belial?—Belial is Satan. Yoking a believer with an unbeliever is like attempting to yoke Christ with Satan. Could there possibly be any accord between Christ and the devil? What is there that belongs to the believer and at the same time to the unbeliever? Not Christ, nor salvation, nor heaven!

temple of God with idols?—How could there possibly be any agreement between the temple where the Spirit of God dwells and a pagan temple where idols are kept? This is the climax of Paul's argument showing that the believers at Corinth were not to be unequally yoked with unbelievers. Paul had warned them of the punishment for destroying the temple of God. See I Cor. 3:16-17. Were they willing to risk destruction of the temple of God by attempting to mix unbelievers and believers in the church?

God had promised Israel that He would be in them and dwell in their midst and be their God. They were to be His people, but on the condition that they separate themselves from every unclean thing.

Then He would be like a father to them and they would be like sons
and daughters to Him. Will God tolerate anything less in the church?

Summary

As an ambassador of Christ, working together with God, Paul
urged the Corinthians not to receive the gracious gift of righteousness as if it were an empty, meaningless thing. He reminded them of
the prophetic word in which God had said to Israel, "At an acceptable
time, I heard you, and in a day of salvation I came to help you."
Paul explained it by saying that the acceptable time is now, and
the day of salvation is now. The whole Christian age that began on
Pentecost and will end when Christ comes again is the day of salvation. But no individual has more than a lifetime in which to accept
it. The Corinthians were in danger of failing to respond to the urgent
plea to be reconciled to God. Paul had been careful not to give
offense to anyone, so that no one could blame him if one should fail
to respond to God's plea to be reconciled to Him.

Paul's ministry was blameless in areas ranging from patience to
power of God. He carried it on by weapons of righteousness, by glory
and dishonor, by evil report and good report. He served as one who
was unknown, yet well known; as one who was dying, but to the
amazement of the disciples, he lived; as one severely punished, but
not killed; as one who knew the meaning of sorrow, yet he always
rejoiced; as having nothing, yet he possessed all things, for he was
a child of the heavenly Father.

Looking back on this frank explanation of his motives and experiences of his ministry in their behalf, Paul plead with the Corinthians
to make room for him in their affections. His mouth was open, for
he had been speaking openly and freely of his love for them. In
his heart there was ample space for all the Christians at Corinth.
Any restriction of affection was on their part, not his. He urged
them to make room for him in their hearts.

Evidently the attack of false teachers on Paul had caused some of
the Corinthians to have an improper regard for him. It became
necessary for him to follow his declaration of love for them with a
sharp warning: "Stop becoming unequally yoked with unbelievers."
The Old Testament regulation forbade yoking animals of different
species together. See Deut. 22:10. Putting an unbeliever in the same
yoke with a believer was as bad as yoking an ox and an ass together.
Believers in Christ are not in the same class with unbelievers.

To assume that this was a reference to the marriage of the Christian and an unbeliever is to miss the main import of the lesson. Some Christians at Corinth were married to unbelievers, and Paul had reminded them of their opportunity to win the unbelieving partner to Christ.

Paul ordered them to stop the practice of being yoked with unbelievers without saying who the unbelievers were. We know he had ordered them to deliver the immoral person to Satan. "A little leaven leavens the whole lump." Those who were denying the resurrection were like "evil companionships that corrupt good morals." False apostles were ministers of Satan; they were to quit associating with such unbelievers.

Paul used a series of contrasts to illustrate what he meant. Righteousness and lawlessness are opposites and cannot be mixed. The same is true of light and darkness. Christ has nothing in common with the devil. God's temple cannot rest on the same foundation as that of the temple of an idol. Believers cannot be linked with unbelievers.

Christians are to be separated from the defilements of sin so that God may dwell in their midst. Then He can be as a father to them, and they as sons and daughters to Him.

Questions

1. What are the two topics discussed in this chapter? How are they related?
2. With whom was Paul working in his ministry of reconciliation?
3. How had he described the relationship between himself and Apollos?
4. What was their relationship to God?
5. What danger did the church at Corinth face that caused Paul to urge them not to receive the grace of God in vain?
6. To what favor from did he refer?
7. How could it be made vain?
8. How does the conduct of Peter and Barnabas at Antioch illustrate Paul's meaning in this context?
9. How had Paul conducted himself so as to avoid making the grace of God vain? See Gal. 2:20.
10. What was the real motivating force in the life and ministry of Paul?
11. What is the first business of the church?
12. Why may the following expressions be considered synonymous:

"Thus saith the Lord," "The Scripture says," and "The Holy Spirit says"?

13. What is the meaning of the text which Paul quoted from Isaiah?
14. How did he apply it to the situation at Corinth?
15. What is the Day of Salvation?
16. When did it begin and when will it end?
17. What did Peter say about the longsuffering of God?
18. Why was Paul eager to have a blameless ministry?
19. How did he accomplish his goal?
20. How had some Jews caused the name of God to be blasphemed?
21. What were some of the stumbling blocks in the pathway of the Corinthian Christians?
22. How harmonize Paul's view of a blameless ministry with the constant criticism brought against him?
23. In what areas was Paul's blameless ministry carried on?
24. By what means did he carry it on?
25. In what manner was it done?
26. What does "patience" mean?
27. In what things did he exercise patience?
28. What does Hebrews say about the trials of the faithful?
29. What did Jesus say about the trials of His disciples?
30. What did Peter say about the trials that were coming upon the brethren?
31. What did Paul mean by "necessities"?
32. What are some of the distressing situations in which he exercised patience?
33. What are some of the situations in which Paul showed patience in stripes?
34. What is the history of Paul's imprisonments?
35. When and how did Paul meet the violence of riotous mobs?
36. How did Paul patiently endure his labors?
37. What were those occasions which Paul called "watchings"?
38. What place did fasting have in the consecration of Saul and Barnabas to their ministry?
39. Why did Paul abstain from food in his blameless ministry?
40. What was the source of Paul's knowledge? How did it help in a blameless ministry?
41. What does longsuffering mean? How does it differ from patience?
42. What place did kindness have in the ministry of Paul?

43. What are two ways to understand the expression "in the Holy Spirit" as it is used in this context?
44. Why did Paul speak of love as being "unfeigned"?
45. What is the message of the word of truth as Paul delivered it?
46. How was Paul's ministry carried on in the power of God?
47. What is the armor of righteousness?
48. Why did he say, "on the right hand and on the left"?
49. How did he use glory and dishonor in his blameless ministry?
50. How did he make use of good and evil reports?
51. How did Paul react when some looked upon him as a deceiver?
52. Who had used the same term with reference to Jesus?
53. Who had considered Paul an unknown?
54. What credentials did he have to prove that he was well known to God?
55. To what incident may Paul have referred when he spoke of himself "as dying, and behold, we live"?
56. Why was Paul subjected to chastening? By whom?
57. How did he face sorrow?
58. In view of his own poverty, how was he making many rich?
59. As one who had nothing, how could he possess all things?
60. How did Paul express his frankness in speaking to the Corinthians?
61. What did he mean when he said, "You are not restricted in us"?
62. What did he ask of them in return?
63. What did he mean by: "Be no unequally yoked with unbelievers"?
64. Why did he mention the absolute contrast between righteousness and lawlessness?
65. How does the lesson to light and darkness teach the same thing?
66. What promise had God made to Israel?
67. What bearing did this have on the issue at Corinth?

For Discussion

1. What are some of the ways in which we may work together to serve God?
2. What are some of the things in the church today that may cause some to stumble?

Analysis

A. Paul appealed to the Corinthians to separate themselves completely from the defilement of the sinful practices of their times, that they might be holy before God (1-3).
  1. He based his appeal on promises of God which he had just quoted (1).
  2. Then he made a strong appeal for them to accept him (2-3).
    a) He asked them to make room for him in their hearts—receive him as a guest in their lives (2a).
    b) He gave his reasons for asking them to do this (2b).
      (1) He had wronged no one.
      (2) He had corrupted no one.
      (3) He had taken advantage of no one.
    c) He explained why he said this: It was not to condemn them, for they were in his heart to live and to die (3).
B. Paul reminded them of his frankness in speaking to them about his comfort and joy (4-13a).
  1. He told them about his great frankness and his pride in them that had resulted in overflowing joy in all his afflictions (4).
  2. He explained about the afflictions which he had suffered (5-7).
    a) In Macedonia, there was no rest for his flesh, but affliction on every side. Without, there were fightings; within, there were fears.
    b) He had received relief and comfort through the presence of Titus, after meeting him in Macedonia (6-7).
      (1) His affliction in Macedonia: No rest for his flesh.
      (2) The comfort from God who comforts the depressed:
        (a) Through the presence of Titus.
        (b) Through the report of Titus about their longing, mourning and zeal.
  3. He explained his attitude toward the letter which he had written, that is, First Corinthians (8-13a).
    a) He did not regret sending the letter, but he did regret that he had caused them sorrow for a while (8).
    b) But he rejoiced in the outcome of the matter (9-11).
      (1) Their sorrow which was according to God had pro-

duced repentance, but resulted in no loss for them.
   (2) He explained sorrow and repentance (10-11).
      (a) Sorrow according to God produces repentance that leads to salvation.
      (b) Sorrow of the world—sorrow that is involved in sin—leads to death.
      (c) Sorrow according to God had produced (11):
         i) Vindication of themselves.
         ii) Indignation toward the sinner.
         iii) Fear or reverance for God.
         iv) Longing for a life of righteousness.
         v) Zeal for a life of purity in Christ.
         vi) Avenging of wrong by reproving the sinner.
         vii) Innocence of further wrongdoing demonstrated by following the instruction of Paul had given them.
   c) He explained why he wrote the letter (12-13a).
      (1) It was not for the sake of the offender nor the one offended, but for their earnest care in the sight of God for the things He had caused to be written by the apostle Paul.
      (2) It was for this reason that he was comforted (13a).
C. Paul told them about his joy and comfort over the way they had received Titus (13b-16).
   1. In addition to being comforted over the response to his letter, he rejoiced over the way they had welcomed Titus (13b).
   2. Paul had not been put to shame for his boasting to Titus about their obedience (14).
   3. Titus' feeling for them overflowed as he remembered their obedience, for they had received him in fear and trembling (15).
   4. Paul rejoiced in the fact that he had been able to depend on them (16).

Appeal for Purity

Scripture

7:1-3. Having therefore these promises, beloved, let us cleanse ourselves from all defilement of flesh and spirit, perfecting holiness in the fear of God.

2 Open your hearts to us: we wronged no man, we corrupted no man, we took advantage of no man. 3 I say it not to condemn you: for I have said before, that ye are in our hearts to die together and live together.

Comments

Having therefore these promises.—Paul now draws his conclusion from the argument which proved the absolute incompatibility between righteousness and iniquity. There follows a two-fold appeal: (1) That which involved cleansing and purity with reverence for God; (2) the appeal for the Corinthians to accept Paul.

The promises as indicated in this context are: (1) that the living God would dwell in them and walk in them; and that He would be their God and they would be His people; (2) that the living God would be their Father and that they would be His sons and daughters. These promises conditioned upon the separation from the defilement of sin were first made to the nation of Israel. The history of that nation shows how God in a remarkable way was in the midst of His people, giving them victories and blessing when they consecrated themselves to Him, but bringing affliction and punishment upon them when they failed to walk according to their agreement with Him. Because that nation, with the exception of a small number of faithful ones, ultimately failed to appreciate the promises that God had made to them, He made a new covenant that involved believers whether Jews or Gentiles. And to this new nation He said, "I will be to them a God and they shall be to me a people" (Heb. 8:10). Then He promised, "I will be merciful to their iniquities, and their sins I will remember no more" (Heb. 8:12). These blessings were involved in the promise that God had made to Abraham. See Gal. 3:8-14, 29. This was made known on the Day of Pentecost to those who repented of their sins and got themselves baptized in the name of Jesus Christ. Peter said, "To you is the promise and to your children, and to all that are afar off, even as many as the Lord our God shall call unto him" (Acts 2:39). Peter speaks of these precious and exceeding great promises by which the Christians have escaped the corruption that is in the world by lust that they may become partakers of Deity. II Pet. 1:4.

let us cleanse ourselves for all defilement of flesh and spirit.—Are

we to assume when Paul says "Let us" that he was guilty of the same
defiling sins which the Corinthians had been practicing? This could
scarcely harmonize with the appeal that he had made for the Corinthians to imitate him even as he imitated Christ. I Cor. 11:1. Nor
does it harmonize with the fact that he had buffeted his body and
brought it into bondage lest after having preached to others he
should become disqualified. I Cor. 9:27. Neither does it harmonize
with his claim that Christ lived in him. Gal. 2:20. Those who hold
that he was defiled just as the Corinthians are fond of quoting his
remarks: "For I know that in me, that is, in my flesh dwelleth no good
thing" Rom. 7:18. But Paul had said in Rom. 6:12, "Let not sin
therefore reign in your body, that you should obey the lust thereof."
The only possible way to harmonize these two statements is to regard
the first one as a reference to Paul before he became a Christian. At
one time he like the Romans before they became Christians had
been a servant of sin, but they became obedient from the heart to
that form of teaching whereunto they were delivered and were made
free from sin that they might become servants of righteousness.
Rom. 6-17-18. Why then does Paul say, "Let us cleanse ourselves?"
Two reasons: (1) because such a thing was possible since he himself
had done so; (2) Paul was aware that it was necessary for him as
well as the Corinthians to be constantly on guard lest he should fall.
He had written to them saying "Wherefore let him that thinketh he
standeth take heed lest he fall" (I Cor. 10:12). But he also indicated
that there is no temptation which they could not endure by following the way which God has provided. With the shield of faith the
Christian can quench all the fiery darts of the evil one. Eph. 6:16.
Not even the apostle Paul could afford to lay down the armor of
God until he had fought the good fight of the faith, being faithful
unto death.

from all defilement of flesh and spirit.—By flesh and spirit Paul
meant the whole life, body and mind. While he used "flesh and
spirit" in a figurative sense as he discussed the works of the flesh in
Gal. 5:16-24, here he is using it in the literal sense referring to the
physical body. The Corinthians lived in an environment of immorality. He had written to them that they should in no way get
themselves mixed up with those who practiced such things. I Cor.
5:8. He had reminded them that their bodies were to be considered
as a temple of the Holy Spirit (I Cor. 6:19-20). Those who hold
that there is inherent sin in the body are at variance with what

Paul teaches on the subject, for one can, and many do, give their bodies to God as instruments of righteousness. Rom. 6:13. In the list of the works of the flesh, Paul not only mentions immorality which defiles the body, but he also lists such things as strife, faction, jealousy, division and the like which defile the spirit. Those who belong to Christ, however, are to be characterized by love, joy, peace, longsuffering, kindness, goodness, faithfulness, meekness, self-control. Gal. 5:22-24. To the Colossians, he said, "Set your mind on the things that are above, not on the things that are upon the earth." (Col. 3:2). To the Philippians, he wrote, "Finally, brethren, whatever things are true, whatever things are honorable whatever things are just, whatever things are pure, whatever things are lovely, whatever things are of good report; if there be any virtue, if there be any praise, think on these things" (Phil. 4:8).

How can the Christian who has become defiled cleanse himself? Is he to be baptized again for the remission of his sins? The case of Simon answers the problem. Along with the other Samaritans, he had been baptized into Christ; but he fell into serious sin when he thought that he could obtain the gift of God with money. Peter said to him, "Repent therefore of this thy wickedness, and pray the Lord, if perhaps the thought of thy heart shall be forgiven thee" (Acts 8:22). John, writing to Christians, says "If we confess our sins, he is faithful and righteous to forgive us our sins, and to cleanse us from all unrighteousness" (I John 1:9). The blood of Christ cleanses us from all sin (I John 1:7-2:2). We have an obligation to one another in this matter. Paul wrote to the Galatians saying, "Brethren, if man be overtaken in any trespass, ye who are spiritual, restore such a one in a spirit of gentleness; looking to thyself, lest thou also be tempted" (Gal. 6:1). James wrote to his brethren to say, "If any among you err from the truth, and one convert him; let him know, that he who converteth a sinner from the error of his way shall save a soul from death, and shall cover a multitude of sins" (James 5:19-20).

perfecting holiness in the fear of God.—Holiness as used in this context is the state of the one who separates himself from sin and its defilement, touching no unclean thing. It clearly means the life of purity that follows the cleansing from sin. The object of the cleansing is a life of purity. Paul urges the Corinthians to make their life complete by conducting themselves in God's sight as His children who refuse to be defiled by sinful practices.

"Perfecting holiness" does not mean perfectionism, for that assumes that it is possible for the individual to reach the state in which it is impossible for him to commit an act of sin. While John makes it clear that it is impossible for a man to go on sinning while he is conducting himself in harmony with the Word of God, he also recognizes the possibility of a sin being committed by any man who does not walk in the light of God's Word (I John 3:9; 2:1).

In this day of low moral standards, the church must not only return to the truth of God's Word but also to the purity of genuine Christian living. In this day it is imperative that Christians present their bodies a living sacrifice, holy, acceptable to God (Rom. 12:1). Peter said, "As God is holy, be ye yourselves also holy in all manner of living" (I Pet. 1:15). Then he explained it, "Putting away therefore all wickedness, and all guile, and hypocrisies, and envies, and all evil speaking, as new born babes, long for the spiritual milk which is without guile, that ye may grow thereby unto salvation" (I Pet. 2:1-2).

Open your hearts to us.—Paul asked the Corinthians to open their hearts to him and welcome him as a guest. He wanted them to let him come in and abide in their affections. There are certain types of people who cannot be welcomed as guests in one's home. Those who would injure, destroy, or cheat cannot be admitted. But Paul declared that he had accused no one unjustly; he had injured no one; he had not corrupted or destroyed anyone; he had not taken advantage of or cheated anyone. There was, therefore, no reason why they should not receive him into their hearts. Some of Paul's enemies may have been making such charges against him, but it is probably better to consider this as a general characterization of unwanted guests which in no way applied to him.

I say it not to condemn you.—This could mean that some had brought these charges against Paul, but, more likely, he was simply showing that he was not the type of individual that would be excluded from the home and heart of a Christian. He had reminded them (6:11) that his heart was enlarged—there was room in it for all the Corinthians. Now he urges them to make room for him in their hearts and affections. He considered the Corinthians as permanent guests in his affections, for they were in his heart to die together and to live together. This was no temporary thing; they were in his heart to stay.

Remembering all that he had done for them as their spiritual father, how could they refuse to open their hearts and welcome him into their lives?

Paul's Frankness

Scripture

7:4-13a. Great is my boldness of speech toward you, great is my glorying on your behalf: I am filled with comfort, I overflow with joy in all our affliction.

5 For even when we were come into Macedonia our flesh had no relief, but we were afflicted on every side; without were fightings, within were fears. 6 Nevertheless he that comforteth the lowly, even God, comforted us by the coming of Titus; 7 and not by his coming only, but also by the comfort wherewith he was comforted in you, while he told us your longing, your mourning, your zeal for me; so that I rejoiced yet more. 8 For though I made you sorry with my epistle, I do not regret it: though I did regret it (for I see that that epistle made you sorry, though but for a season), 9 I now rejoice, not that ye were made sorry, but that ye were made sorry unto repentance; for ye were made sorry after a godly sort that ye might suffer loss by us in nothing. 10 For godly sorrow worketh repentance unto salvation, a repentance which bringeth no regret: but the sorrow of the world worketh death. 11 For behold, this selfsame thing, that ye were made sorry after a godly sort, what earnest care it wrought in you, yea what clearing of yourselves, yea what indignation, yea what fear, yea what longing, yea what zeal, yea what avenging! In everything ye approved yourselves to be pure in the matter. 12 So although I wrote unto you, I wrote not for his cause that did the wrong, nor for his cause that suffered the wrong, but that your earnest care for us might be made manifest unto you in the sight of God. 13 Therefore we have been comforted: and in our comfort we joyed the more exceedingly for the joy of Titus, because his spirit hath been refreshed by you all.

Comments

Great is my boldness of speech.—Some assume that Paul is referring to the great confidence which he had in the Corinthians. While the expression may be translated "confidence" it really refers to one's frankness in speaking out boldly. Paul did speak frankly when he boasted about the willingness of the Corinthians to follow his instructions. See verse 14. Frankness is seen in two issues: (1) he was filled with comfort and (2) he was overflowing with joy in all his afflictions. Paul suffered as anyone else would when he was afflicted. The sting of the lash hurt him as much as it did anyone else. He felt the pain of hunger and cold as anyone else did. But the joy of knowing that he was the servant of God, bearing the message of reconciliation to all who would accept it, caused his joy to overflow like a river out of its banks and cover the ground as far as one could see. *for even when we were come into Macedonia.*—Paul now describes his distress and shows how God had comforted him in it all.

His anxiety over the situation in Corinth had caused him to go to Troas where he was hoping to find Titus and learn from him about conditions in Corinth. But when he got there, "he had no relief for his spirit," so he went on to Macedonia. There, he says, "Our flesh had no relief." In the first instance it was anxiety of mind and heart as he waited for the report of the action of the church on the instruction he had written them in First Corinthians, particularly in chapter five about the sin of the one who had taken his father's wife thus bringing the whole church into disrepute before the pagans. I Cor. 5:1-13. But his distress in Macedonia seems to have been the result of physical hardships which he suffered. He describes them as afflictions, fightings and fears, but gives no details as to their nature. We may assume that those who had been opposing him kept up their steady bombardment of criticism by every means that would bring him distress. Conflicts that were without produced fears within, fears, perhaps, as to whether or not he would be able to complete his mission of reconciling the sinners at Corinth to their God, for this would require repentance and a change of conduct on their part. *He that comforteth the lowly.*—Paul had faced enough to cause him to be depressed, but God who had led him in triumph in Christ in every place had not forsaken him. Although long delayed, God had comforted him by the presence of Titus who he met in Macedonia.

Some have assumed that the section from 2:14-7:6 is a long digression. Paul began it with the reference to his trip to Macedonia to look for Titus without saying whether or not he had found him until he reached 7:6. But we should remember that Paul's meeting Titus and learning from him about the repentance of the Corinthians had filled him to overflowing with joy in all the suffering which he had undergone. It was perfectly logical for him to treat at length his hope and joy and frankness as he told of his love and longing for the Corinthians and urged them to make room for him in their hearts. This, of course, involved their repentance and change of conduct about which he was now ready to write. *and not by his coming only.*—It was not the presence of Titus only that brought comfort to Paul, for two other factors were involved:

139

(1) the fact that Titus himself had been comforted by the Corinthians, and (2) the report Titus made of the attitude of the Corinthians toward Paul. Paul alluded again to their attitude toward Titus in verses 14-15.

while he told us your longing.—The Corinthians had their hearts set on seeing Paul again. While it is true that at one time some arrogant ones among them had suggested that Paul would not come to see them again, every trace of this seems to have been wiped out by the report of Titus. I Cor. 4:18. Titus told him about their lamentation, deep personal mourning, for the things that they had permitted to go on in their midst that had brought the church of God into disrepute before the pagans of their community and caused sorrow to Paul as their father in the gospel. The wrong had been done by disregarding the instruction of the apostle. The Corinthians had shown great zeal for him as their spiritual father by correcting the situation. So while Paul rejoiced at the coming of Titus, he rejoiced even more over the report of their attitude toward him, for that meant their reconciliation to God.

for though I made you sorry with my epistle.—See comment on 2:3-4 as to the identity of this epistle. In the absence of any manuscript evidence to the contrary I assume that this is a reference to First Corinthians. That epistle is full of sharp rebuke for various sins that were being practiced by the church in Corinth. Paul seems now to return to what he had written in 2:5-11 which appears to be a clear reference to the one who was living with his father's wife. See I Cor. 5:1-13. See *Studies in First Corinthians* for comments on that situation.

I do not regret it.—After hearing Titus' report of their reaction to that epistle, Paul writes, "I do not regret it." Then he hastens to add that he had regretted it, that is, not the writing of the epistle but the effect of it for it brought them temporary sorrow. Paul, as their spiritual father, did not take pleasure in causing them sorrow, even though he had to reprove them for their sin with the hope that they might be restored to the life of purity and righteousness in Christ.

I now rejoice.—Again he makes it clear that he was not rejoicing that it had become necessary for him to write so as to bring them sorrow, for his rejoicing was in that which resulted from their sorrow, that is, their repentance. At one point they seem to have been indifferent toward the sin of the one who was living with his father's wife. The instruction which Paul had given had caused them to reverse their attitude and carry out the punishment which had been ordered by the apostle. Repentance is the change of the mind or the reversal of a decision which is brought about through godly sorrow and results in changed conduct. Two other motivating forces are mentioned in the Scriptures which lead to repentance: (1) the goodness of God (Rom. 2:4) and (2) the impending judgment (Acts 17:30-31).

for ye were made sorry after a godly sort.—Literally, "according to God." This means sorrow as God would have it turn out, for it would lead to repentance. Consequently nothing that Paul had written in his epistle had caused them loss. They had corrected the wrong; they were to forgive the sinner; they were not to allow Satan to have the advantage over them. II Cor. 2:11.

For godly sorrow worketh repentance unto salvation.—In accord with God's purpose, their sorrow had produced a reversal of their decision about sin. That, in turn, brought about their salvation, and there was no regret in it.

but the sorrow of the world worketh death.—This bold contrast between godly sorrow and the sorrow of the world justifies Paul's rejoicing over the outcome of his epistle. The sorrow of the world involved shame and disgrace and led ultimately to death, for "the wages of sin is death" (Rom. 6:23).

For behold, this self-same thing.—Paul now calls upon the Corinthians to observe for themselves what had happened as a result of the sorrow that was according to God: (1) *what earnest care it produced in you,* that is, their eagerness to correct the sin that they had so carelessly allowed to go on in their midst; (2) *clearing of yourselves,* that is, the action they had taken under the instruction of the apostle to clear themselves of involvement in such sins as fornication, covetousness, idolatry, reviling, drunkenness, extortion and the like. See I Cor. 5:11; (3) *what indignation,* that is, they were indignant that they had allowed one of their members to bring them such disgrace; (4) *what fear,* that is, reverence for God and the word delivered to them through His apostle, lest they be punished with the wrongdoer; (5) *what longing,* that is, their earnest desire for the purity of life to which they had been called in Christ; (6) *what zeal,* that is, their eager response to the directions Paul had written to them, for they had purged out the old leaven that they might no longer be characterized by malice and wickedness; (7) *what avenging,* that is, they had taken the necessary steps to punish the wrongdoer for the destruction of the flesh that the spirit might be saved in the day of the Lord Jesus. See I Cor. 5:5; II Cor. 2:8-11.

141

Paul was generous on his commendation of the Corinthians, reminding them that in all these things by their swift action they had proved themselves to be innocent of any further wrongdoing.

I wrote not for his cause that did the wrong.—The attitude of the Corinthians which Paul had just described explained his purpose in writing First Corinthians, particularly, chapter five. His purpose was not primarily for the benefit of the one who had done the wrong, nor was it for the one who had suffered the wrong. It was for their concern for the apostle's instruction that had led them to take the necessary steps to clear themselves from guilt of carelessly allowing such practices to go on in their midst. What they had accomplished had been done in the sight of God as they demonstrated their earnest care for Paul.

Another view of this verse assumes that the one who was wronged was Paul, not the father of the man who was living with the father's wife. It assumes that the one who did the wrong was one of his detractors who had sought to discredit him before the Corinthians. This is based on the supposition that the epistle that had caused them sorrow was some other than our First Corinthians. See *Studies in First Corinthians* on chapter five.

Therefore we have been comforted.—Thus Paul closes his remarkable explanation of the effect of Titus' report about conditions in Corinth.

The Joy of Titus

Scripture

7:13a-16.　and in our comfort we joyed the more exceedingly for the joy of Titus, because his spirit hat been refreshed by you all. 14 For if in anything I have gloried to him on your behalf, I was not put to shame; but as we spake all things to you in truth, so our glorying also which I made before Titue was found to be truth. 15 And his affection is more abundantly toward you, while he remembereth the obedience of you all, how with fear and trembling ye received him. 16 I rejoice that in everything I am of good courage concerning you.

Comments

for the joy of Titus.—The magnanimous spirit of Paul is shown in the attitude that he had toward his fellow-workers such as Titus and Timothy. Not only did he write of his own joy at the outcome of the situation in Corinth, but pointed out that he was particularly happy over the joy of Titus because of the manner in which the Corinthians had received him. They had joined in refreshing his spirit. He may have had some misgiving as to the effect of his mission, but the Corinthians had dispelled all doubt about it by the manner in which they received him.

For if in anything I have gloried to him.—The unselfishness of Paul is manifested in his attitude toward the Corinthians for he did not hesitate to boast about their willingness to respond to the inspired instruction which he had written to them. After receiving the report of Titus he could say, "I was not put to shame." What he had said about them to Titus had been found to be the truth.

And his affection.—The generous affection which Paul had for the Corinthians was shared also by Titus. He remembered how they had obeyed the instruction of Paul. They had received him with utmost concern lest they fall short of complete obedience to it.

I am of good courage concerning you.—The battle had been won. Paul had suffered great anxiety over the situation at Corinth. He had rebuked sin. He had plead earnestly that they make room for him in their affections. Now triumphantly, having achieved the victory, he could say, "I am of good courage concerning you.' '

Summary

In the opening verses of this chapter, Paul draws a conclusion from the principles he had just stated in the preceding one. God had called upon His people to separate themselves from every unclean thing and had promised those who did so that He would be their God and they His people. He would be their Father and they His sons and daughters. While Isaiah had written this to Israel, Paul clearly indicates that the same would be true of the Christians at Corinth if they cleansed themselves from those things that were besmearing their lives and defiling their souls. They were to separate themselves from everything that defiles their flesh and spirit—the whole being. Nothing short of complete separation from sin and dedication to a life of purity before God would satisfy the conditions upon which God was to be their Father and they His children.

Paul's concern for the church at Corinth led him to a deep and stirring appeal for them to accept him into their hearts and lives as a guest who was to remain with them. He was the kind of person as their father in the gospel whom they could receive in this manner. They were in his heart to live and to die.

Paul unhesitatingly spoke of his pride in the church at Corinth. In times of distress, the memory of Corinth brought him comfort; in times of sorrow, the thought of them brought him overflowing joy. He suffered in Macedonia, for he had not rest for his flesh. What hardships these were, he does not say, but they were in all probability the results of persecutions from those who everywhere sought to undermine his work of Christ. There were conflicts accompanied by fears. But when he found Titus in Macedonia and learned of their obedient response to the epistle he had written, he was comforted. God who always led him in triumph also comforted him when he was depressed.

This brought him to the discussion of the effect of the letter he had written (First Corinthians). He did not regret writing it, but he did regret that their sins had led to the rebuke that caused them to be made sorry for a while. But he rejoiced that this sorrow had led to repentance, and repentance to salvation. How different the sorrow of the world, for it led to death. Paul could rejoice that they had been saved from such a death. God's purpose in sorrow had led them to change their ways and punish the sinner in their midst. Respect and reverance for God led them to refuse to be mixed up with sinners who practiced things which the Father would not tolerate. They longed for the purity that He praised and zealously sought the life of righteousness in Christ. Paul could give them a clean bill of health, for they were innocent of any further wrongdoing. This was the very purpose of the letter, for it was not for the sake of the offender nor offended, but that they might all show their earnest concern for the things of God.

Titus had told Paul of the wonderful welcome he had received in Corinth. Paul had boasted to him about the kind of people he would find in the church at Corinth, basically good and willing to obey the Word of God. He had not been put to shame, for Titus had found them to be just what Paul had said. Titus had been deeply moved by the warmth of their welcome. Paul rejoiced that he had been able to depend on them.

Questions

1. What promises had God made to His people through Isaiah?
2. On what conditions were the promises made?
3. What were the Corinthians doing that were like the things practiced by Israel? See I Cor. 5:9-13; 6:12-20.
4. What is meant by "defilement of flesh and spirit"?

5. How were they to cleanse themselves from this defilement?
6. Who are the people of God today?
7. To whom does the promise that God made to Abraham refer?
8. What did Peter say about it as reported in Acts 2:39?
9. What did Paul say about it in Gal. 3:8-14 and 29?
10. Why did Paul say, "Let us cleanse ourselves"?
11. How had Paul avoided defilement? See I Cor. 9:27.
12. Can others do so? See I Cor. 10:13.
13. How, then, can we harmonize this with Paul's statement that "in my flesh dwelleth no good thing"?
14. What did Paul say about separation from a life of sin in Rom. 6:17-18?
15. What did Paul say about the shield of faith and the fiery darts of the evil one? See Eph. 6:16.
16. What are the "works of the flesh" as listed in Gal. 5:16-21?
17. What is the fruit of the spirit as listed in Gal. 5:22-24?
18. What obligation do Christians have toward their brethren who may be overtaken in a trespass? See Gal. 6:1.
19. What is holiness? How can it be brought to a state of completion?
20. How did Peter explain the holy life of the children of God?
21. How were the Corinthians to open their hearts to Paul?
22. Why did Paul mention those who injure, destroy and cheat?
23. Is it possible that some may have accused him of these things?
24. Why did Paul speak with great frankness to the Corinthians?
25. On what two issues did he speak frankly at this point?
26. How had Paul become depressed in Macedonia?
27. How had God comforted him at that time?
28. Why did Paul delay mentioning the fact that he had met Titus in Macedonia until 7:6?
29. What in addition to the presence of Titus had brought comfort to Paul?
30. What had been the first effect of Paul's epistle (First Corinthians) on the Corinthians?
31. What did Paul regret about having written the letter?
32. Why did he now rejoice that he had done so?
33. What is "sorrow after a godly sort"?
34. What are the motivating forces that lead to repentance?
35. In what ways is repentance to be shown?
36. To what does repentance lead?

37. What is the difference between the sorrow of the world and godly sorrow?
38. How had the Corinthians cleared themselves?
39. Against what did they show indignation?
40. What had fear led them to do? What is this fear?
41. How had their zeal been shown?
42. What had they done about the wrongdoer in their widst?
43. How had they proved themselves innocent of further wrong-doing?
44. Who is the one who had done the wrong? Who had been wronged?
45. For whose sake, then, had Paul written to them?
46. How did Paul sum up his attitude toward the report that Titus had given of the situation in Corinth?
47. What had happened to Titus while he was at Corinth?
48. What had Paul told him about the church at Corinth?
49. In what ways did Titus share Paul's views of the Corinthians?
50. Why did Paul say, "I am of good courage concerning you"?

For Discussion

1. What is the relation of "perfectionism" to Paul's teaching about the necessity of a pure life?
2. What are some of the sordid things from which church people must separate themselves in order that they may be sons and daughters of the Heavenly Father?

CHAPTER EIGHT

Analysis

A. Paul told about the gracious privilege God had given the Macedonian churches, permitting them to share in helping the saints in Judea (1-6).
  1. The result of God's grace (1-2).
    a) The gracious privilege of sharing had been given by God and was still operating in the churches of Macedonia (1).
    b) Their great joy over this gift, even though they were being put to the test by much affliction and deep poverty, resulted in single-minded devotion expressed in the overflowing wealth of their liberality (2).
  2. Paul's testimony as to their response to God's grace (3-5).
    a) It was according to their ability, even beyond their ability.
    b) It was of their own accord—they chose to do it.
    c) It was with great urgency that they begged for the privilege of sharing in this ministry to the saints.
    d) It was a response beyond anything Paul had hoped for.
    e) It was the result of having first given themselves to the Lord and to Paul by the will of God.
  3. Paul's exhortation to Titus to complete the task he had already begun at Corinth (6).
B. He gave instruction to enable them to determine the amount of their giving (7-15).
  1. Giving in relation to other gracious privileges in which they had abounded (7).
    a) The principle: They abounded in (1) faith, (2) utterance, (3) knowledge, (4) earnestness, and (5) love.
    b) The exhortation: Abound in this gracious privilege also.
  2. Love as the motivating force in giving (8-9).
    a) Paul did not issue a command for them to be generous, but appealed to them to show the sincerity of their love (8).
    b) He reminded them of the example of Christ who, although he was rich, became poor for their sakes that they might become rich (9).

3. Advice about completing the work which they had already begun (10-15).
    a) The advice: Since they were the first to begin, Paul's opinion was that they should complete the task according to their ability (10-11).
    b) The measure:
        (1) Willingness to give makes the gift acceptable, not the amount (12).
        (2) Equality (13-15).
            (a) Not that one should be distressed and another eased (13).
            (b) Equality that balances want and abundance (14).
            (c) Example: Scriptural reference to the manna (15).

C. Paul told them of the mission of Titus and his associates whom he had urged to go to Corinth to assist in this gracious privilege of giving (16-24).
    1. His thanks to God for the concern of Titus for them (16-17).
        a) God had put the same earnest care in the heart of Titus (16).
        b) Titus had accepted the task because of his earnest desire to help them (17).
    2. His commendation of Titus and his associates (18-23).
        a) The first brother (18-21).
            (1) He had been praised for his work in the gospel throughout all the churches (18).
            (2) He had been appointed by the churches to go on this mission (19).
            (3) Paul was thus avoiding any criticism of his handling of the funds (20-21).
        b) The other brother: With Titus and the first associate, Paul also sent another proven brother who had great confidence in the Corinthians (22).
        c) Paul's commendation of Titus and the others (23).
            (1) Titus was his partner and fellow-worker.
            (2) The other brethren were ones who had been sent by the churches to do a work for the glory of Christ!
    3. His plea for them to give a demonstration of the love and justification of his boasting about them (24).

The Privilege of Giving

Scripture

8:1-6. Moreover, brethren, we make known to you the grace of
God which hath been given in the churches of Macedonia; 2 how
that in much proof of affliction the abundance of their joy and their
deep poverty abounded unto the riches of their liberality. 3 For according to their power, I bear witness, yea and beyond their power,
they gave of their own accord, 4 beseeching us with much entreaty
in regard of this grace and the followship in the ministering to the
saints: 5 and this, not as we had hoped, but first they gave their own
selves to the Lord, and to us through the will of God. 6 Insomuch
that we exhorted Titus, that as he had made a beginning before,
so he would also complete in you this grace also.

Comments

Moreover, brethren.—Paul had written with utmost frankness in
defense of his ministry in behalf of the Corinthians and of his deep
affection for them. He had reminded them of his unbounded joy in
learning from Titus that they had complied with the directions
which he had given them in First Corinthians for the correction of
certain sinful practices which they had allowed to go on in their
congregation.

He was now prepared to take up another matter which he had
barely mentioned in the first letter. He had called attention to the
"collection for the saints" and had given them the order, as he had
also done to the churches in Galatia, to begin gathering the funds.
See I Cor. 16:1-2. Chapters eight and nine complete his instruction
on the matter. They constitute a logical progression of thought when
the background of First Corinthians is taken into consideration. The
deep emotional tone of the first section of Second Corinthians is in
perfect harmony with the subject matter with which he dealt. He
had spent so much time with the church at Corinth for it was a
strategic post in the campaign to spread the gospel through the
known world. The threat against the very life of that church occasioned by the sinful practices about which he wrote in First Corinthians was a serious threat to the progress of the gospel in that whole
area. This plus his deep love for those people led him naturally to
write in the deep emotional tone that characterizes so much of the
first seven chapters of the epistle. The mood naturally changes when
he reaches a less personal and far more encouraging situation in

connection with the offering for the saints in Judea, for he knew that the Corinthians had already made a beginning in this matter following the instruction which he had given them. His mood changes again with the defense of his apostleship against the false claims and unfair charges being made by false teachers. They had come to Corinth and were seeking to establish themselves in the life and affection of the people of God whose very existence as Christians had depended upon the ministry of Paul who was the first to bring the gospel to them.

the grace of God which hath been given in the churches of Macedonia.—In the various shades of meaning of the term "grace" the central idea is unmerited favor. The thought that this is some mystical power from God producing unusual liberality in giving is not in harmony with the principles of giving which Paul set forth in these two chapters. But God had been gracious in giving the Macedonian churches the privilege of sharing with those who were in need despite their own deep poverty.

God had miraculously fed the children of Israel on manna from heaven while they were on the wilderness journey. Jesus had miraculously fed the multitudes on the loaves and fishes. In His providence God continually causes the earth to produce an abundance of food, despite the fact that famine has always been common in some areas. Rather than miraculously supplying the needs of the saints in Judea God gave the Gentile Christians the privilege of demonstrating their love for Him by sharing with the saints in Judea.

The earth today produces abundantly. There are many economic and political factors that affect distribution of food in areas where famine strikes. But if men everywhere would respond to the gospel of Christ and recognize the privilege which God had given to men to share with others, the abundance of food which He continually provides could be distributed to the needy by intelligent, Christian people.

This is in no way to suggest any sort of communism or socialism. It is the grace of God functioning in the hearts of men who appreciate the privilege of demonstrating their love for Him by helping the needy. This principle was clearly seen in the church at Jerusalem where the members "sold their possessions and goods, and parted them to all, according as any man had need" (Acts 2:45). The key word in this passage is "need," for there isn't the slightest indication that this action was taken so that every member in the church might be equal in the possession of material things. No where is this made clearer than in the case of Ananias and Sapphira. See Acts 5:1-11. Swift punishment came upon them because Satan filled their heart and caused them to lie to the Holy Spirit about the price of the land which they had sold. But Peter said to them "While it remained, did it not remain thine own? and after it was sold, was it not in thy power?" Very clearly, then, the right of private ownership was upheld by the inspired apostle. The sin of Ananias and Sapphira was not the lack of generosity but of their attempt to lie to the Holy Spirit as they misrepresented their giving before the apostle Peter. It was the widows in the church who were in need of assistance (Acts 6:1). Because some of them were being neglected, the apostles instructed the church to seek out seven men who were given the responsibility of taking care of this ministry. At one time, Agabus, a prophet, speaking under the direction of the Holy Spirit foretold the coming of a famine over all the world. It came to pass in the days of Claudius. The disciples, each one of them according to his ability, decided to send relief to those who dwelt in Judea. They selected Barnabas and Saul—later to be known as the apostle Paul—to carry this relief to the elders in Jerusalem. Acts 11:27-30.

Sometime later when Paul met with the apostles in Jerusalem, he was asked to remember the poor in Judea and he continued his ministry among the Gentiles. But this had always been a matter of deep concern to him. Gal. 2:1-10. His concern that Macedonia and Achaia help the saints in Judea was in accord with his long-standing practice. According to Acts, these churches were Philippi, Thessalonica, and Berea. See Acts 16:12; 17:1, 10.

in much proof of affliction.—The many hardships which Macedonia had endured proved beyond doubt that they understood the situation of the saints in Judea. This and the overflowing of their grace despite their own deep poverty resulted in the wealth of their singleminded devotion and love for God as seen in their liberal contribution to this important cause.

Famines, economic depressions and political oppressions were the common lot of many of the colonies of the Roman Empire. Macedonia's situation was not only known to Paul but, in all probability, to their neighboring province of Achaia also.

Too frequently in this day, Christian people, fall back on their own limited means as an excuse for not sharing with others less fortunate than they. This robs themselves of sharing in the grace of God. Lest Paul be misunderstood, he adds several significant statements governing the thinking and action of those whom he directed to participate in this privilege of sharing with others.

Paul did not hesitate to recognize the poverty of the brethren in Macedonia. It was their single-minded devotion to Christ that made their giving look like a river at floodtide spreading even as far as Judea. Our word "liberality" seems to lose something of its power to describe Paul's view of the generosity of the Macedonian Christians. *according to their power.*—The Macedonians had given according to their ability and, paradoxically, even beyond their ability. Single-minded devotion to God and trust in Him were the underlying causes of this astonishing affect.

their own accord.—Thus Paul makes it clear that the generous giving of the Macedonian Christians was their own gracious response to the favor which God had extended to them to have a share in helping the needy.

beseeching us with much entreaty.—These dedicated Christian people actually had been begging Paul for the privilege of graciously sharing in this ministry to the saints of God.

Too frequently this principle is reversed. Those in charge of the financial program of the church resort to begging the people to give for the support of the work of the church. They often appeal to the legal aspect of giving to break loose portions of the lump with which the supposed parsimonious people grudgingly part. The love of God in the hearts of His people is the most powerful force known in producing generous participation in the program of the church.

the fellowship in the ministering to the saints.—One of the basic issues of Christianity is fellowship or sharing. The apostle John who was an eye-witness of the evidence that established the basic facts of Christianity wrote his first epistle that others might share with him this foundation of their faith, saying, "Our fellowship is with the Father, and with his Son Jesus Christ." See I John 1:1-4. Since Christianity is rooted deeply in fellowship, it should naturally find expression through Christian sharing in service to the saints of God.

not as we had hoped.—Paul, knowing of the deep poverty of the Macedonians, had not hoped for the response which came from them. The secret of their generous response was their dedication to the Lord.

first they gave their own selves to the Lord, and to us through the will of God.—What they did was through the will of God. Paul had made known through his preaching the will of God that had given them the privilege of dedicating themselves to the Lord and of sharing

with Him in the propagation of the gospel and the care of His
saints. Without such dedication churches most likely will always be
struggling to raise the budget. They limp along half-heartedly carrying "the load," but seldom knowing the real joy of generous giving
that springs from devotion to the Lord.

and to us.—Paul did not say that they first gave themselves to the
Lord and then money to him. Rather, they gave themselves to the
Lord and they also gave themselves to Paul. Evidently they volunteered to go with Paul on this mission in behalf of the saints. Luke
gives the list of some who were with Paul on the trip to Jerusalem.
Among them were Sopater of Berea, Aristarchus and Secundus who
were Thessalonians. See Acts 20:4. Paul also mentions the brother
who was selected by the churches to go with him on this mission.
See II Cor. 8:18-19.

we exhorted Titus.—Titus had been Paul's messenger to Corinth to
learn their response to his first letter. Now he reminds them, after
having learned from Titus what their response was, that Titus was
being sent to them again in connection with this ministry to the
saints. Just what Titus at this time had already done in getting them
started on this project is not stated, but Paul indicated that he was
the logical man to help them since he had already begun to do so.

Principles Regulating Giving

Scripture

8:7-15.   But as ye abound in everything, in faith, and utterance,
and knowledge, and in all earnestness, and in your love to us see
that ye abound in this grace also. 8 I speak not by way of commandment, but as proving through the earnestness of others the sincerity
also of your love. 9 For ye know the grace of our Lord Jesus Christ,
that, though he was rich, yet for your sakes he became poor, that ye
through his poverty might become rich. 10 And herein I give my
judgment: for this is expedient for you, who were the first to make
a beginning a year ago, not only to do, but also to will. 11 But now
complete the doing also; that as there was the readiness to will, so
there may be the completion also out of your ability. 12 For if the
readiness is there, it is acceptable according as a man hath, not according as he hath not. 13 For I say not this that others may be
eased and ye distressed; 14 but by equality: your abundance being a
supply at this present time for their want, that their abundance also
may become a supply for your want; that there may be equality:

15 as it is written, He that gathered much had nothing over; and he that gathered little had no lack.

Comments

But as ye abound in everything.—Having commended the Macedonians for their abundant response to the gracious privilege that God had given them to share in the service for His saints, Paul urged the Corinthians to abound in this grace also. He placed this privilege which God had graciously given them on a par with other manifestations of God's grace which they enjoyed and to which they had responded.

faith, and utterance, and knowledge.—Paul had reminded the Corinthians of the grace of God that had been given to them in their relationship to Jesus Christ for they had been enriched in Him in everything and lacked in no gift that would help them as they patiently waited for the coming of the Lord Jesus Christ (I Cor. 1:4-8). Among those gifts, he mentions utterance and knowledge. He also gave a list of nine spiritual powers through the laying on of the apostles' hands that enabled the church to function effectively in the absence of the completed New Testament (I Cor. 12:8-10).

Since Paul lists faith with utterance and knowledge he is in all probability using it in its relationship to the performance of miracles, rather than in its usual sense as belief in the gospel or belief in the Lord Jesus Christ or trust in God. On the other hand, faith in connection with miracles was a tangible demonstration of God's gracious bestowal of power on those on whom the apostles laid their hands. The word of wisdom enabled them to utter the message which God revealed through them. The word of knowledge enabled them to understand this divinely revealed message which we now have in the New Testament.

Paul urged the Corinthians that just as they had an abundant supply of these gracious gifts—faith and utterance and knowledge—so they were to "abound in this grace also."

I speak not by way of commandment.—Paul had reminded the Corinthians that as he had given order for the churches of Galatia so he was also ordering the Corinthians to prepare themselves to make the collection for the relief of the saints. Why does he now say that this was not by way of commandment? The answer seems to lie in the fact that he is here discussing the issue of generosity in giving. As an apostle he did issue the order for the churches to give, but liberality or generosity cannot be ordered; it springs from the single-minded devotion to the Lord of those who first dedicate themselves to Him. He had cited the eagerness of the Macedonians as a standard by which to test the sincerity of the love of the Corinthians. Thus the example of sincere, earnest response to the order to give becomes a strong motivating force to help others to do likewise. Those who fear lest others learn about their giving usually have cause to be ashamed of it themselves. On the other hand, those who give simply to appear generous violate the basic teaching of Our Lord (Matt. 6:2-4; 15:3-9; Luke 21:1-4).

The difference between the command and the motivating force that brings it to reality is seen in the words of Our Lord when He said, "If you love me, ye will keep my commandments" (John 14:15). Those who really love the Lord have only to be told of the need. They have proven their awareness of the command to give by their own dedication to the Lord. How much giving is pointless because of some vague, general appeal! Paul reminded the Macedonians and the Corinthians that what they were giving was to help the poor in Judea. Those who give to the local budget should also be informed as to the items of that budget. Support of missionary projects is lifted to a higher level when the congregation knows the missionary to whom they are giving.

For ye know the grace of our Lord Jesus Christ.—The sincere expression of their love for which Paul was calling found an example in that which had been graciously done by the Lord Jesus Christ. He was rich, yet became poor. No better comment can be found on this issue than Paul's in Phil. 2:5-11. He existed in the form of God and was on equality with God. He emptied Himself, took the form of a servant and was made in the likeness of man. He was found in the fashion as a man and humbled Himself, obediently submitting to the death of the cross. He was crucified through weakness, yet lived through the power of God. See II Cor. 13:4. This does not imply that He lost His deity during His earthly ministry, for there are many examples in the Gospels clearly showing both His deity and His humanity. See *Studies in Luke,* pp. 58-59. The saints are made rich in Him through the salvation which He has so graciously provided. See Eph. 2:1-10; Titus 2:11-14.

And herein I give my judgement.—Another strong motivating force in this matter of giving is the expressed opinion of the inspired apostle. Since the Corinthians were the first to make a beginning in this project, thus showing their willingness to have a share in it Paul urged them to complete the task according to their ability.

if the readiness is there.—God knows the heart of man as well as the size of his bank account. He looks upon the readiness of those whose love leads them to share in relieving the needs of the saints. If this eagerness is present, the amount given is acceptable according to one's ability. It is not determined by what he does not have.

This verse is as much a part of the inspired teaching about giving as the order to give or the appeal based on dedication and love for the Lord. Public appeals overlooking this fact embarrass and often discourage those present who may not be able to give. It was not Paul's intention to do such a thing at Corinth. Jesus' comment about the widow who gave all her living does have some bearing on this issue. See Luke 21:1-4. But it in no way excuses the parsimonious person whose love for money outweighs his love for God.

not that others may be eased.—Paul was not intending to place a burden on the Gentile churches of Macedonia and Achaia in order that the churches in Judea with Jewish background might live in ease. The saints in Judea were in real need. Paul with his Jewish background labored among the Gentiles as the apostle of Christ and everywhere taught that in Christ such distinctions as Jew and Gentile had been removed. But he also recognized the debt which he had to preach the gospel to both Jew and Gentile. He also recognized an obligation toward his Jewish kinsmen, for the faithful among them he said "are Israelites: whose is the adoption, and the glory, and the covenants, and the giving of the law, and the service of God, and the promises; whose are the fathers, and of whom is Christ as concerning the flesh, who is over all, blessed for ever. Amen." (Rom. 9:4-5). Not all Jews could claim this honor but only those who, following in the footsteps of Abraham, had accepted the Lord Jesus Christ. See Rom. 9:6-7; 4:23-25.

but by equality.—The gifts of the Gentile Christians would ease the distress of the saints of Judea.

In the reference to equality, some assume that Paul is indicating that Gentiles who then had the ability to contribute to the relief of the saints of Judea might at some future time suffer distress and be relieved by the saints in Judea, thus bring about equality.

Paul, however, had written to the Corinthians about another phase of equality. He had balanced spiritual things when he had sown for their benefit with his right to reap from their material things. See

I Cor. 9:11. Remembering that the gospel had originated in Judea and that the faithful among the nation of the Jews from Abraham on were like the root out of which the true faith of the gospel had grown, we might also ask whether or not Paul is thinking of that equality that now balanced material things with spiritual things. Paul wrote to the Romans about this trip to Jerusalem on which he was to minister to the saints in connection with the contribution which Macedonia and Achaia were making for the poor in Jerusalem. He said, "Yea, it hath been their good pleasure; and their debtors they are. For if the Gentiles have been made partakers of their spiritual things, they owe it to them also to minister unto them in carnal things" (Rom. 15:25-27).

He that gathered much.—Paul quoted from Ex. 16:18, a reference to the giving of the manna, as an example of the equality about which he was writing. The manna, just as our blessings whether material or spiritual, came from God. God saw to it that no one was able to hoard the manna and thus made everyone equal in that respect. But it is His love and earnest care for others in the hearts of His people that will produce equality in things both spiritual and material.

The Mission of Titus and His Associates

Scripture

8:16-24. But thanks be to God, who putteth the same earnest care for you into the heart of Titus. 17 For he accepted indeed our exhortation; but being himself very earnest, he went forth unto you of his own accord. 18 And we have sent together with him the brother whose praise in the gospel is spread through all the churches; 19 and not only so, but who was also appointed by the churches to travel with us in the matter of this grace, which is ministered by us to the glory of the Lord, and to show our readiness: 20 avoiding this that any man should blame us in the matter of this bounty which is ministered by us: 21 for we take thought for things honorable, not only in the sight of the Lord but also in the sight of men. 22 And we have sent with them our brother, whom we have many times proved earnest in many things, but now much more earnest, by reason of the great confidence which he hath in you. 23 Whether any inquire about Titus, he is my partner and my fellow-worker to youward; or our brethren, they are the messengers of the churches, they are the glory of Christ. 24 Show ye therefore unto them in the face of the churches the proof of your love, and of our glorying on your behalf.

Comments

thanks be to God.—The writings of Paul are full of praise and thanksgiving to God. He was aware that everything that he had been able to accomplish or ever hoped to accomplish had been made possible because God had given him the gracious privilege of serving as the apostle of Christ. He praised God for His comforting care in affliction; he thanked God for leading him in triumph in Christ and making it possible for the gospel to be made known through his efforts. It was God who comforted him through the coming of Titus with the report of improved conditions in Corinth. He thanked God who motivated such men as Titus and his associates to share in the task of assisting the churches to gather funds for the relief of the saints in Judea.

who putteth the same earnest care for you in the heart of Titus.— God made man with the capacity to respond to appeals to relieve the needs of others. He had used Paul to stir up this interest in the heart of Titus. More than that, Titus had seen for himself the desire of the Corinthians to relieve the suffering saints in Judea. People do respond to the cry of their fellowmen for help, for God created them with the capacity to do so. But information about the specific needs must be given if this capacity is to become effective. More than that, this capacity can and should be trained that it might be developed to its fullest extent. Training should begin with children. It should be carried on by the leaders of the church through instruction and example so that the whole family of God might have a wholesome concern for the needs of others. The basic root of all this concern is God's own love for the world demonstrated by the fact that Christ died for us while we were yet sinners. The Lord exhorted men to love their enemies and do good to those who persecuted them.

he accepted indeed our exhortation.—Titus' heart had been stirred by what he had seen in Corinth. They had begun to carry out the order which Paul had given them. He willingly accepted Paul's appeal to continue his assistance to them, for it was in perfect accord with his own decision.

It is a rare thing when effective work in the church is accomplished by those who respond to undue pressure to teach a class, to serve as deacons, or to do the many other things necessary to carry out the total work of the congregation. Unless a man's heart is in it, as in the case of Titus, in all probability it would be better for him not to attempt the task.

with him the brother.—Two others who are designated brothers were to accompany Titus and assist him in this ministry. Their names are not given. Speculation as to their identity has been indulged in through centuries to no profit. Had it been important surely Paul would have given the names. But he does commend them highly Paul never hesitated to commend his fellow-workers such as Timothy, Titus, Apollos and the many others who had proven themselves worthy of such commendation.

This brother had received the commendation throughout all the churches because of his work in the gospel. Paul did not hesitate to pass this information along to the Corinthians. This same principle if followed carefully would save many a church from those whose reputations elsewhere are not good. The leaders of the churches should insist on looking into the reputation of new teachers who come into their midst. Indeed, the Corinthian church could have been saved much grief had they investigated the reputations of the "super-apostles" who had come into their midst attacking the reputation and ministry of Paul. The brethren at Antioch could have been spared a severe split in the church if they had looked into the reputation of those who "came from James." See Gal. 2:11-21.

appointed by the churches.—How these men were selected is not indicated. A good example of how it might have been done is given in Acts 6:1-6. The apostles set forth the qualifications and urged the church to select the men to fit these qualifications. Just how the church went about selecting the men is not indicated but when they had completed the task they brought the men before the apostles who put them in charge of the task. Another example is given in Acts 14:23. Paul and Barnabas appointed elders in every church. The word "appoint" could mean and probably did indicate that this was done with the approval of the church. Titus was given the task of appointing elders in every city in Crete, probably with the approval of the churches as they followed the qualification which Paul had given them. See Titus 1:5-9.

Those selected to travel with Paul and the others in this gracious ministry for the glory of the Lord were men of good reputation among the churches. Paul was eager to have such assistance.

It should be pointed out that these men were selected for a specific task and represented the churches only in the task for which they were selected. In no sense did they become representatives to make decision for the congregations. The New Testament indicates that the congregations were interdependent as well as independent.

avoiding this, that any man should blame us.—Paul was aware of the fact that there were those who would assume that the collections were being made for his own benefit. False charges easily arise making it necessary for those who handle the funds of the congregation to be above reproach in every regard and to be able to prove their honesty against any false charge. Judas even stole from the treasury of Jesus and the apostles. See John 12:6. Why allow the treasurer of a church to be put into a position where he might be accused of such a thing? He should have someone to check his work; his books should be audited and every precaution should be taken for his sake and for the protection of those who contribute to the fund. Paul avoided the possibility of any improper handling of money entrusted to his care. He took "thought for things honorable not only in the sight of the Lord, but also in the sight of men."

this bounty which is ministered by us.—The term "bounty" comes from the word which means thickness or fullness and was used to describe a plant that had reached its full development or its fruit that had become ripe. It aptly describes the generous giving of the church that had been preparing for this effort and were soon to bring it to completion.

Just as time is needed for a plant to grow and produce fruit, so a congregation should be given time to (1) to be adequately informed regarding financial projects and (2) to let their contributions grow to the point where they are adequate for the needs for which they are being given.

we have sent with them our brother.—Paul had urged Titus to undertake this mission, the churches had selected the brother with a good reputation in the gospel to accompany him, and Paul had sent still another proven man on this mission. His earnestness had been proven on many occasions and heightened at this time because of his great confidence in the willingness of the Corinthians to respond generously to this appeal.

Whether any inquire about Titus.—Paul had already written a great deal about Titus, but to make sure that any question about him could be fully answered, he adds, "He is my partner and fellow-worker to you-ward." This is characteristic of Paul's attitude toward those who labored with him. See, for example, his attitude toward Apollos in I Cor. 3:4-9. For his attitude toward Timothy see Phil. 2:19-24.

the messengers of the churches.—As the footnote in some Bibles indicates, the word "messenger" is actually "apostle." It means one who is sent on a mission. It is not to be assumed that they had equal authority with the apostles of Christ, for those men were commissioned by Him and equipped for their task by being baptized in the Holy Spirit. Since the term was one in common use designating anyone being sent on a mission, it becomes absolutely necessary to study each context to learn who the sender is in order to avoid confusion over the use of the term. Here, for that very purpose, it is rendered "messengers"—a word which comes from Latin but means the same thing.

Long usage has accustomed us to use "apostle" to refer to those sent by Christ, but to use "missionary" to designate those who are sent out by churches to proclaim the gospel.

the glory of Christ.—All this—the selection, the commendation, and the sending of the men to protect the reputation of the apostle and the others—was for the glory of the Lord.

Too often this basic principle is forgotten. Many assume that the tasks that they may be performing in connection with the work of the gospel are for their own glory. Evidently there were such in Corinth, for Paul had to write the last section of this epistle to show that such people were in reality servants of Satan.

in the face of the churches the proof of your love.—Paul had not hesitated to remind Corinth of the generosity of the Macedonian churches. Now he urged them to respond in like manner demonstrating before the churches their love for the Lord. This was not to be some hypocritical display (Matt. 6:2-4). It was to be the sincere response of Christian love, the example of which would motivate others to respond in the same manner.

our glorying on your behalf.—Paul had been boasting both to Titus and the Macedonians about the preparation that Achaia had made for this task.

Summary

The collection for the saints in Jerusalem is discussed in chapters eight and nine. The order to make such a collection had been given in the first epistle. The second epistle gave more detailed instruction about that offering.

Paul lifted giving above the level of begging by showing that it is a favor from God. The Macedonians had begged for the privilege of sharing in such a project. Rather than begin with the fact that Corinth was lagging in the matter, Paul told them about the thing that Macedonia was doing despite their affliction and deep poverty. How this must have stirred Corinth to action!

Paul spoke of the riches of Macedonian single-minded devotion to the Lord. This is what made their contribution a thing of liberality. They gave beyond their power; they gave of their own accord; they begged for the privilege of sharing in the ministry to the saints. They gave even beyond the hopes of the apostle Paul. The secret? Macedonia had given themselves first, both to the Lord and to Paul. The latter was done by furnishing men to go with him on the trip to Jerusalem. All this was done through the will of God. Paul did not say that they gave themselves to the Lord and then gave money to him. The money was given for Jerusalem. Dedication to the Lord caused the Macedonians to give to the relief of His saints in Judea.

The Macedonian devotion to Paul stood in contrast to the Corinthian opposition to him. Because of the example of Macedonia, Paul urged Titus to complete the task of collecting funds for Jerusalem, since he had already begun the work, so that Corinth might share in this grace also.

Paul urged Corinth to abound in this favor just as they had in spiritual gifts and Christian character. Giving was commended, but the measure was regulated by love. In love, they were to follow the example of Christ who became poverty-stricken on the cross that he might enable men to share His heavenly riches.

Paul had boasted much about the Macedonians, but he also complimented the Corinthians: they were first to willingly undertake this task. It would be well for them to bring it to completion. When the readiness was present, the gift was acceptable according to one's ability, not according to what he did not have.

Another principle regulating the amount to be given is equality. Material help sent by Corinth would meet Jerusalem's need. What was Jerusalem's abundance that would fill Corinth's need? Some suggest that it was material need at some future date. But Paul's remarks in 9:12-15 may be to the point. Their gift had resulted in thanksgiving to God; they needed to respond to the gracious privilege of sharing as Macedonia had done. Thus material need was balanced by spiritual want. God's miraculous power produced equality in gathering the manna. God's grace produced equality for Jerusalem and Corinth as He met the needs of each.

Paul explained the mission of Titus and his associates. Titus responded to his appeal to complete the work at Corinth, since he had already become interested in it, for God had put it in his heart to do so. To avoid criticism about handling the funds, Paul sent the others to help Titus. One who had a good reputation in the gospel among the churches was selected by them for the task. New Testament churches did cooperate through individuals of good reputation in order to carry out the Lord's work. Paul sent still another brother whom he had tested and found to be earnest many times in many things. Titus, in case anyone inquired, was Paul's partner and fellow-worker. The brethren were sent by the churches. The work to be done was for the glory of Christ.

Paul urged Corinth to give a demonstration of their love before these brethren and a reason for his boasting about their being prepared to share in this task.

Questions

1. What are the three principal topics discussed in this epistle?
2. What chapters are given over to the discussion of the collections for the saints?
3. What characterizes Paul's mood as he wrote about the postponement of his visit to Corinth?
4. How account for the change of mood as he wrote about giving?
5. How did his mood change again as he took up the defense of his apostleship against the charges of false teachers?
6. What did Paul mean by the grace of God that had been given in the churches of Macedonia?
7. In what way does this differ from the usual approach to the subject of giving?
8. How did God provide for the children of Israel in the wilderness?
9. Why didn't He provide for the saints in Judea in the same way?
10. What was the basic principle in the distribution of material goods by the church in Jerusalem?
11. How was it abused by Ananias and Sapphira?

12. Why was it necessary to appoint deacons in the church at Jerusalem?
13. What experience had Paul already had in famine relief in Judea?
14. What had he promised Peter and John with reference to helping the poor in Judea?
15. What does Acts reveal about the churches in Macedonia?
16. What is known about the hardship and poverty which Macedonia was enduring?
17. Is poverty an excuse for not participating in the privilege of sharing with others?
18. What did Paul mean by "liberality"?
19. What caused Macedonia to give even beyond their ability?
20. Who determined what they were to give?
21. What was their attitude toward the privilege of giving?
22. What about the begging approach to budget raising?
23. What is the place of fellowship in the matter of giving?
24. What had Paul hoped for from Macedonia? What happened?
25. What was the secret of their generous response?
26. What did Paul mean when he said that they gave themselves to the Lord by the will of God?
27. How had they given themselves to Paul also?
28. To whom was the money given?
29. What had Titus done to help the Corinthians in the matter of giving for the saints?
30. Why was Paul sending him back to Corinth?
31. What had the grace of God done for the Corinthians?
32. Define faith, utterance, and knowledge? What had these to do with the grace of giving?
33. Why did he say, "I speak not by way of commandment"?
34. How harmonize this with the fact that he had ordered the churches of Galatia to prepare for the relief of the saints?
35. What is the motivating force in generosity?
36. Why did he appeal to the example of the Lord?
37. Why did Paul express his opinion to the Corinthians instead of commanding them to act?
38. What does God look for in the hearts of those who are privileged to give?
39. What was Paul's motive in asking Gentile congregations to help the needy Christians in Judea?

40. In what way were Gentile Christians indebted to those of Jewish background?
41. What are some of the ways in which the offering for the saints in Judea might bring about equality?
42. How does the reference to the giving of the manna explain the issue of equality.
43. What are some of the things for which Paul thanked God?
44. Why did he thank God for Titus?
45. How did God put earnest care for the Corinthians in the heart of Titus?
46. What does the attitude of Titus show as to the essential qualifications of those who may be asked to serve in the church?
47. What did Paul say about the two who were sent with Titus?
48. How can this serve as a guide to churches in selecting workers?
49. How did the churches appoint the brother to travel with Titus?
50. What does this show about cooperation between congregations?
51. What was Paul's concern in handling these funds?
52. What does it suggest to those who handle the funds of the church?
53. Why did Paul use the word "bounty" to describe the offering?
54. What do we know about Paul's attitude toward his fellow-workers? toward Titus? toward Appolos? toward Timothy?
55. What is the literal meaning of the word translated "messenger"?
56. Why not use the literal translation?
57. For whose glory were these messengers to work?
58. What demonstration did Paul want the churches to make?
59. To whom had Paul been boasting about Achaia?
60. What was his purpose in mentioning it at this point?

For Discussion

1. What factors affect the distribution of food to the hungry peoples of the world?
2. How would the evangelization of the world—that's what Jesus said to do—affect the problem of caring for the needy?

CHAPTER NINE

Analysis

A. Paul continued to explain the mission of the brethren who were to help the Corinthians in their minister to the saints (1-5).
   1. His knowledge of their readiness and zeal (1-2).
      a) Because he knew of this, writing to them was not necessary.
      b) He had boasted of their readiness to the Macedonians to stir up their zeal.
   2. Further reasons for sending the brethren (3-5).
      a) He had sent them lest his boasting about their preparedness become an empty thing (3).
      b) In the event that some of the Macedonians should come with him and find them unprepared he—not to mention the Corinthians—would be ashamed (4).
      c) He had urged them to go so that the gift they had promised might be bounteous and not forced (5).
B. He explained the issues involved in generous giving (6-15).
   1. The principle of sowing and reaping in relation to giving (6-7).
      a) The one who sows sparingly reaps sparingly, but the one who sows generously reaps abundantly (6).
      b) In the light of this, each one is to give as he determines in his heart (7).
         (1) He is to make the decision in his own heart.
         (2) He is to do it, not as one who painfully wishes that he didn't have to, but as one who remembers that God loves a cheerful giver.
   2. The ability to give (8-10).
      a) As He makes all grace abound, so he makes the generous giver able to abound in every good work (8).
      b) This is according to Psa. 112:9 (9).
      c) As He supplies seed to sow to produce bread He will supply and multiply the seed for sowing and increase the fruits of righteousness (10).
   3. The results of generous giving (11-14).
      a) Thanksgiving to God (11-12).
         (1) From Paul.

(2) From those whose wants were met. The ministry of this service met their needs and caused them to thank God.
b) Praise to God as they saw the obedience and liberality of those who gave to help them (13).
c) Longing on the part of those who had been helped for those who by God's grace had shared with them (14).
4. The closing word: "Thanks be to God for his unspeakable gift." The full account of the gift could not be put in words (15).

Ministering To The Saints

Scripture

9:1-5. For as touching the ministering to the saints, it is superfluous for me to write to you: 2 for I know your readiness, of which I glory on your behalf to them of Macedonia, that Achaia hath been prepared for a year past; and your zeal hath stirred up very many of them. 3 But I have sent the brethren, that our glorying on your behalf may not be made void in this respect; that, even as I said, ye may be prepared: 4 lest by any means if there come with me any of Macedonia and find you unprepared, we (that we say not, ye) should be put to shame in this confidence. 5 I thought it necessary therefore to entreat the brethren, that they would go before unto you, and make up beforehand your aforepromised bounty, that the same might be ready as a matter of bounty, and not of extortion.

Comments

superfluous for me to write to you.—Paul had spent considerable space in this letter giving direction concerning the offerings for the saints and commending Titus and his associates for the part they were to have in assisting the Corinthians in preparing their offering. Indeed it was superfluous to go on writing to them about the matter, for he knew that they were eager to do their part. He had been boasting to the people of Macedonia saying, "Achaia has been ready for a year." Just how many months had gone by since they had begun to make preparation is not clear, but the Corinthians knew exactly. The zeal of Achaia had aroused many of the Macedonians to action. *But I have sent the brethren.*—While it was not necessary to go on writing to them about their offering, it was necessary to say some additional words about the mission of Titus and his associates. He was sending them to make sure that his boasting about their preparedness had not been in vain. He did not want the Macedonians, some of whom had volunteered to go with him to Corinth, to find the Corinthians unprepared. This would embarrass him, to say nothing about what it would do to them.

as a matter of bounty and not of extortion.—The word translated "bounty" is commonly, within proper context, translated "blessing." It meant words that were well spoken about praise that was well deserved; it meant blessings that benefitted those who received them. Out of this concept comes the thought of bountiful giving that brings benefit to others. Paul had clearly indicated that this was the type of gift that Macedonia was preparing and he did not hesitate to suggest that Achaia's gift should be of the same kind. He did not want a poor showing on their part to demonstrate an attitude of greediness that would keep them from parting from their material wealth.

Stingy, miserly people do not give in such a manner as to suggest that their giving is a blessing to either themselves or to others.

Generous Giving

Scripture

9:6-15. But this I say, He that soweth sparingly shall reap also sparingly; and he that soweth bountifully shall reap also bountifully. 7 Let each man do according as he hath purposed in his heart: not grudgingly, or of necessity: for God loveth a cheerful giver. 8 And God is able to make all grace abound unto you; that ye, having always all sufficiency in everything, may abound unto every good work: 9 as it is written,

He hath scattered abroad, he hath given to the poor;
His righteousness abideth for ever.

10 And he that supplieth seed to the sower and bread for food, shall supply and multiply your seed for sowing, and increase the fruits of your righteousness: 11 ye being enriched in everything unto all liberality, which worketh through us thanksgiving to God. 12 For the ministration of this service not only filleth up the measure of the wants of the saints, but aboundeth also through many thanksgivings unto God; 13 seeing that through the proving of you by this ministration they glorify God for the obedience of your confession unto the gospel of Christ, and for the liberality of your contribution unto them

and unto all; 14 while they themselves also, with supplication on your behalf, long after you by reason of the exceeding grace of God in you. 15 Thanks be to God for his unspeakable gift.

Comments

He that soweth sparingly shall reap also sparingly.—Now Paul enlarges upon what he had said about bounty and extortion with the illustration of sowing and reaping. Sowing sparingly explains his remark about extortion, for the one who holds back the seed instead of putting plenty on the ground is like the miserly person who would hold back his wealth rather than look to blessing that comes both to him and those whom he might help through generous giving. On the other hand, the one who anticipates a bountiful harvest by scattering an abundance of seed is like the generous giver who will be blessed in his giving as well as benefitting those to whom he gives. It was Paul who reminded the elders of the church at Ephesus about the words of the Lord Jesus who said, "It is more blessed to give than to receive" (Acts 20:35). James denounced the miserly rich and warned them about the miseries that were about to come upon them. He said, "Your riches are corrupted, and your garments are moth-eaten. Your gold and your silver are rusted; and their rust shall be for a testimony against you, and shall eat your flesh as fire. Ye have laid up your treasures in the last days" (James 5:1-3).

Let each man do according as he has purposed in his heart.—Because giving has a double blessing, first to the giver and then to the one who receives each one was to decide in his own heart what he would do before making the gift. Guidelines had already been given by the apostle by which the decision was to be made. He added still others at this point.

not grudgingly, nor of necessity.—It was not to be done out of sorrow in parting with his coveted wealth; it was not to be of necessity, that is, not being forced to give rather than suffering the embarrassment of not joining with the generous people who were making up the liberal offering for those who were in want.

Since giving is to benefit the giver, the leaders of the churches should avoid methods of forcing people to give as if God were poverty stricken and had to have their help. These are they who give grudgingly and painfully and constantly complain that the church is "always after money."

for God loveth a cheerful giver.—God has demonstrated that He has bountifully given for the benefit of all mankind. He did not spare His own Son, but delivered Him up for us all. Paul asks, "How shall He not also with Him freely give us all things?" (Rom. 8: 31-32). All this, God gladly gives in bountiful measure; He loves the cheerful giver.

Pressure methods used to force people to give who really do not want to give are wrong from every point of view: (1) God doesn't have to have the money. The case of Ananias and Sapphira proved it. (2) The benefit to the giver is nullified. (3) The principle of spontaneous, generous giving as a blessing to the giver is violated.

God is able.—This seems to be Paul's answer to the one who says "I can't." Although he had recognized the principle that if a man has the right attitude, what he does is acceptable to God according to what he has and not according to what he has not. The supply of the seed for sowing and the multiplying of that seed in the harvest is all from God. Man cannot produce seed that will grow and multiply. With this principle clearly stated, Paul indicated that God graciously makes it possible for one to give for the benefit of others and to multiply the blessing. Paul quoted from Psalm 112:9 which tells of the righteous man who is not afraid to trust God as he gives to the poor.

God promised Noah that "while the earth remains, seedtime and harvest, cold and heat, summer and winter, day and night, shall not cease" (Gen. 8:22).

And he that supplieth seed to the sower and bread for food.—Those who trust in the Lord, rely on His promise, and sow generously will go on reaping the abundant harvest. This is not to say that there will be no famines, but that the principle of planting and harvesting is guaranteed by the Lord. Distribution of the harvest of the land may depend on the generousity of those who love the Lord. Hence the gospel that transforms the hearts of men is the key to the world food problem. Jesus said, "But seek ye first His kingdom, and His righteousness; and all these things shall be added unto you" (Matt. 6:33).

worketh through us thanksgiving to God.—Among the benefits of generous giving are not only those to the giver and the receiver, but the motivation of men to thank God for His blessings and for those who generously share with others.

seeing that the proving of you by this ministration.—This ministry on behalf of the saints gave the Gentile Christians an opportunity

170

to prove that they were glorifying God and being obedient to their commitment to the gospel of Christ.

your confession unto the gospel of Christ.—Those who accept the privileges of the gospel of Christ openly acknowledge their indebtedness to others. See Rom. 1:14-15. They had received the blessings of Christ's gospel and were obligated to make these blessings known to other and to share their material things with all the family of God.

long after you.—Those who received the material blessing prayed for those who gave. Their hearts were stirred with deep longing for the welfare and even the presence of those who had been moved by the grace of God to help them.

Thanks be to God for his unspeakable gift.—Paul closed the subject of giving with thanks to God for His gift which no words could adequately describe. The context indicates that that gift had produced in the hearts of the saints in Judea prayers to God for the Gentile Christians and a deep longing for fellowship with those whom they now accepted as fellow-heirs of the inheritance of the saints.

This marvelous gift, of course, comes out of the gift of His Son through whom fellowship among God's people was made possible.

Commentators have long been divided on these two points. Strict adherence to the context indicates that the gift is the result of the grace of God in the hearts of those who longed for the fellowship of their fellow-Christians. But in no way does this ignore the gift of God's love in the Person of His Son.

Summary

Paul began the discussion of the offerings for the saints in Judea with a word of praise for the Macedonian churches. Now he shows the Corinthians that he had boasted of their readiness to the Macedonians. The example of Ahaia had stirred up the zeal of the Macedonians.

In this chapter, Paul continues to explain the mission of the brethren who had been sent to help the Corinthians in their effort to relieve the usffering of the saints. Although he knew of their readiness and zeal, he thought it necessary to write to them to explain still another reason for sending the brethren to help them. He wanted to make sure that his boasting would not turn out to his embarrassment, not to mention their shame if the brethren should come from Macedonia and find them unprepared. The brethren would help them prepare a generous gift, but would not force anyone to give beyond his ability.

Paul explained the principle of generous giving by referring to sowing and reaping. The one who sows sparingly reaps a poor harvest; the one who sows generously reaps an abundant harvest. Thus he drew attention to the results of giving which provide strong motivation for giving generously. Forced giving may help the needy, but it robs the giver of the blessing that should come to him. Let each one make up his own mind and so let him give out of love, for God loves a cheerful giver.

But how could they give? Macedonia was burdened with deep poverty. The Corinthians may have been but little better off. Paul's answer was: God is able! He is able to supply the seed for sowing and bring about the increase at harvest time. He is able to do the same in the spiritual realm, making it possible for his people to share with those less fortunate in material things.

The bountiful harvest resulting from generous giving was the thanksgiving to God in the hearts of those whose needs had been met. But there was another remarkable feature to that harvest: the longing in the hearts of the saints with Jewish background for the welfare of their brethren in Christ with Gentile back-ground. God's unmerited favor in permitting Macedonia and Achaia to share had resulted in this abundant harvest.

"Thanks be to God for his unspeakable grace." The full account of this abundant harvest could not be put into words.

Questions

1. In what way is the thought of this chapter related to the preceding one?
2. Why did he say that it was superfluous to write to them?
3. What had he told Macedonia about Achaia?
4. What had the zeal of Achaia done for the Macedonians?
5. What was the additional reason for sending Titus and his associates?
6. What embarrassment to the Corinthians was he anticipating?
7. How can one word be translated "bounty" in one context and "blessing" in another? What does the word denote?
8. What did Paul mean when he said that the offering was not to be a matter of extortion?

9. How does the example of sowing and reaping explain the principle of generous giving?
10. What did the Lord Jesus say about the blessing involved in giving?
11. What did James say about those who misuse riches?
12. Who is to determine the amount to be given?
13. In what way are some people forced to give?
14. Why does God love the cheerful giver?
15. How did He demonstrate His willingness to freely give us all things?
16. What did Ananias and Sapphira do that was wrong?
17. How was it possible for poverty-stricken Macedonia to give for the relief of the sains in Judea?
18. How did God multiply the harvest of their giving?
19. How had their giving glorified God?
20. How had it shown their obedience to their commitment to the gospel?
21. How are those who accept the privileges of the gospel under obligations to others?
22. What is unusual about the fact that the saints of Judea longed for their brethren among the Gentile congregations?
23. What is God's unspeakable gift to which Paul refers?
24. Why was he unable to put into words a full account of this gift?

For Discussion

1. In what way do pressure methods force some to give who would rather not do so.
2. How has God made it possible to give to the needy?

CHAPTER TEN

Analysis

A. Paul appealed to the Corinthians for understanding in his defense of his apostolic authority (1-6).
   1. He made it a personal appeal (1-2).
      a) It was made in the meekness and gentleness of Christ (1a).
      b) Parenthetically, he let them know that he was aware of the charge that he was meek when present but bold when he was absent (1b).
      c) He begged that he might not have to deal boldly with some who assumed that he was acting in mere human manner (weak and fearful before the enemy) (2).
   2. He corrected the false notion about the nature and effectiveness of his kind of warfare (3-6).
      a) Although he was living in the world, he was not waging war in a worldly manner (3-4).
         (1) His weapons were not of this world—not spears of slander, nor arrows of defamation and lies, etc., but the truth of God's Word!
         (2) They were powerful before God—that is, as God considers them.
         (3) They effectively destroyed strongholds.
      b) He described the stronghold which his weapons were capable of destroying (5a).
         (1) Imaginations or speculations.
         (2) Every high thing that is exalted against the knowledge of God.
      c) He explained the effectiveness of his warfare (5b-6).
         (1) Every thought was made captive to obedience to Christ (5b).
         (2) He was prepared to punish all disobedience when their obedience was complete—that is, when they had been given ample time to obey (6).
B. Paul defended his boasting about the authority which the Lord had given him (7-12).
   1. He charged the Corinthians with taking a superficial view of the issues before them (7-8).

a) They were looking at the things that were before them but failing to see that the basis of another's claim to belong to Christ was the same as Paul's.

b) He reminded them that his authority about which he may have boasted too much (from the view point of his critics) was from the Lord.

c) He intended to use this authority to build up and not to cast down.

2. He answered those who had criticized his letters (10-12).

a) The critics said his letters were weighty and strong, but his bodily presence was weak (10).

b) He declared that his action when present would match his words by letter (11).

s) He was not like those who compared themselves with themselves and measured themselves with themselves— that is, by their own standards—and conseqeuntly were without true understanding (12).

C. He defended the standard by which his boasting was to be judged (13-18).

1. He boasted only in the limits God had set for his work that reached even to Corinth (13).

2. He did not overextend himself but reached even to Corinth in the work of the gospel of Christ (14).

3. In doing so, he had not been boasting in other men's labors (15-16).

a) He kept within the appointed measure which the Lord had set.   . . . .

b) He hoped for further progress of the gospel through their mature faith.

c) This would mean preaching the gospel in areas beyond Corinth and still not boasting in another's field of effort.

4. He explained his basic principle in boasting (17-18).

a) It was to "the glory of the Lord."

b) In boasting, he sought the approval of the Lord—not men.

Defense of Paul's Apostolic Authority

Scripture

10:1-6. Now I Paul myself entreat you by the meekness and gentleness of Christ, I who in your presence am lowly among you, but being absent am of good courage toward you: 2 yea, I beseech you, that I may not when present show courage with the confidence wherewith I count to be bold against some, who count of us as if we walked according to the flesh. 3 For though we walk in the flesh, we do not war according to the flesh 4 (for the weapons of our warfare are not of the flesh, but mighty before God to the casting down of strongholds); 5 casting down imaginations, and every high thing that is exalted against the knowledge of God, and bring every thought into captivity to the obedience of Christ; 6 and being in readiness to avenge all disobedience, when your obedience shall be made full.

Comments

Now I Paul myself.—This chapter begins the third and last section of the epistle. It is Paul's defense of his apostolic authority which had been given him to build up and not to tear down. In it he answers the false charges of the super-apostles who in his absence had come to Corinth and were seeking to undermine his influence and destroy the work which he had done.

There is a distinct change in the tone in this part of the letter. Since his apostolic authority was under attack and since this was the very foundation of the relation of the church to the Lord, it became necessary for him to deal sharply with the enemy and to remind all that unless false teachers were abandoned he would necessarily deal harshly with them on his forthcoming visit. Some have imagined that Paul could not have changed his mood so abruptly. As a result they have also imagined that this rebuke must have been from some other epistle. But the change of his mood is perfectly understandable in the light of the change of subject matter. There is no good reason for assuming that Second Corinthians is a synthetic epistle made up of sections from several other epistles of Paul. In the light of the sound reasons for Paul's change of mood as well as complete lack of manuscript support for the theory that attacks the unity of the epistle, we may be assured that we now have the epistle as Paul wrote it to the Corinthians.

In a most emphatic manner Paul lets his readers know that this defense is coming from him. He has frequently used the plural in his writings. In doing so, he is usually considering himself in connection with the rest of the apostolic group. But since this is an answer to the attack that had been made on him and his apostolic authority he emphatically declared that the appeal he was making to them was his own personal appeal. And since he wrote as an apostle, this was written under the control of the Holy Spirit as were all of his writings.

by the meekness and gentleness of Christ.—Although Paul's tone grew harsh as he dealt with the false teachers who had wrought such havoc in Corinth and had so unfairly attacked his apostlesip, he began this section in the same gracious manner in which he had sought to win the approval of the Corinthians on all the issues about which he had written.

We note the exalted view of the church which is presented in the opening words of First Corinthians, but which had to be followed by severe condemnation of the sinful practices that had been permitted to go on. The temple of God was being destroyed by them. In this section, Paul does not suddenly lash out at the enemy, but by gracious reasoning and encouraging appeal he urged his readers to look at the real facts of the case. Finally, he warned them of the result of failure to heed his appeal. He was coming to them a third time, and just as he had promised in his first letter (I Cor. 4:18-21) so he made it clear again that he would not spare the wrong doer when he arrived.

Paul proceeded in all his dealings with man in the courteous and gracious manner that had characterized the ministry of our Lord. Isaiah prophecied of Him in these words "He shall not strive, nor cry aloud; neither shall anyone hear his voice in the streets. A bruised reed shall he not break, and a smoking flax shall he not quench, till he send for judgment unto victory" (Matt. 12:19-20). He was gentle in dealing with the erring, urging them to sin no more. He reasoned with His critics who condemned Him for "receiving sinners." But when compelled to do so by hardhearted hypocrisy on the part of those who would not listen to reason, He did not hesitate to pronounce severe judgment upon the willfully disobedient.

The Corinthians were familiar with our Lord's methods of dealing with men. Paul had preached nothing among them save Jesus Christ and Him crucified. He had upheld the Word of the Cross which is a symbol both of the love of God expressed toward those who repent and of awful judgment upon those who persisted in willful disobedience.

I who in your presence am lowly among you.—Paul, parenthetically, reminded his readers that he was fully aware of the attitude of the false teachers toward him. It was they who were saying that Paul was lowly when he was with them but when he was absent he made a show of courage. Genuine humility is to be commended on the part of anyone at any time. Paul did not lack this virtue. The thought that is implied by the remark of his critics was that he was a person of low status and not to be compared with those whom he later designated as "super-apostles." They considered themselves elevated above such as Paul because of their professional status as orators and teachers of wisdom. Paul prepared his readers to anticipate his answer to such unfair insinuations.

that I may not when present show courage.—Now Paul's plea becomes more intense as he begs his readers to listen to his gracious appeal that he might not have to show boldness which he fully intended to do on his arrival against those who were claiming that he was conducting himself "according to flesh." He did not conduct himself on the same basis as worldly-minded human beings. The description of his weapons of warfare shows how mistaken his enemies were.

we do not war according to the flesh.—Paul never claimed to be other than a human being, but he did not conduct himself in the manner of the false teachers who were disturbing the brethren at Corinth. He did not carry on a campaign nor wage a war in the manner of men. While he does not specify at this point the nature of that warfare, it is easy to see what he meant by the description of the action of those who had arrayed themselves against him. They had resorted to unfair tactics. They had not hesitated to stoop to falsehood, boastful claims of importance, and hypocritical pretense of relation to Christ while in reality they were servants of Satan.

the weapons of our warfare.—In carrying on his campaign for Christ, Paul did not use such weapons. By contrast, they were powerful in the sight of God. His mighty weapon, as the Corinthians well knew, was the truth of the revealed wisdom of God (I Cor. 2:6-16). They had seen it demolish the claims of Greeks who placed their confidence in their own wisdom and of Jews who demanded signs. But both of these had rejected the Word of the Cross that exalted Christ who was "made unto us wisdom from God."

Paul wrote to the Ephesians about the warfare against the spiritual hosts of wickedness in the heavenly places. He urged them to take up the whole armor of God that they might be able to withstand the attack of the devil. He named the elements of that armor: truth,

righteousness, peace, faith, salvation, and the Word of God. See Eph.
6:10-18.

casting down strongholds.—The Corinthians were familiar with the
engines of war in use in their day. They enabled conquering armies
to demolish fortresses that stood in the pathway of their progress
toward victory. Paul likened the gospel to such instruments of victory.

casting down imaginations.—The gospel which Paul preached was
able to demolish the clever systems of thought that had been devised
by the Greeks.

We need to turn the light of that same gospel upon the systems of
thought devised by men in our day, for some have disregarded God's
wisdom which came down from above. Too frequently we strive to
test the message of God's Word by the theories of men. A careful
reading of the first chapter of Romans in the light of the tragic things
that are happening all over the world today will show the folly of
such procedure. And a careful reading of the third chapter of Romans
will indicate the remedy which we so desperately need. Paul wrote
to the Philippians reminding them that he had at one time been led
astray from the truth, but had long since considered everything loss
that he had once held dear that he might gain Christ and know Him
and the power of His resurrection. See Phil. 3:10-11.

every thought into captivity to the obedience of Christ.—With full
confidence in the truth of the knowledge of God with which he was
armed, Paul expected to capture the thought of men as a victorious
army would take prisoners in battle and lead those thoughts to
obedience to Christ.

and being in readiness to avenge all disobedience.—Paul knew that
there were those who would not submit to the truth of God and he
was prepared to deal with such disobedience. This was a direct
reference to the false teachers who had been disturbing the church
at Corinth as well as those in the congregation who had sided with
them. All disobedience would be punished as he had warned in
I Cor. 4:18-21 and as he was about to repeat the warning in II
Cor. 13:2. Paul was not bluffing; he intended to punish those who
were attempting to destroy the church of God at Corinth.

when your obedience shall be made full.—Once again he is indicating
what he had plainly stated before that he had delayed coming to
Corinth in order to give them ample time to comply with all that he
had instructed them to do. He is now anticipating the necessity of
dealing with the super-apostles. Those who had insinuated that his

absence implied lack of courage to deal with the situation were reminded that he would delay sufficiently long for them to correct their
ways, but that he would punish the disobedient upon his arrival.

A Defense Of His Boasting About His Authority
Scripture

10:7-12. Ye look at the things that are before your face. If any
man trusteth in himself that he is Christ's, let him consider this again
with himself, that, even as he is Christ's, so also are we. 8 For though
I should glory somewhat abundantly concerning our authority (which
the Lord gave for building you up, and not for casting you down), I
shall not be put to shame: 9 that I may not seem as if I would terrify
you by my letters. 10 For, His letters, they say, are weighty and
strong; but his bodily presence is weak, and his speech of no account.
11 Let such a one reckon this, that, what we are in word by letters
when we are absent, such are we also in deed when we are present.
12 For we are not bold to number or compare ourselves with certain
of them that commend themselves: but they themselves, measuring
themselves by themselves, and comparing themselves with themselves,
are without understanding.

Comments

Ye look at the things that are before your face.—Paul began the
defense of his apostolic authority against those who had attacked his
person and methods. He reminded those, of readers who had been
in sympathy with his enemies, that they were taking a superficial view
of things that were before their very eyes. These men were in their
midst, their claims were well known, and their motives should have
been understood. But lest there be any doubt about it, Paul explained
it to them in plain language. See 11:20-33.

If any man trusteth in himself that he is Christ's.—This seems to
be directed against anyone who was attacking Paul while claiming to
belong to Christ. But there is really only one way by which anyone
can belong to Christ, and that is the way of complete surrender to
Him. As Paul had done when he asked on the Damascus way, "Lord,
what wilt thou have me to do?" so must every one obey Him. Paul
obeyed the instruction of the Lord through Ananias whom the Lord
sent to tell Paul what to do and got himself baptized into Christ.
From that time on, he conducted himself as a Christian, for Christ
lived in him (Gal. 2:20). By this standard the brethren at Corinth
could judge the teachers who at that time were disturbing them.

Had they actually obeyed from the heart that form of teaching which led them to be crucified with Christ and be buried with Him in baptism and walk with Him in the new life? Had they demonstrated by their conduct that they had been transformed so that their thinking and action conformed to the truth revealed in God's Word?

For though I should glory somewhat abundantly concerning our authority.—In the light of the claims of these false teachers, it was necessary for Paul to boast about his authority. This was his apostolic authority which he received from the Lord Jesus when He appeared to Paul on the Damascus road. Paul quoted the words of the Lord Jesus in his trial before Agrippa, "But arise, and stand upon thy feet; for to this end have I appeared unto thee, to appoint thee a minister and witness both of the things wherein thou hast seen me, and of the things wherein I will appear unto thee; delivering thee from the people, and the Gentiles, to whom I send thee, to open their eyes, that they turn from darkness to light and from the power of Satan unto God, that they may receive remission of sins and an inheritance among them that are sanctified by faith in me" (Acts 26:16-18). Which of these false teachers had received such a commission from Christ? The brethren at Corinth knew that Christ had commissioned Paul as an apostle, for the signs of an apostle had been performed in their midst. See 12:12. Who among those who were seeking to tear down the apostolic authority of Paul could produce divine credentials to support their claims?

which the Lord gave for building you up.—The apostolic commission and the miraculous powers that accompanied it were not given to Paul for his exaltation nor to be used to destroy others. The intention of the Lord had been made clear in His instruction to Paul, for the ultimate goal was to bring men to the inheritance among them that are sanctified by faith in Christ.

Paul's authority was not given him for the purpose of destroying the church at Corinth. But these servants of Satan were doing so.

I shall not be put to shame.—Paul had perfect confidence in the message which as an apostle of Christ he had delivered to the church at Corinth. He was confident in the ultimate victory in the struggle to overcome the destructive false teaching to which some were apparently willing to listen.

that I may not seem as if I would terrify you by my letters.—These were not idle threats designed to strike terror in the hearts of those who read his letters; they were the solemn warnings of one whose love for them had been demonstrated time and again, for he was their father in the gospel.

His letters.—So far as we know, Paul had written only one letter to the Corinthians. He had written other letters to other churches with which the people at Corinth may have been familiar. It is best however, to take the plural as a general reference to his writings rather than use it in support of theories about the "lost letter" or the "severe letter." See comment on I Cor. 5:9 and II Cor. 2:3.

The critics had pointed to the threatening tone of Paul's writings such as given in I Cor. 4:18-21. They had been attempting to destroy the effect of these warnings by resorting to a personal attack on the apostle. His bodily presence may not have been that of a strong, robust individual. He mentioned, "an infirmity" in connection with his preaching the gospel to the Galatians. See Gal. 4:13-14. He mentions "the thorn in the flesh" in II Cor. 12:7. But after reading the account of the things which he had endured as given in 11:23-33, it would be difficult indeed to believe that he was a physical weakling. In all probability this was a vicious attack without any foundation. It was designed to destroy the confidence of the brethren in the one who had led them to Christ.

and his speech of no account.—Paul readily admitted that he did not belong to the order of professional orators. See 11:6. When he came to Corinth the first time, it was "not with excellency of speech or of wisdom," for he had but one message and that was Jesus Christ and Him crucified. The Athenians had looked upon his preaching of Jesus and the resurrection with utter scorn, for to them it compared in no way with the systems of wisdom taught by their philosophers. See Acts 17:16-22. But there is no eloquence or system of thought that surpassed Paul's when he spoke on Mars Hill revealing the God whom the Athenians had worshipped in ignorance. He said, "the time of ignorance therefore God overlooked; but now He commands men that they should all everywhere repent: in as much as he has appointed a day in which he will judge the world in righteousness by the man whom he hath ordained; whereof he hath given assurance to all men, in that he hath raised him from the dead" (Acts 17:30-31).

Paul hastened to assure his readers that his deeds when present with them would coincide exactly with what he had said in his letters in his absence.

For we are not bold to number or compare ourselves.—In boasting about the authority which the Lord had given him, Paul was in no way attempting to compare himself with the false teachers at Corinth. He had urged his readers to be aware of the fact that his authority had been given him by the Lord. On the other hand, the false teachers had set up their own standards and had measured themselves by them and, consequently, were without proper understanding of the true basis of relationship to Christ which was to be found only in the authoritative Word proclaimed by His apostles.

The Standard By Which The Apostle Boasted

Scripture

10:13-18. But we will not glory beyond our measure, but according to the measure of the province which God apportioned to us as a measure, to reach even unto you. 14 For we stretch not ourselves overmuch, as though we reached not unto you: for we came even as far as unto you in the gospel of Christ: 15 not glorying beyond our measure, that is in other men's labors; but having hope that, as your faith groweth, we shall be magnified in you according to our province unto further abundance, 16 so as to preach the gospel even unto the parts beyond you, and not to glory in another's province in regard of things ready to our hand. 17 But he that glorieth, let him glory in the Lord. 18 For not he that commendeth himself is approved, but whom the Lord commendeth.

Comments

beyond our measure.—When the Lord appointed Paul to the apostleship He clearly defined the limits of his activities, sending him to the Gentiles. When he was at Troas on his second journey, in a vision, the Lord gave him specific instruction to go to Macedonia. Paul's policy was, and this seems to be within the limits the Lord had set for him, to preach the gospel where Christ was not already known, thus avoiding building upon another man's foundation. See Rom. 15: 18-21. Paul planted, but Apollos watered. This division of labors was approved by Peter and James and John when they gave Paul and Barnabas the right hands of fellowship as they went to the Gentiles while the others continued their ministry among the Jews. Their only request was that Paul and Barnabas should remember the poor of Judea which, of course, he was willing to do. See Gal. 2:6-10.

In the history of Paul's first visit to Corinth given in Acts 18, no specific direction of the Lord is mentioned indicating that he should preach the gospel there. On other occasions, when emergencies arose, Luke does record the fact that the Lord gave Paul specific instruction as for example when He told him that he would go to Rome. See Acts 23:11. It is quite possible, then, that Paul's journey to Corinth to preach the gospel of Christ came under the general order to preach the gospel to the Gentiles.

The point that Pual is making is that he was under the orders of God to carry out his ministry in Corinth. This raises a serious question about his critics who came later and who were disrupting the progress of the gospel among those who had been converted to Christ through Paul's preaching. From whom did they receive direction to go to Corinth? Paul makes it very clear that they were not ministers of Christ but ministers of Satan. See 11:14-15.

For we stretch not ourselves over much.—Paul and his associates had not over extended themselves when they came to Corinth, for he was within the limits that God had set for him. He came in his capacity as an apostle of Christ preaching the gospel that had been revealed to him. In no way was he violating the limits which the Lord had set for him; he was not encroaching on other men's labors. He very definitely implies that the false teachers who were disturbing the church at Corinth were imposters. Indeed, they were not true teachers as Apollos had been, for he built on the foundation which Paul had laid (I Cor. 3:10-11); but they were endeavoring to destroy that very foundation by perverting the gospel and destroying the confidence the people had in the one who had led them to Christ.

but having hope.—Paul, appealing to the sound judgment of those who knew the history of the work in Corinth, expressed his hope that as the faith of the Corinthian brethren increased his place in their affection and his opportunity to work among them might be greatly enlarged. It was also his hope that he might be able to preach the gospel in areas beyond Corinth, but without the need of boasting about work already done by others.

Since the gospel was to be taken into all the world there was no need for duplication of effort even on the part of the faithful gospel ministers, not to mention the imposters who had sought to disrupt Paul's work at Corinth. This raises a serious question about the duplication of work in many areas today, a duplication which has in many cases been brought about by the sin of division. Corinth is a good example of what happens when through strife and faction men seek to propagate their own theological opinions rather than dedicate themselves to the sincere proclamation of the truth as God gave it to be presented to all the world.

But he that glorieth.—Paul called attention to a basic principle of his ministry: glorying in the Lord, referring to Jer. 29:4 in support of his view.

False teachers were commending themselves as they measured themselves by their own standards, but Paul was concerned that he have the approval of the Lord.

Summary

This third and last section of the letter is a defense of Paul's apostleship. It is a series of appeals in which he answered charges of his enemies. It closes with an explanation of his intended visit.

The first appeal is humbly presented in the spirit of gentleness and meekness of Christ who endeavored to win men to the truth which the Father had sent Him to reveal. Paul had preached Christ to the Corinthians, and they were familiar with His gentleness and deep concern for the erring.

Evidently Paul's enemies had remarked disparagingly about his humility as opposed to what they said was a show of courage through his letters when he was away. Paul begged them to accept the evidence of his apostleship so that he might not be forced to use this courageous boldness in dealing with them as he confidently expected to do against his critics who were saying that he was motivated by base principles.

Taking up the charge, he said, "Although we may be walking in the flesh, we are not waging war according to the principles and methods of men." His weapons were mighty, for they were spiritual and capable of demolishing every stronghold in the way. He spoke the truth as an inspired apostle of Christ. Exalted imaginations and arrogant thoughts of men were brought as prisoners to obey Christ. Paul stood ready to avenge every disobedience when they had been given ample opportunity to obey.

Paul charged that they were taking a superficial view of the issues before them. The basis of anyone's claim to be Christ's applied to Paul also. If he had boasted somewhat of his authority, they were to remember that it had been given him by the Lord to edify and not to tear down. But he intended to use this authority if necessary when he came to Corinth, for he was not merely frightening them by the letter. His enemies had said that while his letters were weighty and strong he was weak in person and should be despised. He warned them that what he was in his letters he would be in reality when present.

As to his right to instruct the Corinthians, he was not like some who were setting up their own standards comparing themselves with themselves and who, consequently, were without understanding. He conformed to the standard of measurement which God had established for him. It gave him the right to be the first to come to Corinth to preach the gospel. His enemies evidently, had attempted to take credit for work he had done. Still, he hoped to be assisted by the Corinthians in carrying the gospel to regions beyond them. He did not want to boast about work done by others as if he had done it. "Let one's glorying be within the Lord's approval. It is not the one who commends himself, but whom the Lord commends, that is approved." Paul's self-commending critics were not approved by the Lord.

Questions

1. Why did Paul turn to the defense of his apostleship in this third and last section of the epistle?
2. Why was it necessary to again mention his forthcoming visit?
3. Why is there such a distinct change in Paul's attitude in this section of the letter?
4. What defense is there for the unity of the epistle in view of the harsher tone expressed in this section?
5. Why did he use the expression "I Paul myself" instead of his usual "we"?
6. When Paul uses the plural pronoun, to whom does he usually refer?
7. What is meant by the meekness and gentleness of Christ?
8. Why would the Corinthians be expected to understand it?
9. Why did Paul first appeal to them in this manner?
10. Why did he assume a somewhat harsh manner in his later effort to get them to look at the facts before them?
11. Why did he speak of himself as lowly in their presence but courageous when he was absent from them?
12. How did he confidently expect to use his apostolic authority upon his arrival? Against whom?
13. Who had been making these disparaging remarks about Paul?
14. How did Paul indicate that his critics had misjudged him?
15. What did he mean when he said that he did not war according to the flesh?

186

16. What had been the tactics of those who arrayed themselves against Paul?
17. What weapons did Paul use in carrying on his campaign for Christ?
18. How had he demonstrated their effectiveness to the Corinthians?
19. How did Paul describe the whole armor of God when he wrote to the Ephesians?
20. What stronghold were standing in way to victory for the gospel?
21. What was Paul's view of the outcome of the clash which he anticipated with the false teachers upon his arrival?
22. What did he mean by the expression, "when your obedience shall be made full"?
23. What did he mean when he said, "Ye look at the things that are before your face"? To whom did he refer?
24. What is the only way by which anyone can belong to Christ?
25. How did this apply to Paul as well as those who were claiming to be His?
26. How had Paul demonstrated the meaning of this standard to the Corinthians?
27. Measured by that standard, what could be said of the super-apostles who were attempting to discredit Paul?
28. What had it become necessary for Paul to boast somewhat about his authority?
29. From whom had he received his authority? When?
30. What could the false apostles at Corinth say about any commission they may have claimed as a reason for their being there?
31. What proof did he give that the Lord had commissioned him as an apostle?
32. What was the purpose of this authority?
33. Why, then, did he say that it was not for tearing down?
34. Why did he say, "I shall not be put to shame"?
35. How did all this answer the charge that he was attempting to terrify them by his letters?
36. If Paul had written only one letter to the Corinthians prior to this one, how explain the reference of his critics to "his letters"?
37. What possible evidence could the critics present to establish their claim that Paul was weak?
38. What did they mean when they said that his speech was of no account?

39. How does this compare with what Paul had written to the Corinthians? See I Cor. 2:1-5.
40. How had the Athenians looked upon his preaching about Jesus and the resurrection?
41. By what standard had the false teachers been measuring themselves? With what result?
42. By what standard was Paul's work to be judged?
43. Who authorized Paul's mission to Corinth?
44. What was Paul's policy in his missionary work?
45. How was this seen in the work that he and Apollos had done at Corinth?
46. What, then was the basic difference between the work of Apollos and the false teachers at Corinth?
47. What was Paul implying when he said that he had not encroached upon other men's labors?
48. What did Paul hope that the Corinthians might do to help him?
49. Whose approval was Paul seeking?
50. From what Scripture did he take this basic principle?

For Discussion

1. How can the light of the Word of God be turned on some of the widely accepted views of men that ignore God and His Word?
2. What can be done about the duplication of effort to preach Christ that is occasioned by division among His followers?

Analysis

A. Paul appealed to the Corinthians to understand his position in respect to their relation to Christ (1-5).

    1. He began with an ironical appeal for them to "bear with a little foolishness" (1-6).

        a) He made the appeal even though he aware that they were bearing with him (1).

        b) He stated his position in respect to their relation to Christ (2-3).

            (1) He was the one who had betrothed them to Christ.

                (a) As such, he was jealous of others who might usurp his position.

                (b) He wanted them to remain as a pure virgin betrothed to Christ.

                (c) He reminded them that Christ was to be their one husband.

            (2) He expressed his fear that they might be led away from this pure relationship to Christ.

                (a) Just as the serpent deceived Eve, they were being deceived by false teachers.

                (b) They were actually in danger of being led away from sincere devotion to Christ.

        c) He pointed out the conditions under which they were ready to listen to other teachers (4).

            (1) They would listen if some came preaching another Jesus.

            (2) They would listen if they received a different spirit than that which they had received when they accepted the gospel that Paul preached—this is a part of the "foolishness" about which he wrote.

            (3) They would even listen to a different gospel which was not the one they accepted when he led them to Christ.

        d) He defended his apostleship against these deceivers (5-6).

            (1) He was in no way inferior to these "super-apostles."

            (2) He admitted that he was no professional orator, but

defended his knowledge which he had in every way shown to be from God. They had seen the evidence that this was true.

2. He contrasted his ministry at Corinth with that of the false teachers (7-15).

   a) He asked, "Did I sin in lowering myself that you might be exalted?" (7-11)

     (1) This issue was based on the fact that he had preached the gospel to them without charge (7).

     (2) Ironically, he stated that he had "robbed" other churches—he had accepted support from them—in order to preach the gospel without charge to the Corinthians. (8)

     (3) The brethren of Macedonia had supplied his needs when he was at Corinth and in want. (9a).

     (4) He determined not to be a burden to them and that no one would stop him from boasting about this in Achia (9b-10).

     (5) Why was this? It was to show his love for them, for God knew that he did love them (11).

   b) He explained his reason for continuing this policy in Achia (12-15).

     (1) It was to prevent others from making the claim that they were on the same footing as Paul in relation to the Corinthians (12).

     (2) It was to show the real motive of others (13).

       (a) He revealed what they really were:

         i) False apostles.

         ii) Deceitful workers.

         iii) False apostles of Christ.

       (b) He revealed their relation to Satan (14-15).

         i) Satan disguises himself as an angel of light.

         ii) His servants disguise themselves as servants of righteousness. See Rom 6:16 ff.

       (c) He revealed what their end will be: It will be according to their deeds.

B. Paul ironically asked to be allowed to boast a little (16-33).

  1. He asked that no one think him foolish; yet if they did, he wanted them to allow him to boast a little (16-21a).

a) He asked them to accept him even if he was boasting foolishly (16).

b) This approach was not the manner in which the Lord had appealed to His hearers (17a). See 10:1.

c) He had confidence in his grounds for boasting about these things (17b).

d) Since others gloried in the flesh—their human accomplishments—he would also, for the Corinthians seemed to be willing to listen to this foolishness. They thought of themselves as being wise. (18-19).

d) He described the type of man they were willing to put up with (20).

    (1) One who enslaved them.

    (2) One who devoured them.

    (3) One who took advantage of them.

    (4) One who exalted himself.

    (5) One who struck them in the face.

f) Judged by such standards Paul admitted that he was weak (21a).

2. He compared his grounds for boasting—his labors and sufferings—with that of others (21b-29).

a) In relation to the fathers, he was their equal (21b-22).

    (1) Are they Hebrews? So was he.

    (2) Are they Israelites? So was he.

    (3) Are they Abraham's seed? So was he.

b) In relation to Christ, he excelled them (23).

    (1) To call them ministers of Christ is to speak as one who is mad.

    (2) Paul excelled them in labors, imprisonments, beatings, and death for Christ.

c) In relation to the things he suffered as a minister of Christ, he was far beyond them (24-29).

    (1) Beatings, stonings, shipwrecks (24-25).

    (2) Journeys and perils (26).

    (3) Labors, travail, watchings, hunger, thirst, fastings, cold and nakedness (27).

    (4) Anxiety for all the churches (28).

    (5) Identity with the weak and stumbling (29).

3. He presented an example of the solemn truth about his boasting in weakness (30-33).

a) The truth of this account was known to the God and Father of the Lord Jesus. (30-31).

b) As evidence of his weakness, he related the story of his escape from persecution at the hands of the governor under Aretas (32-33).

An Ironical Appeal

Scripture

11:1-6 Would that ye could bear with me in a little foolishness: but indeed ye do bear with me. 2 For I am jealous over you with a godly jealousy: for I espoused you to one husband, that I might present you as a pure virgin to Christ. 3 But I fear, lest by any means, as the serpent beguiled Eve in his craftiness, your minds should be corrupted from the simplicity and the purity that is toward Christ. 4 For if he that cometh preacheth another Jesus, whom we did not preach or if ye receive a different spirit, which ye did not receive, or a different gospel, which ye did not accept, ye do well to bear with him. 5 For I reckon that I am not a whit behind the very chiefest apostles. 6 But though I be rude in speech, yet am I not in knowledge; nay, in every way have we made this manifest unto you in all things.

Comments

in a little foolishness.—It was really unnecessary for Paul to defend his apostleship since it had been established by the signs which he had performed in their midst. More than that, the Corinthians were thoroughly aware of the fact that their relation to Christ depended on the message which Paul had preached to them and which they had accepted. See I Cor. 9:1-2 and II Cor. 3:1-3. Consequently, Paul could say, "I wish that you would bear with me in a little foolishness." That is, let him go on defending his apostleship which had come under attack from false leaders who had come to Corinth after his departure. *but indeed ye do bear with me.*—Paul knew from the report of Titus that the Corinthians had responded to the directions he had given them in his first letter. They's why he said, "Of course, you do bear with me. But in this particular issue in which my apostleship is being attacked by the super-apostles, I want you to let me restate the facts in answer to the charges that are now being brought against me." *For I am jealous over you.*—Paul's position in the Corinthians' relation to Christ was that of a father who had espoused his daughter to the bridegroom. Paul had espoused them to Christ. Just as a father would

192

be jealous of anyone seeking to usurp his position in such a case, so Paul expressed his jealousy over the fact that some of the Corinthians were listening to the Satanic teachers who were interfering with the arrangements that he had made in commiting the Corinthian Christians to Christ.

a godly jealousy.—Paul's attitude was like that of God toward those who would lead His people away from Him.

Jealousy can be, and often is, an evil thing. This is true when it becomes an expression of selfish envy. But no such element enters into the attitude of Paul in his relation to the church at Corinth.

The Old Testament frequently represents God as the jealous husband of a faithless wife who has forsaken her husband for another man. Israel kept forsaking God for the gods of the pagans. She was like a faithless wife, and God is said to be jealous in such cases. "Thou shalt have no other gods before me" is the basic principle on which the Law of God for the Israelites rested. He would not tolerate Israel's running after idols and getting involved in all the sinful practices accosiated with idolatry.

The apostle of Christ with Godlike jealousy resented the defection of the Corinthian Christians to the false teachers whose true character Paul was about to point out as being Satanic.

to one husband.—The marriage relationship presented a perfect illustration of the point Paul was making. From the beginning, the divine plan was that there should be one husband for one wife. See *Studies in First Corinthians,* chapter seven, for the instruction Paul had given the Corinthians on the divine standard of marriage. With that letter before them, they knew exactly the meaning of Paul's words when he said that he had espoused them to one husband that is, to Christ. In the Ephesian letter, Paul referred to the relationship between the church and Christ and called upon wives to be faithful to their own husbands as unto the Lord. See Eph. 5:22-23.

John wrote about the marriage supper of the Lamb as he anticipated the coming of Christ and the gathering of the saints unto Him. "Let us rejoice and be exceeding glad, and let us give glory unto him: for the marriage of the Lamb is come, and his wife hath made herself ready. And it was given unto her that she should array herself in fine linen, bright and pure: for the fine linen is the righteous acts of the saints. And he saith unto me, Write, Blessed are they that are bidden to the marriage supper of the Lamb. And he saith unto me, These are true words of God" (Rev. 19:7-9).

193

a pure virgin to Christ.—Paul indicates that the purity of the bride who anticipates her wedding should symbolize the purity of the church as it anticipates the coming of Christ and the privilege of being with Him in the heavenly kingdom. Purity, of course, meant loyalty to Him and none other, abiding by the truth of His gospel, rejecting all falsehood, and keeping themselves unspotted from the sinful practices of the world. It meant faithfulness to Christ and His word in the Christian life which is the period of preparation for the marriage supper of the Lamb.

The term "virgin" in our language denotes purity. Since it had other connotations in the language of the Greeks, it became necessary for Paul to define his meaning by saying "pure" virgin so that no member of the church could mistake his meaning.

To further insure his readers against any possible misunderstanding, he illustrated exactly what he meant by calling their attention to Satan's complete deception of Eve in the Garden.

But I fear.—Paul had grounds for his fears, for the Corinthians were in real danger. They were gladly listening to the false teachers who were endeavoring to undermine the work of the apostle of Christ who had preached the gospel to them. And it was that gospel that had converted them to Christ.

as the serpent beguiled Eve.—There isn't the slightest indication that the inspired apostle Paul believed that the account of Satan's effort to deceive Eve was some mythological explanation of the presence of evil in the world. He presented it in exactly the same way that Moses did in the third chapter of Genesis, that is, as an historical fact. To complete his account, he identified Satan, the troublemaker at Corinth, with the serpent. John does the same thing when he refers to the old serpent as the one who is called the devil and Satan. See Rev. 12:9.

his craftiness.—Paul had already warned the Corinthians against the schemes of the devil as he tried to take advantage of God's people. His craftiness had succeeded in Eve's case. Paul had his fears that Satan might also succeed in some instances at Corinth.

corrupted from the simplicity and purity that is toward Christ.—In the epistle to the Romans Paul tells what happens to men who turn from the knowledge of God to the worship of idols and the sins that accompany such worship. When they did so, God gave them up to an unapproved mind. See Rom. 1:18-32. But since God has provided the means by which sins are blotted out, Paul could exhort his readers to be not fashioned according to this present age, but to be transformed by the renewing of their minds, so that they might approve the will of God, the thing that is good, acceptable to God, and complete. See Rom. 12:2. The plea of the message of the Bible is for men to straighten out their thinking in the light of the truth of God revealed Word.

Some of the Corinthians were in danger of having Satan corrupt their minds from the simplicity and purity of the truth by which their relationship to Christ was governed. The word "simplicity" suggests the single-minded devotion to the things God wants man to do. It is translated "liberality" in 8:2. This singleness of purpose had led the Macedonians to give generously for the relief of the saints in Judea. But in 11:3 it suggests the sincere dedication of mind and purpose to the service of Christ. It is coupled with purity of heart and mind in all this vital relationship.

Paul had good reason to fear that some of the Corinthians were being led astray from this devotion to Christ through the craftiness of Satan. Every Christian must be constantly on guard against this happening to him. Some things that help prevent it are: (1) A real knowledge of the Word of God. Jesus illustrated this when He said to Satan, "Thus it is written, Man shall not live by bread alone, but by every word that proceedeth out of the mouth of God." That individual who does not know what God has written may fall easy prey to the devices of Satan cleverly presented by false teachers. (2) Not only must one know the Word but he must also translate it into life. Anything short of active participation in the total program of Christ for His church places the Christian in jeopardy. Paul had written that it was necessary for him to buffet his body and bring it into bondage lest by any means after he had preached to others, he might be rejected. See I Cor. 9:27. There is more to Christianity than being present in the assembly on the Lord's Day, keeping the Lord's supper, and hearing the Word taught. The first business of the church is to seek and save the lost. Every Christian should be busily engaged to the extent of his ability in this work of Christ. The untaught, idle church member needs to be brought to the realization of the peril which he faces, the very real danger of being lost.

For if he that cometh preacheth another Jesus.—Paul had been sent to Corinth to preach the Lord Jesus Christ. "Lord" indicated, in all probability, that Jesus was identified with the eternal living God. "Jesus" means "Savior." "Christ" refers to the fact that He is prophet, priest, and king. Could the super-apostles who had come to Corinth preach another Jesus who was superior to Jesus whom Paul preached? It is true that they were preaching another "Jesus" but the Corinthians needed to learn that Jesus whom Paul preached was the only one in whom there is salvation, for there is no other name given among men in whom they must be saved. See Acts 4:12.

if ye received a different spirit.—This is not a reference to the Holy Spirit. The Galatian churches had been corrupted by false teachers just as the Corinthians were being corrupted by the super-apostles. Paul asked them, "Did you receive the Spirit that is, the Holy Spirit— by the works of the law or by the hearing of faith" (Gal. 3:2)? By "receiving the Spirit" in that context, Paul referred to the miraculous power which had been granted to those upon whom the apostles had laid their hands. This demonstration of power showed the Galatians that they should not follow the false teachers who wanted them to observe the works of the Law. Paul encountered a similar situation in the case of the disciples of John whom he found at Ephesus. They knew only what John had taught about Jesus. Paul asked them, "Did ye receive the Holy Spirit when ye believed?" They had heard nothing of the Holy Spirit, so Paul commanded them to be baptized in the name of the Lord Jesus. After he had laid his hands on them the Holy Spirit came upon them in the manifestation of miraculous power that enabled them to speak in foreign languages and to prophesy. See Acts 19:1-7.

Since Paul was referring to a different spirit which the Corinthians received through the work of false teachers who in no way could impart the miraculous power of the Holy Spirit, it becomes necessary to determine the meaning of his question in the light of what he has taught in his epistles. Paul wrote to the Romans explaining that those who are led by the Spirit of God, that is, led through the things said by the inspired apostles, are sons of God. Then he added, "For ye received not the spirit of bondage again unto fear: but ye received the spirit of adoption—that is, sonship—whereby we cry Abba, Father" (Rom. 8:14-15). The spirit that is received as a result of obeying the gospel is that frame of mind of the one who knows he is a child of God and can give expression to this knowledge by calling God "Father." See also Gal. 4:4-7. It was this spirit which the Corinthians had received as a result of their obedience to the gospel which Paul preached.

What, then, was the different spirit which they received when they submitted to false teachers? It was a spirit of faction, jealousy, and deception that characterizes the children of the devil. See John 8:44. It is no wonder that Paul was afraid lest they be corrupted from the simplicity and purity that is toward Christ.

a different gospel.—Paul marveled at the Galatians who so quickly after their conversion to Christ were transferring their allegience to a different kind of gospel which was not another gospel of Christ. See Gal. 1:6. The super-apostles were preaching a different kind of gospel to the Corinthians. It was not the Word of the Cross that had saved them when they believed in Christ.

ye do well to bear with him.—A fine touch of irony in the same vein as that regarding "foolishness of his boasting."

For I reckon.—As Paul considered the issues, he was convinced that in no way was he inferior to these super-apostles.

But though I be rude in speech.—An unfortunate translation, misleading in every way. Paul was never rude in our understanding and use of the term. This does not mean that he did not denounce false teaching in the severest of terms. Jesus had done the same thing in the case of the hypocrites with whom He dealt, but He was never rude.

The word translated "rude" simply means one who does not belong to the class of professional people, in this case orators. It is to be doubted, however, that the professionals were ever able to match the eloquence of Paul as he preached the gospel. He openly set forth Jesus Christ crucified before the eyes of his listeners. See Gal. 3:1. Festus, listening to his defense of the gospel, cried out, "Paul, you are mad. Your much learning has turned you mad." Even the king said, "With but little persuasion thou wouldest fain make me a Christian." While there are differences of opinion as to the interpretation of Agrippa's words, it is evident that the eloquent defense of the gospel which Paul made that day really stirred the minds of all who heard him. See Acts 26:24-29. Not infrequently in Paul's writings do we find examples of his ability to express himself in excellent style. See Rom. 11:33-36; I Cor. 13:1-13; and I Cor. 15:51-58. Examples are also to be found in Second Corinthians.

not in knowledge.—His knowledge came through the ability given him as an apostle by the Holy Spirit to understand the deep things which he received by revelation from God. See I Cor. 2:6-16. No super-apostle nor false teacher was superior to Paul in knowledge pertaining to the gospel of salvation through Jesus Christ.

we made this manifest to you in all things.—When he was present

197

with the church at Corinth and through his letters, Paul had clearly demonstrated the fact that his wisdom and knowledge came from God. See I Cor. 1:18-31; 2:1-5, 10, 16.

Paul's Defense Of His Ministry At Corinth

Scripture

11:7:15. Or did I commit a sin in abasing myself that ye might be exalted, because I preached to you the gospel of God for nought? 8 I robbed other churches, taking wages of them that I might minister unto you; 9 and when I was present with you and was in want, I was not a burden on any man; for the brethren, when they came from Macedonia, supplied the measure of my want; and in everything I kept myself from being burdensome unto you, and so will I keep myself. 10 As the truth of Christ is in me, no man shall stop me of this glorying in the regions of Achaia. 11 Wherefore? because I love you not? God knoweth. 12 But what I do, that I will do, that I may cut off occasion from them that desire an occasion; that wherein they glory, they may be found even as we. 13 For such men are false apostles deceitful workers, fashioning themselves into apostles of Christ. 14 And no marvel; for even Satan fashioneth himself into an angel of light. 15 It is no great thing therefore if his ministers also fashion themselves as ministers of righteousness; whose end shall be according to their works.

Comments

did I commit a sin?—This is a continuation of the ironical appeal in defense of Paul's ministry. The Corinthians knew that Paul had refused to accept support from them in order to avoid criticism from those who might say that he was preaching the gospel for material gain. See I Cor. 9:12-18.

They were also aware of the fact that as a teacher Paul had a right to receive support from them. He did not hesitate to work with his hands at tent-making when he first came to Corinth while awaiting the help that later came from the churches of Macedonia. It was a custom that every Jewish boy be taught a trade and learn the dignity of work. Paul was no exception. The only reason that he said that he had humbled himself by working with his hands is that it was not in accord with the custom of that day to let teachers do so.

I robbed other churches.—This is also said in irony, for it was actually a privilege for those who had received the gospel through the ministry of Paul to share with him as he went elsewhere preaching the Lord Jesus Christ. He had taken wages from them that he might preach to the Corinthians. His needs had been met by others, and he kept himself from being a burden to any man at Corinth.

when they came from Macedonia.—The church at Philippi began supporting Paul when he was at Thessalonica. At that time they were the only ones helping him. More than once they responded to his needs. See Phil. 4:14-18. For some reason not stated by Paul, the line of supply was broken when Paul came to Corinth. This caused him to fall back on his trade to make a living. In the light of his own statement about the matter, we can be reasonably sure that Paul was entirely too busy spreading the gospel to continue working at a trade any longer than necessary for the support from Macedonia to reach him. But he had kept himself from being a burden to the churches of Achaia and he was determined to hold steadfastly to that policy. As the inspired apostle of Christ he spoke the truth when he preached, and what he was now saying was equally true. No one, not even the super-apostles who may have been pressing the issue, could stop him from boasting about this in the regions of Achaia.

Wherefore?—Such a statement called for an explanation. The teachers who had come to Corinth after Paul left were evidently aware of the fact that he had received no support from the Corinthians. Apparently they were endeavoring in some manner to get him to do so, or to insinuate that he had done so, in order that they might have the opportunity to receive support or to justify the support they had already been accepting. Since they were false teachers, Paul absolutely refused to allow them any such opportunity to boast about their work.

because I love you not?—Paul's attitude toward the churches of Achaia in no way indicated that he loved the less than the churches of Macedonia from whom he had received support. God knew his love for them. Since Paul had demonstrated it to them time and again and had openly declared it in his letters, the Corinthians knew that he loved them.

For such men are false apostles.—Paul boldly labeled those who had been attacking him and attempting to undermine his work at Corinth. They were not apostles of Christ; they were false apostles, deceitful workers who were attempting to appear as apostles of Christ. Where they came from or who had sent them is not known, but the Corinthians must have known about it.

for even Satan.—Paul clearly implies that Satan was back of the work of those whom he called false apostles. Since Satan could fashion himself into an angel of light, his minsters had no difficulty in masquerading as ministers of righteousness. Their destructive work only served to indicate the ultimately destruction that would be visited upon them.

Satan had appeared in an attractive form when he completely deceived Eve. His true character is indicated by such figures as those used by Peter and others. Peter refers to him as a roaring lion seeking to devour his victims. See I Pet. 5:8. John refers to him as a great dragon and calls him the old serpent and deceiver of the whole world. See Rev. 12:9. Jesus said he is a murderer and the father of the lie. See John 8:44. Being warned by such clear description the enemy of all righteousness, the people of God ought not to listen to his ministers.

Boasting A Little As One Counted Foolish

Scripture

11:16-21a.   I say again, Let no man think me foolish; but if ye do, yet as foloish receive me, that I also may glory a little. 17 That which I speak, I speak not after the Lord, but as in foolishness, in this confidence of glorying. 18 Seeing that many glory after the flesh, I will glory also. 19 For ye bear with the foolish gladly, being wise yourselves. 20 For ye bear with a man, if he bringeth you into bondage, if he devoureth you, if he taketh you captive, if he exalteth himself, if he smiteth you on the face. 21 I speak by way of disparagement, as though we had been weak.

Comments

Let no man think me foolish.—Paul had begun this ironical appeal as if speaking in foolishness. The evidence he gave in his defense was based upon truth; the element of foolishness lies in the fact that the Corinthians knew that he was an apostle of Christ for he had performed the signs of an apostle in their midst and God knew that he loved the brethren in Christ. It should not have been necessary, therefore, to defend his apostleship against the charges of the ministers of Satan. But since it had apparently become necessary, he continued the defense of his apostleship.

I speak not after the Lord.—This does not indicate that Paul was

200

setting aside his power to speak under the direction of the Holy Spirit. He had begun his appeal by speaking in the meekness and gentleness of Christ. But there is no example in Our Lord's ministry of the type of defense which Paul was now forced to make because of conditions in Corinth resulting from charges and false claims of the super-apostles. They were boasting from a purely human point of view. They were boasting of their professional status. They were boasting of their wisdom which, of course, was the wisdom of the world. It would be foolish for the apostle to come to that basis in order to offset their claims. But he was more than a match form them even on their own grounds.

Seeing that many glory after the flesh.—Since others were boasting about their human achievements, Paul would do so also. The Corinthians considered themselves wise and gladly listened to this type of boasting. They did so even though they were being enslaved by it, even though such persons were taking unfair advantage of them, even though the false teachers were exalting themselves while striking them in the face.

I speak by way of disparagement.—It was a shame for the apostle to be forced to follow this line of reasoning; but since he was compelled to do so, he spoke of his weakness as demonstrated by all the things which he suffered in his service for Christ.

Paul's Labors and Sufferings

Scripture

11:21b-33.   Yet whereinsoever any is bold (I speak in foolishness), I am bold also. 22 Are they Hebrews? so am I. Are they Israelites? so am I. Are they the seed of Abraham? so am I. 23 Are they ministers of Christ? (I speak as one beside himself) I more; in labors more abundantly, in prisons more abundantly, in stripes above measure, in deaths oft. 24 Of the Jews five times received I forty stripes save one. 25 Thrice was I beaten with rods, once was I stoned, thrice I suffered shipwreck, a night and a day have I been in the deep; 26 in journeyings often, in perils of rivers, in perils of robbers, in perils from my countrymen, in perils from the Gentiles, in perils in the city, in perils in the wilderness, in perils in the sea, in perils among false brethren; 27 in labor and travail, in watchings often, in hunger and thirst, in fastings often, in cold and nakedness. 28 Besides those things that are without, there is that which presseth upon me daily, anxiety for all the churches. 29 Who is weak, and I am not weak? who is caused to stumble, and I burn not? 30 If I must needs glory, I will glory of the things that concern my weakness. 31 The God and Father of the Lord Jesus he who is blessed for evermore knoweth that I lie not. 32 In Damascus the governor under Aretas the king guarded the city of the Damascenes in order to take me: 33 and through a window was I let down in a basket by the wall, and escaped his hands.

Comments

Yet whereinsoever any is bold.—It was foolish to be forced to compare his sufferings for Christ with anything the false teachers had suffered, for they were preying on the church at Corinth and endeavoring to lead the people away from Christ. In relation to God's ancient people, Paul was their equal; but certainly in relation to Christ he excelled them. In relation to the things he suffered for Christ, he was too far beyond them for comparison.

Are they Hebrews?—Although Paul was born in Tarsus of Cilicia, his parents were Hebrews and on that score he was easily equal to any of the false teachers who were claiming to be true teachers since, in all probability, they had come from Jerusalem.

Are they Israelites?—The ancient chosen people of God bore the name which was given to Jacob after he had wrestled with the Angel of the Lord and had been blessed by him. The name symbolized the transformation that had taken place in his life. It appropriately applied to the nation that had been chosen from among all the nations of the world as "a royal nation, a holy priesthood, a people that belonged to God." Were these teachers at Corinth Israelites? So was Paul.

Are they seed of Abraham?—The Jews proudly looked to Abraham as their father. They argued with Jesus despite their intention to put the Son of God to death that they were the seed of Abraham. Literally, of course, they were; but their hatred for Jesus proved that they were the offspring of Satan. See John 8:31-44. The Jewish teachers who troubled the church at Corinth claimed to be Abraham's offspring. Paul could substantiate his right to be called a child of Abraham for he was of the stock of Israel and of the tribe of Benjamin. More than that, He had surrendered his life to the Lord Jesus Christ.

Are they ministers of Christ?—While one would have to be out of his mind to admit their claim to be ministers of Christ was true, Paul was prepared to compare his ministry with theirs and to demonstrate that he far excelled them in relation to Christ. He had labored more abundantly than they. He had been imprisoned as a result of his service to Christ more than they. He had undergone countless beatings and had constantly faced death for Christ. What had they done for Him?

Of the Jews five times received forty stripes save one.—This list of the things that Paul had suffered in his ministry for Christ is a challenge to the false teachers at Corinth to compare the things that they had done with the things Paul had endured. The Corinthians who certainly must have known much of what Paul had undergone were well aware of the fact that the super-apostles were in no way a match for him.

He mentioned the beatings which he had received, the time when he was stoned, and the times that he had suffered shipwreck. Although he was a Roman citizen, he had been beaten and imprisoned at Philippi. He was stoned and abandoned for dead at Lystra. He suffered shipwreck three times. At one time, probably because his ship went down far from shore, he spent a full twenty-four period in the deep.

in journeyings often.—Paul listed the perils which he had faced on his many travels. He had risked his life in crossing rivers, in traveling through bandit infested areas, in the things he had suffered from the hands of his own countrymen as well as Gentiles. He had faced perils in the cities, in the wilderness and at sea. He knew what it meant to be among false brethren. His experience with them was enough to justify his warning the church against them.

in labor and travail.—Paul did not have an easy life; it was one filled with labor, hardship, and suffering. It meant standing guard during periods of distress; it meant being without food and drink; it meant fasting often in order that he might give all his time to the task before him; it meant enduring cold and nakedness.

Besides those things that are without.—Paul gave the list of the things he had suffered for the cause of Christ. It was adequate to establish his claim to have undergone suffering for beyond anything the false teachers at Corinth had ever done. Aside form all this, there was one thing that had not been mentioned: the thing that brought daily pressure upon him, anxiety for all the churches. If there had been any question in the mind of anyone regarding all that he had said in refutation of the claims of the false teachers, there could be no doubt whatever about this climactic issue, for Corinthians knew very well about Paul's anxiety for them. But he was just as concerned for the

Philippians and the brethren at Thessalonica. They all knew of his deep concern for the saints in Judea.

Who is weak?—The meaning of anxiety is indicated in Paul's attitude toward the weak. He understood and desired to help as if he were that weak person himself. It is doubtful if any more Christlike attitude toward the weak can be found. As he thought of the brother in Christ who for some cause had stumbled, he so identified with that one that he burned with the shame that should have been felt by the erring one. The Corinthians knew about his concern for the weak and erring. Did they see anything like it in the teachers who were attempting to discredit Paul by saying that he was weak in their presence even if he was bold in his writings?

If I must needs glory.—Since the situation at Corinth had forced Paul into this line of defense, he insisted in boasting not about his power but about his weakness. The secret of this weakness is revealed in 12:9. The God and Father of the Lord Jesus Christ knew that Paul was not lying when he related the incident by which he was to prove his weakness and humility and through which he had been forced to put is trust in God alone. The incident had taken place in Damascus. A guard had been thrown around the city to prevent his escape, but his friends had let him down through an opening in the wall, and he had escaped the hands of those who were bent on killing him. See Luke's description of the incident in Acts 9:23-25. The providence of God had watched over him; the faithful messenger of the gospel went on his way preaching Christ.

Summary

As Paul continued the defense of his apostleship, he began a long, ironical appeal for them to bear with him in a little foolishness. Irony is seen in the fact that he appeared to boast, but in reality he wasn't. His sincere purpose in coming to Corinth was to preach the gospel that he might espouse them to Christ as a pure virgin. He was afraid lest false teachers should lead them away from the simplicity and purity that ought to mark their relation to Christ. Eve had been completely deceived by the serpent. They were in danger of having the same thing happen to them through the work of the ministers of Satan in their midst.

In each of the examples given to support the charge, Paul assumes that the thing was being done. Someone had come to them and had preached another Jesus. Paul had preached Jesus Christ and Him crucified. He had preached the resurrection of Christ as the foundation of hope of resurrection from the dead. But some in Corinth had denied that there is a resurrection, despite the evidence Paul had given to prove it. Just what the super-apostles were saying about another Jesus is not stated, but no other Jesus could have them from their sins.

The second example had to do with the spirit they had received. What was the different kind of spirit which they had not received through his ministry? It may have been the spirit of slavery as opposed to the spirit of freedom found in the spirit covenant.

His third example had to do with the gospel. They were accepting a different kind of gospel. It may have been some such perversion of the gospel as mentioned in Gal. 1:6-8. Paul said, "You bear beautifully with this kind of thing." The irony lies in the fact that they could not put up with his gospel as he preached the truth about Christ.

In defense of his ministry as an apostle of Christ Paul said, "I consider that I do not fall short of the chiefest apostles." Who were they? Not Peter nor John, for there was no such distinction among the apostles of Christ. Paul had in mind those who were preaching another Jesus, those whom he labeled "false apostles." Paul freely admitted that he did not belong to the class of professional orators, but this implied no inferiority in his message. Our word "rude" denoting a lack of artistic or refined expression misses the point, for no uncultured crudeness or unpolished, inelegant speech can be attributed to Paul.

Paul continued to speak in irony as he asked, "Did I commit a sin by preaching to you without pay, robbing other churches that I might be able to do so?" Macedonia had supported him in Corinth. He had been a burden to no one. He was determined to maintain this policy in order to prevent false apostles having an excuse to receive support from the church. They had boasted of the right to support and apparently would have been glad for Paul to receive it in order to justify their doing so. Paul was determined to give them no grounds for such a thing.

In irony he said, "Let no one think that this attitude of mine is foolish." But even if they did, he was going to boast a little about it. This was not through the gentleness and meekness of the Lord, that is, the Lord had not used this approach in dealing with false teachers in His day. Paul was not saying, however, that he was substituting his opinion for the inspired message of the Lord.

He intended to boast in the flesh—as a human being—since others were doing so and the Corinthians were gladly listening to them. They thought this was permissible since they were wise—irony again!

Paul compared his racial and religious background with that of the false apostles. He compared his service for Christ with that of the false apostles, even if it was foolish to think of them as ministers of righteousness.

After telling of his labors, his sufferings, and his trials, there was one more thing to mention: his anxiety for all the churches. Even the foolish ones at Corinth would know better than to attempt to compare the super-apostles with Paul on this point.

His experience in Damascus was another example of his weakness in which he boasted, since boasting seemingly had to be done.

Questions

1. Why did Paul ask that they bear with him in a little foolishness?
2. Why did he say that they were bearing with him? What evidence did he have to prove this?
3. Why did Paul say, "I am jealous over you"?
4. To what kind of jealousy did he refer? How did he illustrate it?
5. What were the Corinthians doing to make him jealous?
6. What was Paul's position in their relation to Christ?
7. How does marriage explain the relation of the believer to Christ?
8. What had Paul written to the Corinthians on the subject of marriage that would cause him to recall this point?
9. What had Paul written to the Ephesians illustrating the same point?
10. What is suggested in Revelation on the subject?
11. Why was it necessary for Paul to use the word "pure" in connection with the word "virgin?"
12. What was he implying by the use of these terms as to the conduct of the Corinthians?
13. How had Satan completely deceived Eve?
14. What grounds did Paul have for his fears that the Corinthians were being deceived?
15. What did John say about the old serpent?

16. How is the craftiness of Satan illustrated in his deception of Eve?
17. What is meant by the simplicity and purity that it showed toward Christ?
18. Explain how the word translated "simplicity" can also be translated "liberality."
19. How can the Christian guard himself against the crafty deception of Satan?
20. What is the first business of the church?
21. What comparison can be made between Jesus whom Paul preached and the Jesus whom the false apostles were preaching?
22. What was the different spirit which they were receiving?
23. What did Paul mean when he asked the Galatians, "Did ye receive the Spirit by the works of the law or by the hearing of faith?"
24. What did he mean when he asked the disciples at Ephesus "Did ye receive the Holy Spirit when ye believed?"
25. What did the Christians at Rome receive that enabled them to call God "Father"?
26. What, then, was the different spirit which the Corinthians received when they listened to the super-apostles?
27. How did the gospel which Paul preached compare with the different gospel preached by the false apostles?
28. Why did he say that they did well to bear with such false teachers?
29. What did Paul say about himself in comparison to such teachers?
30. What is meant by the word that is translated "rude" in some of our Bibles?
31. What may be said of Paul's style and manner of speech and writing?
32. What claim did Paul make as to his knowledge? Why?
33. Why did Paul ask, "Did I commit a sin?" by not taking wages from the Corinthians?
34. How had Paul demonstrated to the Corinthians that his message was from God?
35. How had he been supported when he was at Corinth?
36. How are we to understand his statement that he "robbed other church"?

37. What did Paul say to the Philippians about the support of his ministry?
38. Why did he say that no one could stop him from boasting about this policy in the regions of Achaia?
39. Why did he raise the question of his love for them in this connection?
40. In what terms did Paul describe these false teachers?
41. In what terms did he describe Satan's activity?
42. In what terms did Jesus and Peter describe Satan?
43. How explain the irony in Paul's reference to foolishness?
44. Why did he say, "I speak not after the Lord"?
45. What were the false teachers at Corinth boasting about?
46. Why did Paul feel a sense of shame in having to boast about the things he had suffered in his ministry for Christ?
47. How did Paul compare with the super-apostles in relation to the Israelites? the Hebrews? the ministry for Christ?
48. What is the meaning of "Hebrews" and "Israelites"?
49. Who are the seed of Abraham?
50. Into what categories did Paul put the things he had suffered as an apostle of Christ?
51. What did he mean by anxiety for all the churches?
52. What had been his attitude toward the weak?
53. Why did he insist that he would boast only in his weakness?

For Discussion

1. What are some of the crafty ways in which Satan is attempting to deceive the church today?
2. What can the church do to demonstrate its faithfulness to Christ?

CHAPTER TWELVE

Analysis

A. Paul continued boasting in his weakness (1-13).
   1. He reminded the Corinthians of the visions and revelation of the Lord (1-10).
      a) He was compelled to boast because it was forced upon him by the claims of the false apostles, although nothing was gained by it (1a).
      b) He came to the matter of visions and revelations of the Lord, that is, given to him by the Lord (1b).
      c) In an impersonal manner he told of the experience in which he was caught up to the third heaven (2-4).
         (1) He said "I know a man in Christ." This happened to such a one—it was, of course, Paul himself.
         (2) This happened some fourteen years before his writing Second Corinthians.
         (3) He said, "Whether in the body I know not; God knows." He had no way of knowing whether he was taken up bodily or just in spirit.
         (4) Such a one was caught up to the third heaven.
         (5) He was caught up to Paradise.
         (6) He heard words not lawful for man to utter.
      d) Boasting about this experience emphasized his own weakness (5-10).
         (1) On behalf of one who had such an exalted experience, he boasted; but as to himself he boasted in his weakness (5).
         (2) This actually happened to Paul, so it was not foolish to boast about it, except that some might tend to overrate him because of it (6).
         (3) To keep him from self-exaltation, Paul was given "a thorn in the flesh, a messenger from Satan to buffet him" (7).
         (4) He asked the Lord three times to remove it, but the answer was: "My grace is sufficient for thee" (8-9a). God's favor had already granted him strength to endure it. Cf I Cor. 10:13.
         (5) Paul gladly, therefore, boasted in his weakness

209

that the power of Christ might rest upon him or cover him (9b).

(6) It was for that reason that he took pleasure in weakness, injury, necessity, persecution, and distress for Christ's sake for while he was weak in in himself, he was strong in Christ (10).

2. Paul concluded the defense of his boasting by admitting that he had become foolish (11-13).

a) He had become foolish, but they had compelled him to do so by their attitude toward the super-apostles (11).

(1) He should have been commended by the Corinthians.

(2) Even though he was nothing in himself, he was in no way inferior to these false apostles.

b) He reminded them that he had performed the signs of a true apostle before them (12).

(1) These signs were done in all patience.

(2) They were signs and wonders, and mighty works.

c) Since the Corinthians had received all these benefits, Paul asked, "In what sense were you inferior to the other churches?" The implied answer was: "In no way."

d) Then he referred to the only possible thing in which they were not on the same footing at the other churches: He had not been a burden to them. Ironically, he added, "Forgive me this wrong."

B. As Paul neared the end of the epistle, he turned again to the matter of his inttended visit (14-21).

1. He reaffirmed his intention not to be a burden to them (14-18).

a) He explained his reasons for this position (14-15).

(1) He did so because of his impending third visit.

(2) He laid down his basic principle in dealing with them: "I seek not yours but you."

(3) He explained the issue involved: "Children ought not to lay up for the parents but the parents for the children."

(4) As their father in the gospel, he said, "I will most gladly spend and be spent for your souls."

(5) Then he asked, "Since I love you more, am I to be loved less?"

b) He answered a possible charge of crafty dealing (16-18).
   (1) He stated the issue involved in the charge (16).
   (2) Then he asked, "Did I or any of those whom I sent (Titus and the brother) take advantage of you?" (17-18a).
   (3) Didn't these co-workers act exactly as he had done? (18b) These questions would force the Corinthians to admit that he had dealt with them in a thoroughly Christian manner.
2. He reminded them of his reason for the delay in making this third visit (19-21).
  a) It was for their own good (19).
   (1) Did they think that he was making exuses for himself?
   (2) He solemnly declared as an apostle of Christ that it was for their upbuilding.
  b) Then he explained his fears that he might find them acting as he would not want and as they might not want him to find them (10-21).
   (1) He again named the conditions that he feared might exist: Strife, jealousy, wraths, factions, backbitings, whisperings, swellings, and tumults. These were the very things about which he had written in his first epistle.
   (2) He had delayed lest God should humble him before them in mourning over their sins and failure to repent.
   (3) He listed these sins: Uncleanness, fornication, and lasciviousness. He had spoken of them in detail in his first epistle.

Visions and Revelations of the Lord

Scripture

12:1-10. I must needs glory, though it is not expedient; but I will come to visions and revelations of the Lord. 2 I know a man in Christ, fourteen years ago (whether in the body, I know not; or whether out of the body, I know not; God knoweth), such a one caught up even to the third heaven. 3 And I know such a man (whether in the body, or apart from the body, I know not; God knoweth), 4 how that he was caught up into Paradise and heard unspeakable words, which it is not lawful for a man to utter. 5 On behalf of such a one will I glory: but on mine own behalf I will not glory, save in my weaknesses. 6 For if I should desire to glory, I shall not be foolish; for I shall speak the truth: but I forbear, lest any man should account of me above that which he seeth me to be, or heareth from me. 7 And by reason of the exceeding greatness of the revelations, that I should not be exalted overmuch, there was given to me a thorn in the flesh, a messenger of Satan to buffet me, that I should not be exalted overmuch. 8 Concerning this thing I besought the Lord thrice, that it might depart from me. 9 And he hath said unto me, My grace is sufficient for thee: for my power is made perfect in weakness. Most gladly therefore will I rather glory in my weaknesses, that the power of Christ may rest upon me. 10 Wherefore I take pleasure in weaknesses, in injuries, in necessities, in persecutions, in distresses, for Christ's sake: for when I am weak, then am I strong.

Comments

I must needs glory.—Paul had been forced by existing circumstances at Corinth to boast about his weakness. Although there was nothing to be gained by it, since he had demonstrated through the miracles which he had performed as an apostle that the approval of God rested upon him, he nevertheless, proceeded to relate an incident that had happened in the life of one on behalf of whom he could boast.

visions and revelations of the Lord.—Paul had been given the privilege of seeing the risen Christ at the time of his appointment to the apostleship, but the incident to which he was referring had to do with the visions and revelations which the Lord had permitted him to see and hear after his conversion.

I know a man in Christ.—Although there can be no doubt that Paul was speaking of himself, he did so in an entirely impersonal manner for the simple reason that this was something that the Lord had done in contrast to the long list of weaknesses which he had experienced.

fourteeen years ago.—The incident was so vivid that it remained in the mind of Paul even after all those years. There is no point in trying to fix the date when this occurred, since Paul chose to point out the significant fact that it had remained in his mind throughout this long period of his labor and suffering for Christ.

whether in the body.—While Paul knew exactly when the incident had occurred and what had happened at that time, he could not say whether it happened to him bodily or in the spirit. But he knew that he had been caught up even to the third heaven. It made no difference whether bodily or spiritually, for it was something the Lord had done and it had left this lasting impression upon him.

the third heaven.—This expression has caused much speculation on the part of commentators. Some even suggest that after he was caught up to the third heaven he was again elevated to an even higher position called Paradise. It seems better to assume that the third heaven was Paradise where Paul heard "unspeakable words."

I know such a man.—Paul again emphasized the impersonal aspect of the incident. He did not know whether it was bodily experience or not, nor did it matter, for he said, "God knows."

Paradise.—Jesus said to the thief on the cross, "Today, shalt thou be with me in Paradise." It is safe to say, then, that Paradise is the place where the Lord is. We do not know all things about the future state, but we do know that absence from the body is at home with the Lord. As to Paul's experience, he knew that he had been caught up into Paradise and had heard things that could not be revealed. See *Studies in Luke,* pages 278-279 and 380.

It is impossible to put into human language the glories that shall be revealed for the saints of God at the coming of Christ. John says, "Beloved, now are we children of God, and it is not yet made manifest what we shall be. But we know, that when it shall be manifested, we shall be like him; for we shall see him even as he is" (I John 3:2). This was enough to make Paul "willing rather to be absent from the body, and to be at home with the Lord" (II Cor. 5:8).

On behalf of such a one I will glory.—In face of the boastful claims of the false teachers at Corinth, Paul had lowered himself to that which should have been entirely unnecessary: the giving of a detailed account of the sufferings which he had undergone as an apostle of Christ. But he was determined to limit his boasting to his weakness. There is no inconsistency between this and his boasting on behalf of the one to whom the Lord had given such visions and revelations, for it was a thing the Lord had done, not Paul. Furthermore, it was something that could not possibly have happened to those who were boasting about their power and position among the Corinthians for they were ministers of Satan, not of Christ. Paul occupied an unassailable position when he restricted his boasting to the things done by the Lord and his own weakness.

I shall not be foolish.—It was not foolish to boast in the thing which the Lord had done. Paul spoke the truth about what the Lord had done with him and limited his remarks to this lest anyone should exalt him above what they saw in him and heard from him.

And by reason of the exceeding greatness of the revelations.—Paul was now ready to relate the incident about which he had boasted. Such an exalted experience could easily tempt one who was less dedicated to Christ to distort its meaning and lead others praise him rather than the Lord. To prevent this thing from happening, there was given Paul a thorn in the flesh.

thorn in the flesh.—Paul identifies this as a messenger of Satan to buffet him. Much speculation has been indulged in in an effort to identify the thorn in the flesh. No one really knows what it was, except for the things Paul said about it. It was in the flesh as a messenger of Satan and acted as an opponent in the boxing ring that kept him from being too elated over what had happened. It kept him from using what the Lord had done for him as a means of self-glory.

a messenger of Satan.—Paul wrote to the Ephesians indicating that the forces of Satan are like an opposing army against which the followers of Christ must wage war. The church has been equipped with the whole armor of God with which to stand against the wiles of the devil. See Eph. 6:10-18.

God permitted Satan to afflict Job with great bodily suffering. But Job remained steadfast and faithful to the Lord through all of it. Paul reminded the Corinthians that God would not permit them to be temped above their ability to endure, for He would with the temptation make the way of escape that they might be able to endure it. See I Cor. 10:13. In this life, the people of God constantly face the enemy who will destroy them unless they remain faithful to the Lord.

I besought the Lord thrice.—Whatever this thorn in the flesh was, it brought such distress to Paul that he asked the Lord three times that it might depart from him. The answer was: "My grace is sufficient for thee: for my power is made perfect in weakness."

God does not always answer our requests in the manner in which we might expect. Certainly He was not deaf to the plea that Paul made. The favor that He had already bestowed on him in commissioning him as an apostle of Christ, in endowing him with all the signs of an apostle, in providentially watching over him through all the things he suffered for the sake of Christ, was sufficient to assure him that he could triumph over this thing even though it had brought him great distress. He had written to the Corinthians in the first letter about his apostleship despite his having persecuted the church of God. He said, "By the grace of God I am what I am: and his grace which was bestowed upon me was not found vain; but I labored more abundantly than they all: yet not I, but the grace which was with me" (I Cor. 15:10).

for my power is made perfect in weakness.—Paul's reason for relating this experience is now made clear. The thorn in the flesh symbolized human weakness. There were some things that he could not do; only the Lord could have caught him up to the third heaven. Thus the power of the Lord stood in bold contrast to the weakness of Paul even though he was a true apostle of Christ.

that the power of Christ may rest upon me.—Jesus had promised the eleven that they would receive power when the Holy Spirit should come upon them. See Acts 1:8. On the Day of Pentecost they were baptized in the Holy Spirit and were empowered to speak in other languages that those who heard the message on that day might know that it came from God. More than that, they were enabled to perform miracles that demonstrated that the Spirit of God was speaking through them. See Acts 2:43 and Heb. 2:3-4.

All of the signs of an apostle were done by Paul in the midst of the Corinthians. God's providential protection had covered him like a tent that protects the desert traveler from the burning sun. For all this, Paul gladly boasted in his own weakness.

I take pleasure in weakness.—Paul had listed the weaknesses that were his, the injuries he had sustained, the wants in which he had found himself, the persecutions which he had endured and the distresses which he had undergone for Christ's sake.

for when I am weak, then I am strong.—This is the remarkable climax of the boasting that was forced upon Paul. Being aware of his weakness, he had committed himself to the providential care of the Lord. Knowing his weakness, he determined to preach Christ and Him crucified, for therein lay his strength.

Admission of Foolishness

Scripture

12:11-13. I am become foolish: ye compelled me; for I ought to have been commended of you: for in nothing was I behind the very chiefest apostles, though I am nothing. 12 Truly the signs of an apostle were wrought among you in all patience, by signs and wonders and mighty works. 13 For what is there wherein ye were made inferior to the rest of the churches, except it be that I myself was not a burden to you? forgive me this wrong.

Comments

I am become foolish.—Paul did not hesitate to remind the Corinthians that he should have been commended by them. Their very position in relation to Christ depended upon the gospel which he had preached to them. Through his preaching and their obedience he had become their father in Christ and they were his children. His credentials as an apostle were well known to them. Through them they had been given spiritual gifts involving the word of wisdom and knowledge as well as the powers by which these were proven to be the revelation from God. See I Cor. 12:8-10. It is difficult to understand how they could have forgotten all this and gladly listened to the claims of false teachers in the absence of Paul.

though I am nothing.—Paul readily admitted that in himself he was nothing. The favor that God had granted him had enabled him to do the work of an apostle. He had therefore refused to boast in anything save his own weakness. But though he was nothing, he maintained that he was in no way inferior to the super-apostles who had attacked him in order to gain power over those whom he had converted to Christ.

by signs and wonders and mighty works.—These were the credentials of the apostles through which the Lord demonstrated His approval on their ministry. They were guided by the Holy Spirit into all the truth pertaining to life and godliness. What credentials could the super-apostles present? Empty claims and boastful pretensions!

inferior to the rest of the churches.—The Corinthians knew that they had been "in everything enriched in him, in all utterance and all knowledge; even as the testimony of Christ was confirmed among them" (I Cor. 1:5-6). They lacked no gift that would enable them to conduct themselves as true followers of Christ while awaiting the coming of the Lord Jesus Christ. Paul had preached the same gospel to them that he had preached to all the churches. He had performed the same apostolic signs in their midst that he had shown in all the churches.

except it be that I myself was not a burden to you?—This is an

216

ironical thrust at those teachers who were seeking, if indeed they had not already been receiving, support from the church at Corinth. *forgive me this wrong.*—In the height of irony, Paul begged for their forgiveness! They knew that there was nothing to forgive. Did they burn with shame when they remembered how he had labored in their midst while insisting on preaching the gospel of Christ to them for nothing?

Paul's Intended Visit

Scripture

12:14-21. Behold, this is the third time I am ready to come to you; and I will not be a burden to you: for I seek not yours, but you: for the children ought not to lay up for the parents, but the parents for the children. 15 And I will most gladly spend and be spent for your souls. If I love you more abundantly, am I loved the less? 16 But be it so, I did not myself burden you; but, being crafty, I caught you with guile. 17 Did I take advantage of you by any one of them whom I have sent unto you? 18 I exhorted Titus, and I sent the brother with him. Did Titus take any advantage of you? walked we not in the same spirit? walked we not in the same steps? 19 Ye think all this time that we are excusing ourselves unto you. In the sight of God speak we in Christ. But all things, beloved, are for your edifying. 20 For I fear, lest by any means, when I come, I should find you not such as I would and should myself be found of you such as ye would not; lest by any means there should be strife, jealousy, wraths, factions, backbitings, whisperings, swellings, tumults; 21 lest again when I come my God should humble me before you, and I should mourn for many of them that have sinned heretofore, and repented not of the uncleanness and fornication and lasciviousness which they committed.

Comments

this is the third time I am ready to come to you.—The first time Paul had visited the Corinthians was when he first preached the gospel to them and established the church. The second time was when he was present in spirit as they obeyed the instructions he gave in his first letter for them to follow in dealing with the sinful practices which they had allowed to grow up in their midst. He had delayed coming again, as he had explained in the beginning of the letter, that they might have an opportunity to carry out those instructions. News had been brought to him by Titus that they had gladly obeyed. The section of this letter beginning in chapter ten, however, clearly indicates that false teachers whom Paul had designated "super-apostles" and who were actually servants of Satan had come to Corinth seeking to undermine his influence and insinuating that he was interested in the money he might obtain from them. It is possible that they had been distorting his purpose in connection with the collections for the saints in Judea. It is evident that their own motive was a desire for financial gain as they pretended to serve as ministers of righteousness.

and I will not be a burden to you.—Paul defended his position on this issue from every standpoint, since it seems to have been the chief point of attack of the false teachers who were opposing him.

for I seek not yours, but you.—There is an implied thrust in this remark at the false teachers to whom the Corinthians had so readily listened. Their ministry was being carried out for what they could get out of it in contrast to the unselfish devotion to Christ that characterized all of Paul's work on their behalf. It was not their possessions, but themselves that Paul sought. He wanted their understanding and love and, above all, their faithfulness to the Lord.

for the children ought not to lay up for the parents.—Paul had repeatedly reminded them that the relation which they sustained to him was as children to parents. As their father in the gospel he had done everything in his power to protect them from the erosion of sinful practices which they had allowed to go on. He had sought to warn them against the encroachment of the false teachers who had come to them and to protect them from the subtle attack of Satan whose goal was their destruction. Just as parents lay up for their children, so Paul had done all this for their benefit, for they were dear to him in the Lord.

for your souls.—Paul reminded them of what they must have known: he was willing most gladly to spend and be spent for their souls. He was following the pattern set by Our Lord who came not to be ministered unto but to minister and to give His life a ransom for many. See Mark 10:45. This must ever be the position of the true minister of Christ.

am I loved less?—Was this demonstration of Paul's overflowing love for them to result in their loving him less? As this letter was being read to them, one wonders if many present hid their faces in shame for failing to respond in kind to the love of the apostle whom Christ had sent to them with the message of His love?

being crafty.—Again Paul reminded them that he had not become a burden to them. He had anticipated possible difficulties which might arise in connection with his preaching the gospel to them. He had written to them in the first letter telling them that he was willing to forgo his right to support in order to avoid any criticism of his ministry. He was "being crafty." He had caught them unawares. They had not seen through his reason for refusing to accept support from them, although he did receive support from others. But the thing that Paul feared had happened. Now, perhaps, they would understand his position and his determination to maintain it.

Did I take advantage of you?—Having called attention to a fact which they well knew, for he had not been a burden to them, he came to the defense of Titus and the brother who was sent with him to carry on the work of the gospel in his absence. Did Titus take any advantage of you? They knew that he had conducted himself in exactly the same spirit of devotion to Christ that had characterized all of Paul's labors in their behalf. He had walked in Paul's footsteps leaving no ground for criticism of himself or of Paul.

Ye think all this time that we are excusing ourselves unto you.—It is possible that Paul put this in the form of a question as the footnote in some Bibles indicates. But the punctuation makes little difference, since the point that Paul was making was that all this defense was not a matter of excusing himself in connection with the delay of his intended visit. He was aware that he lived and acted in the sight of God and that what he said was spoken as an apostle of Christ. Instead of making excuses for himself, he was sounding the warning and giving instructions for their benefit. Christ's purpose in his ministry was that they might be built up and not torn down. If they should follow his directives they would be built up in the faith; if they failed to do so, they would certainly be punished when he arrived.

For I fear.—Paul had a right to fear the consequences of the presence of false teachers in Corinth. He knew that they were listening to them gladly. He knew how they had permitted sinful practices to go on in their midst which had all but destroyed the church of God. The false teachers and indifferent leaders would have accomplished their goal if the church had not responded to Paul's instruction in his first letter to them. Titus had reported their obedience to this instruction; but as this had happened before, there was real possibility that they might again fall victims to the influence of the false teachers.

when I come, I should find you not such as I would.—Paul longed to see them break with these false teachers who were ministers of Satan and discontinue their sinful practices. He wanted them to reach maturity so that they might function to the fullest capacity as members of the body of Christ.

lest by any means there should be strife.—Those of the household of Chloe had reported to Paul the divisions, factions, jealousies, and wraths that had existed among them. Would they slip back into this sinful practice? Would they give themselves again to slander, gossip, conceit and disorder, acting in a manner unbecoming to the saints of God?

Lest again when I come my God should humble me before you?—Paul had written of his anticipation of a joyful visit both in his first letter and in the beginning of this second letter. Now he wonders if it will be necessary for God to humble him before them when he comes again. Will they reject the apostle whom Christ is sending to them for the ministers of Satan? They had been led into sin before, and that had caused great grief to Paul. He had told them in the beginning of the letter about his sorrow. He repeated the warning at the close of the letter, for he did not want them to forget it. Would those who had sinned fail to repent of their impurity, immoral conduct, and licentious practice?

Summary

Paul continued to boast in his weakness, since it had been forced upon him by the claims and false charges of his critics. But nothing was to be gained by it, since none of the critics could possibly match the experience about which he was to tell. He took up the matters of visions and revelations which the Lord had permitted him to have. The Lord had granted visions and revelations to Paul on various occasions, but this one was different. Its purpose was to emphasize the power of the Lord and the weakness of the apostle.

The incident which he related occurred fourteen years before the writing of Second Corinthians. No information is available that would enable us to fix the exact date of the incident or the place where Paul was when it happened. The vivid impression which it had made on Paul had remained with him through all those years.

Paul said that he was caught up to the third heaven, caught up to Paradise. There he heard words not to be uttered by man. He did not know whether this had been a bodily experience or just one that had occurred in the spirit. This may have some bearing on the intermediate state of the dead, since the term "Paradise" is used elsewhere in that connection. If so, it would indicate that Paradise existed after the resurrection of Christ. Although it is interesting, the theory is not vital: freedom of opinion should be observed in connection with it. The purpose of the vision was clear, as well as Paul's reason for relating it. After such an experience, Paul was given a thorn in the flesh to keep him from arrogant boasting. We do not know what that sharp thing was; there is no use to speculate on the matter. Paul said that it was a messenger from Satan. Perhaps Job's experience may shed some light on its meaning. It did serve to remind Paul of the power of the Lord and of his own unfinished task. Three times he asked to have it removed, but the Lord said, "My grace is sufficient for thee." The unmerited favor of the Lord Jesus had made him an apostle. His providential protection had been with him in all the hardships which he had endured for the sake of Christ. Paul boasted in his weakness, for then the protecting power of Christ was spread over him like a tent.

As he looked back at what he had just written about the divine approval of his apostleship, Paul said, "I have become foolish." They had compelled him to mention these things in order to answer the false charges against him. The evidence of his apostleship, however, was to be seen in the miracles which he had performed in their midst. The Corinthians were in no way inferior to the rest of the churches in this regard. But there was one difference: He had not been a burden to them. Ironically, he said "Forgive me this wrong."

Paul was determined not to be a burden to them on this third visit. Speaking ironically, he said, "Being crafty, I caught you with guile." He had anticipated the possibility of some charging him with the guilt of preaching the gospel for the sake of money. Although he had a right to receive support, he had not used it. His purpose was to preach the gospel to win men to Christ. He had worked with his own hands when he was in Corinth and in want. He had received help from the brethren in Macedonia, but he had not and would not become a burden to Achaia.

Paul was not making excuses for himself. He had delayed his visit to give them time to set their house in order. But he was fearful lest upon his arrival he might find things not as he would have them to be. He knew that false teachers were present and that some of the people had gladly listened to them. Would God humble him again by letting him find strife, jealousy, wrath, faction, backbiting, whispering, swelling, and tumults among them? It had happened once; would they see to it that these things were not present again when he arrived on this impending third visit?

Questions

1. Why had it become necessary for Paul to boast in his weakness?
2. Why did he say that nothing was to be gained by it?
3. What are some of the visions and revelations in which the Lord had appeared to Paul?
4. Why is this one different?
5. Why did he write about it in an impersonal manner?
6. What evidence is there that he was the man who had actually experienced this thing?
7. What is the point in his having mentioned the fourteen years that had elapsed since this happened?
8. Why did he say that he did not know whether it had been in the body or just in spirit?
9. What is the third heaven?
10. What is Paradise? What are some of the things said about it in the Scriptures?
11. Why was Paul permitted to hear things which man was not permitted to speak?
12. What are some of the things which Paul and other New Testament writers were permitted to reveal about heaven?
13. Why could Paul boast about "such a one" while refusing to boast about himself?
14. Why did he indicate that he was not foolish in boasting about this one?
15. Why was he given a thorn in the flesh?
16. What is meant by the messenger of Satan?
17. How may the story of Job help to explain this?
18. What is shown by the fact that Paul asked the Lord three times to remove this thing?
19. What was the answer to his prayer?
20. In what way had the grace of God been with Paul?
21. What was it to do for him under these circumstances?
22. How is the Lord's power made perfect in human weakness?
23. What special power had the Lord given to the apostles?
24. In what way had He providentially watched over Paul?
25. Why did Paul take pleasure in his weakness?
26. Why did Paul finally say, "I am become foolish"?
27. Although Paul said he was nothing, how did he compare with the super-apostles?

28. What were the apostolic credentials which Paul presented to the Corinthians?
29. What credentials could the super-apostles present?
30. How had Paul shown that the Corinthians were in no way inferior to the other churches?
31. What difference had he made between them and others?
32. Why did he say, "Forgive me this wrong"?
33. What are some of the views by which attempts have been made to explain the number of times Paul visited Corinth?
34. Why are such matter, while interesting, unimportant?
35. Why did Paul insist on continuing his policy of not being a burden to the churches in Achaia?
36. What was his real interest in them?
37. How did he use the relationship of parents to children to illustrate his meaning?
38. In what way was Paul following the example of the Lord in thus dealing with the brethren at Corinth?
39. Why did he ask, "Am I loved the less?"
40. Why did he say that he had been crafty?
41. Why did he ask if he or Titus had taken advantage of them?
42. What point was Paul making when he said, "You are thinking that we are excusing ourselves".
43. What grounds did Paul have to fear that the Corinthians might be found in sinful practices upon his arrival?
44. What sins did he think he might find?
45. How would God humble him before them?

For Discussion

1. The providence of God as seen in His gracious dealing with His people.
2. How can the church prevent backsliding such as Paul feared might occur at Corinth?

223

CHAPTER THIRTEEN

Analysis

A. Paul reminded the Corinthians of the things he intended to do when he came to them on this third visit (1-4).
   1. He stated the basis on which any testimony would be accepted (1).
   2. He warned that he would not spare those who had sinned (2).
      a) He had told them about this in the first epistle, and was repeating it for their benefit.
      b) He had warned them when he was present the second time (that is, through his first epistle to them).
      c) He was repeating it in his absence, warning them that he would not spare those who had sinned or the rest when he came again.
   3. He gave his reasons for this intended action against sinners in their midst (3-4).
      a) They had desired proof that Christ was speaking through him (3a).
      b) Christ is not weak, but powerful in His dealing with them (3b).
      c) Explanation of the issue of weakness and power (4).
         (1) He was crucified in weakness—voluntarily submitting to death on the cross—but He lives by the power of God as demonstrated by His resurrection.
         (2) In the same way, Paul declared that he was weak in Him, but lived with Him by the power of God. God's power raised him from death in sin and enabled him to live for their sakes.
B. He urged them to settle their problems in the light of the truth (5-10).
   1. The issue to be settled was their relation to Christ (5-7).
      a) They were to examine their relation to the faith (5a).
      b) They were to test their relation to Christ (5b).
         (1) Were they in Christ?
         (2) Were they rejected? Had they failed to pass the test of true relationship to Him?
      c) Paul expressed his hope and prayer for them (6-7).

224

(1) He hoped that they would not fail in their relation to Christ (6).

(2) He prayed that they might do no wrong (7).

    (a) This was not that he might appear to have been vindicated.

    (b) He wanted them to do what was right.

2. He was writing to help them do this very thing (8-10).

   a) In doing so, he must act according to truth.

   b) He rejoiced in his own weakness when they were strong.

   c) He prayed that they might settle their problems.

   d) He wrote while absent that he might not have to use the authority which the Lord gave him to build up and not to tear down (10).

C. He closed the epistle with words of admonition, promise, greeting, and benediction (11-14).

  1. Admonition (11a).

   a) Rejoice (good-bye).

   b) Settle your own problems—put things in order.

   c) Be comforted—accept his help.

   d) Straighten out your thinking—think the same thing.

   e) Live in peace.

  2. Promise: The God of love and peace will be with you (11b).

  3. Greeting (12-13).

   a) Greet one another with a holy kiss.

   b) All the saints greet you.

  4. Benediction: "The grace of the Lord Jesus Christ, and the love of God, and the fellowship of the Holy Spirit be with you all" (14).

Paul's Intended Action on His Third Visit

Scripture

13:1-4. This is the third time I am coming to you. At the mouth of two witnesses or three shall every word be established. 2 I have said beforehand, and I do say beforehand, as when I was present the second time, so now, being absent, to them that have sinned heretofore, and to all the rest, that, if I come again I will not spare; 3 seeing that ye seek a proof of Christ that speaketh in me; who to you-ward is not weak, but is powerful in you: 4 for he was crucified through weakness, yet he liveth through the power of God. For we also are weak in him, but we shall live with him through the power of God toward you.

225

Comments

This is the third time.—See comment on 12:14. Anticipating the long delayed third visit, Paul kept reminding the Corinthians that he was coming. In the above paragraph, he had indicated his determination not to be a burden to them. He also pointed out his intention of dealing with any sinful practices of which they might not have repented. *At the mouth of two or three.*—Quoting from Deut. 19:15, Paul cited the Law as the standard by which he intended to deal with sinful practices mentioned in 12:20-21. There is no good reason to assume that this quotation was being applied to his own statement about his forthcoming visit.

as when I was present the second time.—Paul had been present with the Corinthians, not in body but in spirit through his authoritative apostolic epistle in which he had given specific instructions for dealing with sinful practices which the Corinthians had allowed to develop in their congregation. He had received adequate evidence to establish the fact that parties and divisions actually existed in their midst. He had not written to them on the basis of mere hearsay. Reliable testimony had been furnished by those of the household of Chloe. In the case of immoral conduct involving the man who was living with his father's wife, the evidence was so clear that even the pagans were condemning the church for condoning such a thing. In the matter of lawsuits among brethren, the evidence against them was such that the pagan judges looked disparagingly upon the churches for allowing such a condition to exist.

Although Titus had reported their obedient response to the instruction Paul had sent in his first letter, the presence of false teachers at Corinth was sufficient grounds for his fear that some of them might have sinned again, or that some may never have repented.

Upon his arrival, he intended that every charge should be supported by adequate testimony. Those among them with Jewish background were thoroughly familiar with this procedure and would surely assent to the fairness of Paul as he anticipated the possibility of being forced to use the authority which the Lord gave him to build up and if need be, to destroy the sinful practices that were opposing the gospel of Christ.

to them that have sinned heretofore.—Paul had asked in his first letter: "What will ye? Shall I come unto you with a rod, or in love and a spirit of gentleness?" (I Cor. 4:21). While the church as a whole had responded to his warning, he kept repeating it for the sake of some who may not have heeded it and the rest who might have become involved again in such sins as he had listed in 12:20-21.

seeing that ye seek a proof of Christ that he speaketh in me.—Apparently some had begun to question whether or not Christ had been speaking through Paul as he had written to them warning them of the consequences of their sins. Some had gladly listened to those false teachers who said, "His letters are weighty and strong, but he is weak when present." Clearly, the false teachers had implied that Christ was not speaking through Paul and that he would not be able to carry out such punishment as he had promised. Yet the Corinthians knew that their very relation to Christ depended upon the gospel which Paul had preached to them. Furthermore, they knew that he had exhibited the credentials of his apostleship in the miracles which he had performed in their midst. All this points to the fickleness of the human heart. We do not wonder that Paul was afraid that the Corinthians might lapse into their old sins, for he knew how quickly the Galatians had turned from the gospel as he preached it to a different kind of gospel that would enslave them in false teaching.

who to you-ward is not weak, but is powerful in you.—Paul had constantly boasted in his own weakness and in the power of Christ that had raised those who were dead in trespasses and sin to sit with Him in the heavenly places. That power had been channeled into their lives through the gospel which Paul preached. False teachers had no such power. As ministers of Satan teaching false doctrine, they were corrupting men and making them slaves of unrighteousness. Only through the power of the gospel can men be transformed into the glorious image of the Lord. See II Cor. 3:18.

for he was crucified through weakness.—Christ Jesus who existed in the form of God and was on an equality with God took upon Himself the form of a servant and was made in the likeness of men. He humbled Himself by becoming obedient to the death of the cross. See Phil. 2:6-8.

Jesus said, "I lay down my life, that I may take it again. No one taketh it away from me, but I lay it down of myself. I have power to lay it down, and I have power to take it again. This commandment received I from the Father" (John 10:17-18). Although He could have called twelve legions of angels to defend Him, He meekly submitted to arrest in the Garden and suffered the indignities that were heaped upon Him by His tormentors at the time of His trial and, finally, allowed them to crucify Him. From the human point of view no greater symbol of weakness could be found than the cross. But myopic men have failed to see that in His death He destroyed him who has power of death, that is, the devil. See Heb. 2:14.

yet he liveth through the power of God.—The resurrection of Christ is the foundation of Christian faith. The world has not known a greater demonstration of power than that which raised Christ from the dead and caused Him to sit at the right hand of the Majesty on high. It was to this power that Paul directed the thinking of the Corinthians who had been saved from sin through the power of the gospel, but who, if they insisted on returning to the old sinful ways, were facing eternal destruction from the face of the Lord and from the glory of His might. See II Thes. 1:8-9.

For we also are weak in him.—In his first letter, Paul had written: "God hath set forth us apostles last of all, as men doomed to death" (I Cor. 4:9). From the human point of view, Paul readily admitted his weakness, but he refused to boast in anything except the power of Christ that had saved him from sin. He had been crucified with Christ, but he was living in faith, that is, he believed the gospel of Christ and conducted himself in accord with it. He was anticipating the life with Him in the eternal kingdom made possible through the power of God.

Problems Settled In The Light of Truth

Scripture

13:5-10. Try your own selves, whether ye are in the faith; prove your own selves. Or know ye not as to your own selves, that Jesus Christ is in you? unless indeed ye be reprobate. 6 But I hope that ye shall know that we are not reprobate. 7 Now we pray to God that ye do no evil; not that we may appear approved, but that ye may do that which is honorable, though we be as reprobate. 8 For we can do nothing against the truth, but for the truth. 9 For we rejoice, when we are weak, and ye are strong: this we also pray for even your perfecting. 10 For this cause I write these things while absent, that I may not when present deal sharply, according to the authority which the Lord gave me for building up, and not for casting down.

Comments

Try your own selves.—The Corinthians had been wanting Paul to prove to them that Christ had spoken through him. He had given them adequate proof of it, reminding them that he would again demonstrate it when he arrived on his third visit. He also reminded them that it was their responsibility to put themselves to the test with regard to their own faith and to determine, by testing it, whether or not they were living a life of faith in Christ. Such a test could only be carried out in the light of the authoritative message of the gospel that had been delivered to them by Christ's apostle. It couldn't be done by measuring themselves by the standards of the false teachers who "measured themselves by themselves and compared themselves with themselves, and were without understanding" (II Cor. 10:12).

Paul was recommending to the Corinthians an exercise by which every Christian should continually check his relation to the Lord. Only a diligent study of the Word and a sincere effort to put into practice can assure one that he is living in harmony with the true faith in the Lord Jesus Christ.

prove your own selves.—Paul had written in his first letter that a man was to prove himself in the light of the meaning of the loaf and cup in the Lord's supper. He was to determine what there was in his life that met the approval of Christ. The bread represented the body of Christ and the true relation of each member of that body to Christ the Head. The content of the cup symbolized the blood of Christ which was the means of blotting out all sin. No better place could be found for the Corinthians to examine their own lives than at the Lord's table as they meditated on the meaning of the death of Christ for their salvation.

Or know ye not as to your own selves, that Jesus Christ is in you?— Paul did not hesitate to declare that Christ lived in him because he had been crucified with Christ. See Gal. 2:20. He also made it very clear that those who belong to Jesus Christ have crucified the flesh— a symbol of sinful conduct—with its passions and longing desires for things that are evil. See Gal. 5:24. He had written to the Corinthians in his first letter to remind them that their bodies were temples of the Holy Spirit which was in them which they had from God. They did not belong to themselves, for they were bought with the price of the blood of Christ. Therefore, Paul urged them to glorify God in the body. See I Cor. 6: 19-20. If they were actually glorifying God in the things that they were doing, they could be sure that Christ was in them. If the test which he had directed them to make proved otherwise, they could know that the Lord did not approve their conduct. Had they failed by the standard of measurement which the Lord had given them through His faithful apostle?

But I hope that ye shall know that we are not reprobate.—Since the test of their faith and the presence of Christ in them depended upon the standard of the gospel which Paul preached, he hoped that they would know that he and all the apostles through whom Christ had spoken were not rejected by the Lord. This, of course, was something that the super-apostles had insinuated, if indeed they had not openly declared it. Since they were ministers of Satan, nothing they said could possibly be used by the Corinthians to test their relationship to Christ.

Now we pray to God.—The earnestness of Paul as he thought of the tragic fate of those who were about to reject the gospel of Christ led him to express his views in his prayer to God that they do no evil. His concern was not for himself nor for what the false teachers might say about him. He did not want to be guilty of joining with them in false teaching that he might merely appear to be approved by Christ. His concern was that they, as his children in the gospel, might do the thing that was right before the Lord even though false teachers might attempt to discredit him and show that he did not have the approval of the Lord.

For we can do nothing against the truth, but for the truth.—As an apostle of Christ, Paul spoke the truth. And as one who had been crucified with Christ and had committed himself wholeheartedly to the Lord, he acted in accord with the truth.

For we rejoice, when we are weak.—It did not matter to Paul that false teachers were calling him weak. He had gladly admitted it, because the secret of his life was to be found in the power of Christ who had raised him from death in trespasses and sin to the place where he could truthfully say that Christ lived in him. He did not make void the grace of God. Although he could rejoice in his own weakness, Paul rejoiced that his children in the gospel were strong. Their strength, too, depended upon their relation to Christ. It depended upon their being in the faith; upon their living by the standard of the gospel; upon their putting on the whole armor of God, that they might withstand the crafty work of the devil through his ministers who had fashioned themselves into ministers of righteousness.

even your perfecting.—Paul uses this interesting term again in verse eleven. He had used it in I Cor. 1:10. See *Studies in First Corinthians* on the various usages of the term.

In this context, Paul is urging them to settle their problems, to get rid of their sinful practices, to rearrange their lives that they might be in harmony with the truth of Christ as delivered to them by His inspired apostle.

For this cause I write these things while absent.—Once again Paul called their attention to his purpose in writing this epistle. What he said to them about sin and its punishment was no idle threat. It did, however, give them an opportunity to correct their ways and avoid the punishment which would otherwise be meted out to them through the authority which the Lord had given to Paul.

They had joined with Paul in punishing, according to his instructions, the one who had been guilty of immoral conduct. That had meant delivering the guilty one to Satan for the destruction of the flesh, with the fond hope that the spirit might be saved in the day of the Lord Jesus. Paul was hoping and praying that it might not be necessary to again use his authority against sinners in their midst who refused to repent.

Closing Admonition And Benediction

Scripture

13:11-14. Finally, brethren, farewell. Be perfected; be comforted; be of the same mind; live in peace: and the God of love and peace shall be with you. 12 Salute one another with a holy kiss. 13 All the saints salute you. 14 The grace of the Lord Jesus Christ, and the love of God, and the communion of the Holy Spirit be with you all.

Comments

Finally, brethren, farewell.—Despite the fears which he held that they might again be corrupted through the efforts of the false teachers, Paul addressed the Corinthians as brethren when he told them goodbye.

This was characteristic of his letters, for in the first epistle he had adressed them as the church of God, although he was aware of their divisions by which they were destroying the temple of God. He called them "brethren" although he was aware of the spiritual immaturity that marked them as men. The term "brethren" implied that they were members of the family of God. But it in no way implied approval of practices unbecoming to a child of God. It did indicate Paul's love and hope for them that they might settle their problems in the light of the gospel so that they might be in the family of God in heaven. For that reason he urged them to be perfected. He urged them to

231

accept the help that he as their father in the gospel offered those who were like beloved children to him. He wanted them to be united in their expressed opinions regarding their relation to Christ, by basing their conclusions on the truth which he had taught them. He wanted them to live in peace with one another, but peace must be preceded by purity in teaching and conduct. Their factions, jealousies, and backbitings could all be abolished by bringing their lives up to the standard of conduct which Christ had set for them. Only by doing so could the peace of God guard their hearts and thoughts in Christ Jesus.

and the God of love and peace.—Paul served the God of love and peace. He demonstrated His love in giving His Son to die for us. He made peace possible through the blood of the cross. Those who have found peace at the cross should be able to live at peace with their brethren in Christ.

Salute one another with a holy kiss.—This was the usual greeting among brethren. Brotherhood is determined by relationship to Christ. Brethren in Christ should follow the apostolic injunction to greet one another even if local customs suggests that it be done through the handshake rather than the holy kiss which was the custom in Paul's day.

All the saints salute you.—Saints are those who have separated themselves from the things of the world by washing their robes and making them white in the blood of the Lamb. They have dedicated themselves to the pure service of God. Paul had addressed this epistle to "the church of God which is at Corinth, with all the saints that are in the whole of Achaia." He lifted high this holy standard as he closed the letter even though in it he had warned the impenitent sinners about the punishment that would be visited upon them in his forthcoming visit.

The grace of the Lord Jesus Christ.—In this sublime benediction, Paul expressed his fondest hope and deepest longing for those whom he loved as his children in the gospel. He prayed that the grace of Christ, His unmerited favor, might be with them. He knew from experience how that grace had saved him and had continued in providential protection to be with him in all his trials and labors for Christ. He prayed that the grace of Christ by which they too had been saved through their faith expressed in obedience to the gospel might also providentially protect them from from the destructive power of Satanic false teaching that they might be presented in purity and victory before Christ when He comes.

and the love of God.—He prayed that God's love which had been the compelling force in his life might motivate them to obey His Word so that they might not be chastized with the disobedient. This was God's love for them. His love made forgiveness through Christ available to the believer. But they were not to presume upon the love of God, for those who will not walk with Christ in the new life shall suffer punishment, even destruction from the presence of the Lord. See II Thes. 1:8-9.

and the communion of the Holy Spirit be with you all.—This was the fellowship or partnership of the saints which had been made possible through following the wisdom of God revealed by the Holy Spirit through the inspired apostles. Paul prayed that it might be a reality in their lives as they worked together for Christ at Corinth and joined with the brethren in Macedonia to help the saints in Judea.

As these solemn words were being read to the church, the brethren must have realized that they were far more than a mere formal closing. This was an earnest prayer that had come from the heart of the one who had led them to Christ and who continued to love them as a father. The sublime benediction embodied the apostle Paul's hope and prayer for the saints of God at Corinth.

Summary

Paul had mentioned his forthcoming return visit to Corinth in his first letter. Much of the second epistle centers in the explanation of his delay in coming. It had been necessary to postpone the trip until he had given them time to act upon the instruction given in the first epistle about the tragic sins which they had permitted to go unreproved in their midst.

While he had written with loving care for those whom he considered his children in the gospel, he again, as he closed the letter, called attention to the necessity of getting themselves straightened out in the light of the truth of the gospel which they had learned from him. He was coming. And he would not spare those who were guilty of conduct unbecoming a Christian. But he assured them that all would be done in fairness for every charge would be established by adequate testimony.

Under the influence of false teachers, they had been led to question his authority. Did Christ really speak through him? Since they had asked for proof, Paul gave them ample evidence to support his authority which the Lord had given him to build up the church, not to tear it down as the false teachers were doing.

Since they sought proof of him, he suggested that they put themselves to the test and find out in the light of the truth whether or not they were in accord with the faith in Christ. Was Christ in them? He was, unless they failed to pass the test of conducting themselves according to His gospel. Out of his love for them, Paul expressed his hope that they would not fail, even though false teachers attempted to disqualify him as an apostle of Christ. He boasted only in his weakness and in the power of Christ by whose death and resurrection he, as well as the believers at Corinth, had been saved.

Paul prayed to God that they would do no evil, but he reminded them he was guided by the truth in all his dealings with them. As an apostle of Christ, he could do nothing against the truth. Lest they miss the point, he reminded them again that the purpose of his writing was to give them time to take care of their problems so as to avoid being punished upon his arrival.

The letter was finished. Reluctantly, it seems, Paul said "good-bye" to the brethren whom he loved in Christ. But once more he urged them to straighten out their problems, to take courage, to hold the same views of the gospel, and to live in peace. "Do this," he said, "and the God of peace will be with you."

Gathering up all his hope and prayer for them in one sublime benediction he wrote: "The grace of the Lord Jesus Christ, and the love of God and the communion of the Holy Spirit be with you."

Questions

1. Why did Paul repeat his statement that he was about to make a third visit to Corinth?
2. What had he expected them to accomplish before he arrived?
3. Why did he insist that everything was to be established by two or three witnesses? To what things did he refer?
4. How had Paul dealt with the charges against them when he was present in spirit?
5. What punishment had been meted out by the church to those who had sinned?
6. What may this suggest as to the action Paul intended to take through the authority the Lord had given him?
7. Since Titus had reported that they had obeyed the instructions of the first letter, why did Paul anticipate the possible need for further disciplinary action on this third visit?
8. What proof were some demanding of Paul? Why?
9. How had Paul responded to this demand?

10. In what sense was Christ crucified through weakness?
11. How was the power of God demonstrated in Him?
12. What effect did this have on the Corinthians? on Paul?
13. What was the nature of Paul's weakness about which he boasted?
14. How will the power of Christ be used against the disobedient when He comes?
15. What does it mean to be crucified with Christ?
16. What does it mean for Christ to live in the Christian?
17. Why did Paul tell the Corinthians to try themselves?
18. How were they to do this?
19. How were they to know that Christ was in their midst?
20. What would demonstrate that they were unapproved by Christ?
21. Why did he say "I hope that you will know that we are not unapproved"?
22. Whom did he include in this expressed hope? Why?
23. Who had been suggesting that Paul did not have the approval of Christ?
24. Why did Paul say, "We can do nothing against the truth"?
25. Why did Paul rejoice when false teachers called him weak?
26. In what did he rejoice in the lives of the Christians at Corinth?
27. What did he mean by "your perfecting"?
28. Did Paul teach "perfectionism"—the doctrine that holds that it is possible to reach a state in this life in which it is impossible to commit an act of sin?
29. What are some of the ways in which the word translated "perfect" was used in Paul's time?
30. Why did Paul, in his closing words, refer to the Corinthians as "brethren" after having just warned them about their sins?
31. Why is God called "the God of love and peace"?
32. What is the Christian's obligation and privilege in the matter of greeting others?
33. What did Paul mean by "the grace of the Lord Jesus Christ"?
34. What did he mean by the "love of God"?
35. What did he mean by "the communion of the Holy Spirit"?

For Discussion

1. In the light of Paul's instruction for the Corinthians to try themselves, how can the Lord's supper be made a meaningful experience to the conscientious Christian?
2. What is the place of the grace of the Lord Jesus Christ in the life of the faithful Christian.